"Not all of us are called to be journalists, but every American—whether he likes it or not—has his thinking shaped by journalism. *Prodigal Press* will help you to understand both the blatant and the subtle ways in which journalists promote liberal and anti-Christian ideas, and what you can do to protect your family from that influence."

—**Gary Bauer,** President, American Values

"Here—in the tradition of Calvin, Edwards, and Machen— is a tough-minded call to spiritual renewal directed to the most tough-minded of our democratic institutions. The impact of this book will be likened to David's meeting Goliath, with the outcome postponed."

—**Dr. Mark Fackler,** Professor of Communication Ethics and African Studies, Calvin College

"The most important book about journalism I have ever read. *Prodigal Press* is must reading for all Christians and for all reporters, editors, journalism professors, and students."

—**Dr. Clifford Kelly,** Professor of Communication Studies, Liberty University; Founding Director, Institute of Public Affairs Journalism

"The twenty-fifth anniversary edition of *Prodigal Press* is a book that I wish every American would read. Olasky and Smith, veteran journalists themselves, provide an honest and thorough critique of their trade. Well argued and meticulously footnoted, the original edition was a landmark of exposé and insight. This edition—showing what American journalism was, has become, and could be—is needed now more than ever."

—**Alex McFarland,** Director for Christian Worldview and Apologetics, North Greenville University

"This is a great day: two of my favorite journalists from my all-time favorite newsmagazine, *WORLD*, have issued a twenty-fifth-anniversary edition of one of the truly inspirational books that I remember reading as a young believer. *Prodigal Press* is a captivating narrative chock-full of fascinating stories and historical insight—but it is more than a story; it is a call to redeem journalism from the bias, spin, and propaganda that masquerade as reporting these days. There has never been a more important time for truth-believers to become truth-tellers. Thanks to Olasky and Smith, we know how to do it."

—**Jeff Myers,** President, Summit Ministries

"I loved *Prodigal Press* when it was first published. As someone who became a Christian while working as a journalist, it really helped to crystallize things for me. It's important and strategic to have this book updated and expanded for a new generation."

—**Lee Strobel,** former legal editor, *Chicago Tribune*; author, *The Case for Christ*

"At a time of declining newspaper readership and falling TV ratings, the media's discrimination against people with a Christian worldview is a form of professional suicide. In this updated version of his 1988 book, Marvin Olasky gives new examples of anti-Christian bias, which ought to motivate more Christian young people to consider careers in journalism instead of cursing the growing darkness made worse by the absence of their light."

—**Cal Thomas,** America's #1 nationally syndicated columnist

"*Prodigal Press* is a masterpiece of historical research, Christian analysis, and practical application. Much change has taken place in journalism and the media since the first edition was published in 1988—much of which was predicted in the book—with the growth of both anti-Christian bias and pro-Christian alternatives. This updated edition adds new examples, addresses contemporary issues, and takes up the new information technology. But the original insights are as fresh as ever. They will make you a more perceptive reader and possibly inspire you to be a more perceptive writer, whether the medium is the printed page or a computer screen."

—**Gene Edward Veith,** Professor of Literature and Provost, Patrick Henry College

PRODIGAL PRESS

PRODIGAL PRESS

Confronting the
Anti-Christian Bias of the
American News Media

Revised and Updated

Marvin Olasky
Warren Cole Smith

P U B L I S H I N G
P.O. BOX 817 • PHILLIPSBURG • NEW JERSEY 08865-0817

Unless otherwise indicated, all Scripture quotations are from The Holy Bible, English Standard Version, copyright © 2001 by Crossway, a publishing ministry of Good News Publishers. Used by permission. All rights reserved.

Scripture quotations marked (NIV) are from the HOLY BIBLE, NEW INTERNATIONAL VERSION®. NIV®. Copyright © 1973, 1978, 1984 by International Bible Society. Used by permission of Zondervan Publishing House. All rights reserved.

Italics within Scripture quotations indicate emphasis added.

ISBN: 978-1-59638-597-9 (pbk)
ISBN: 978-1-59638-598-6 (ePub)
ISBN: 978-1-59638-599-3 (Mobi)

Printed in the United States of America

Abstract background © iwanara / Fotolia.com

Library of Congress Cataloging-in-Publication Data

Olasky, Marvin N.
  Prodigal press : confronting the anti-Christian bias of the American news media / Marvin Olasky, Warren Cole Smith. -- Revised and updated edition.
    pages cm
  Includes bibliographical references and index.
  ISBN 978-1-59638-597-9 (pbk.)
  1. Religion and the press--United States--20th century. 2. Religion and the press--United States--21st century. 3. Christianity--Controversial literature. 4. Humanistic ethics. 5. Journalism--Objectivity--United States. I. Smith, Warren Cole. II. Title.
  PN4867.O45 2013
  302.23'0973--dc23
                    2013019785

To all our colleagues at *WORLD* who are not only
hearers of the Word but doers
and producers of new words that reflect biblical teaching.

Contents

Acknowledgments

Olasky

My wife, Susan, listened to the ideas of this book's first edition during long walks; her intellect and insight improved every chapter. *Prodigal Press* owed its existence to the vision of Christian worldview publishing shared by Howard and Roberta Ahmanson. Special thanks go to Herbert Schlossberg.

Smith

When I first read this book, it changed the trajectory of my life. I am therefore profoundly grateful to Marvin Olasky for writing this book, and for allowing me to collaborate with him on its revision. Marvin Padgett, now retired editorial vice-president at P&R, gave us the green light for this 25th anniversary edition. To him I return the benediction with which he closed every conversation I had with him: grace and peace to you.

Introduction to the 25th Anniversary Edition

Marvin Olasky

Prophecy is of two kinds. We read in the Bible about God giving some individuals specific knowledge of events to come. We see others who lack that specific knowledge but realize that once we forget the initial commandments—"I am the LORD your God. . . . You shall have no other gods before me" (Ex. 20:2–3)—everything else falls apart. First we hammer the nails into Christ's palms. Then we hammer them into our own.

J. Gresham Machen was a prophet of the second kind. In 1924 he wrote a great book, *Christianity and Liberalism*, which exposed theologically liberal Christianity as no Christianity at all. He knew that once we stop believing in God's sovereignty and the efficacy of Christ's atonement, we slip-slide into breaking commandments not to kill, not to commit adultery, etc.

Machen would not have been surprised to find Protestant denominations that went liberal on theology in the 1920s embracing abortion in the 1970s and same-sex marriage in these latter days. Aristotle said that man without society is either beast or God;[1] but Machen would have agreed with Communist-turned-Christian Whittaker Chambers, who said, "Man without God is

---

1. Aristotle, *Politics*, Book 1, Section 2: "He who is unable to live in society, or who has no need because he is sufficient for himself, must be either a beast or a god."

a beast, and never more beastly than when he is most intelligent about his beastliness."[2]

Twenty-five years ago I wrote *Prodigal Press: The Anti-Christian Bias of American News Media* and punctuated my analysis of journalism's descent with that quotation from Chambers. One chapter title, "Spiking the Spiritual," referred to the tradition of copy editors having a large spike on their desks: stories that didn't pass muster ended up impaled. I showed how mainstream journalism had abandoned its Christian roots—and the result was fear, loathing, and a wide variety of journalistic, legal, ethical, and economic problems.

P&R Publishing is reprinting this book, with added material from my friend Warren Smith, because some say *Prodigal Press* was prophecy of the second kind. But it was easy to prophesy, as the American journalistic elite had abandoned and scorned Christian press antecedents. The train was already off the rails, and a smashup was inevitable. Technology would soon help alternatives to liberal daily newspapers move from infancy to vigorous adulthood, and in a game of computer/scissors/paper, computers would win.

Prodigal Press in the 1980s received some positive and some negative reviews. The negative critics typically stated that I was exaggerating the problem. They said *Newsweek* might occasionally tilt left, but network newscasts still played it down the middle and the Associated Press was rock-solid in its adherence to objectivity in the sense of balancing subjectivities, with liberals and conservatives receiving equal space and editors vigilantly removing loaded adjectives from their young reporters' prose.

Evidence of bias was exceptionally clear on questions such as how we should treat unborn children, so I followed up *Prodigal Press* with *The Press and Abortion*. But on current coverage of some political and economic issues I had to grit my teeth and

2. Whittaker Chambers, *Witness* (Random House, 1952), 13.

say to hostile reviewers, wait and see. Since what we believe about God inevitably affects what we say about man, watch the cloud on the horizon that then seemed, to some, smaller than a man's hand.

That cloud has now has filled the sky and is pelting us with not only rain but hail. I can say this because *WORLD*, the magazine I edit, is a member of the Associated Press, so I read lots of AP stories. In June and July 2011, three interns and I began every weekday by reading a half-dozen stories on controversial political, economic, and social issues. We asked: Are they balanced enough to put on our website? Or—because of their bias, their superficiality, or both—do they need lot of work prior to publication?

A list of the lowlights would be long, and I will mention only a few. It was no surprise that Associated Press reports during those months were highly tilted in favor of same-sex marriage, with AP regularly connecting battles for racial equality with those for redefining marriage. Conservatives received treatment like that of segregationists fifty years ago. One AP reporter on June 21 called conservative legislators "the last hurdle" to be jumped and didn't balance that with the view that they could be considered "the last defense" against societal breakdown.

The AP reports were not balanced, and it would be silly to expect them to be when mainstream journalists see critics of the gay movement as defenders of social cancer. No one sees the need to balance news of a new anticancer drug with statements by pro-cancer proponents. But AP's liberal bias on political and economic questions was also evident. Think of it algebraically, with AP standing for coverage of person A, who who has a problem, and person P, the politician who purports to have a solution. The Associated Press typically did not bother to cover person F, the one paying taxes so that person P can gain glory for sending aid to person A.

In the nineteenth century, Yale professor William Graham Sumner had offered a similar equation and called person F "the forgotten man." In the twenty-first century, AP regularly broke its pledge to be evenhanded by highlighting person A and forgetting Mr. F. For example, early in July AP covered Minnesota's brief government shutdown by noting, "Poor families are scrambling after the state stopped child care subsidies. . . . Minnesota's most vulnerable residents and about 22,000 laid-off state employees began feeling the effects on Friday." True enough, but in 1,200 words the AP reporter didn't bother to ask a Mr. F what he thought about paying for all the programs.

Another AP story from the July Fourth weekend told us, "California college students are bracing for higher tuition bills and fewer courses and campus services under a new state budget that once again slashes spending on higher education." The state budget inflicted "the latest blow" on California higher education, which has already seen "deep cuts" that have "eroded" instructional quality. The reporter did not mention taxpayers' death by a thousand cuts, or that tens of thousands of Californians have moved to Texas, Idaho, or other states.

Week after week my interns and I saw these types of stories. A May 25 AP story, "Broken Budgets, Struggling Schools," quoted ten teachers, administrators, or union executives decrying budget trends and no one—no taxpayer, no conservative legislator—providing a different perspective.

AP reporters did not question the assumption that Washington should be deciding the sugar content of cereal and saying, in essence, "Silly rabbit, Trix aren't for kids." AP could have asked whether a Congress debating trillion-dollar deficits and authorizing funds for three wars should be debating whether eight or ten grams of sugar per serving makes a cereal grrrreat.

The interns and I saw AP reporters exuberantly praising the politically and environmentally correct. For example, a plan to install solar pancls on the White House meant "returning the power of the sun to the pinnacle of prominence." AP's adjectives indicated its position on abortion. A June 26 story complained about South Dakota's "new restrictive state law" on abortion that imposed "stringent counseling requirements." (A different perspective could have noted "a new protective state law" requiring "thorough" or "comprehensive" counseling requirements.)

AP's basic assumptions were readily evident: the federal government should be involved in every problem that arises, and federal spending should increase. A July 17 story included typical drumbeating: "Time is running out for Washington to raise the country's borrowing limit and avoid a default. Wall Street isn't panicking yet. But if the unthinkable happens, a default could strike financial markets like an earthquake."

In February 2011, I interviewed Tom Kent, AP's deputy managing editor and standards editor, and asked him about studies showing that conservatives are rare in major mainstream news organizations and conservative Christians nowhere in sight. Kent responded, "I don't see this as an issue because we don't focus on it. There are people whom I've worked with for twenty, thirty years, and I don't know how they vote. That would not be useful information for me to know." It seems to me that the lack of discussion indicates this should be an issue. When an organization includes a diversity of views, people know it.

The liberal bias of Associated Press and other major mainstream organizations has grown worse, but the past quarter-century has also seen an expansion of conservative alternatives— talk radio, blogs, and Fox News—and Christian alternatives. In 1987 I was writing from theory, but in 1990 I joined WORLD's board, and in 1992 became its editor, and have now been able to put theories into practice.

Now, I continue to recommend biblical crusading and biblical sensationalism (chaps. 11 and 12), but I've learned more about the joy of journalism. In what other endeavor do craftsmen get front row seats at a different circus every week?

I've learned the pleasures of reporting not just because it's fun but because of the fun of glorifying God. As John Piper writes, "Every joy that does not have God as its central gladness is a hollow joy and in the end will burst like a bubble." Piper points out that we should aspire "to study reality as a manifestation of God's glory, to speak and write about it with accuracy, and to savor the beauty of God in it."[3] Our goal at WORLD is to discover and communicate the reasons that exist for honoring Christ in all things and above all things. The Bible teaches us that God created this world to be his theater, so the more we report accurately what happens in it, the more we will praise him.

WORLD sometimes highlights good news, and that praises God, for our natural selfishness means we readily see what is good as coming from him. We cover compassionate ministries because God most showed his glory when Christ lowered himself to live among us and then suffer and die for us. Since Christ so amply displayed compassion, our trying to follow in some of his steps glorifies God. We also praise Christ by showing bad news about the results of sin—because the bad shows how desperately we need him.

We try to have zeal for God's glory characterize all our editorial decisions. Why do we praise marriage and hate abortion? Our natural tendencies are toward selfishness—so when a mom sacrifices her freedom to care for a child and when a dad sacrifices his freedom to provide for his family, that glorifies God. Some of our news and feature articles praise God without specific mention. They take after the biblical book of Esther, which never speaks of God explicitly but shows God's sovereignty in every chapter. Other stories specifically refer to God, as did the

3. John Piper, *Think: The Life of the Mind and the Love of God* (Wheaton, IL: Crossway, 2011).

early American newspapers and magazines discussed in part one of *Prodigal Press*.

I've learned more from editing *WORLD* about the importance of provocative and evocative news stories that come out of pavement-pounding rather than thumb-sucking. We make mistakes, but we stand for factual accuracy and biblical objectivity, trying to see the world as best we can the way the Bible depicts it. Journalistic humility for us means trying to give God's perspective. We distinguish between issues on which the Bible is clear and those on which it isn't. We also distinguish between journalism and propaganda: we're not willing to lie because someone thinks it will help God's cause.

Over the past quarter-century I've learned more about the importance of offering salt, not sugar. We print what we believe to be true, not what we'd like to be true. *WORLD* is generally conservative; but we try to be biblical first, conservative second, which means taking positions on compassion, immigration, prison reform, and other issues which don't always fit within the conservative box. We practice journalism, not public relations, which means we are willing to criticize prominent Christians when they are hurting the cause of Christ.

We try to speak up for those it's convenient to forget: the unborn, the unemployed (during a Democratic administration, since the mainstream media cover this issue relentlessly during Republican administrations), the uneducated (victimized by poor schools), and the politically unfashionable. We see government as often the problem rather than the solution, yet we honor those who are in authority over us and recognize the God-given place of the state. We are fallen sinners, but we aim to present sensational facts with understated prose. In a high-decibel society we try to have a no-scream zone.

We value on-the-ground reporting from Africa, Iraq, Afghanistan, China, and U.S. inner cities, and we put less trust in abstract essays. We emphasize the human touch by spending less time inside the Beltway and more on the prairie. We are willing to pass by some geopolitical analysis so as to emphasize the lives of harassed or persecuted Christians. We try to cover cultural developments beyond Christian ghettos and comfort zones.

WORLD began publishing as I was writing *Prodigal Press*, and I mentioned the new publication. Happily, *WORLD* founder Joel Belz and I had a similar sense of how Christian journalism should develop: the *WORLD* mission statement states well the need "to report, interpret, and illustrate the news in a timely, accurate, enjoyable, and arresting fashion from a perspective committed to the Bible as the inerrant Word of God." Beginning in 1992 Joel graciously allowed me to put ideas into practice. To me *WORLD* is a dream walking, and *Prodigal Press* explained why we had to dream.

My colleague Warren Smith began reading *WORLD* about the time I became its editor. After four years as first an occasional and then regular freelance writer, he joined *WORLD* full-time in 2010. He has written most of the new material for the second edition of this book. When I published the first edition of *Prodigal Press* in 1988, the Internet was in its infancy and cable news, dominated by CNN, was only a slightly more mature toddler. We are still much closer to the beginning than the end of the media revolution created by these new technologies, but we are now far enough along to have much new to say.

Some of what I said before is now outdated, so our updating includes a revision of chapter 8, "Perceptive Media Watching," and a much more substantial revision of chapter 9, "Network News and Local Newspapers." We also have an entirely new chapter— chapter 10, "The Devil in the Electrons"—that highlights both the promise and opportunity provided by electronic media, but also identifies how new manifestations of anti-Christian bias appear.

Chapter 13, "A Christian Journalism Revival?," also has significant new material, some of it related to our experiences at *WORLD*.

Introduction to the First Edition

One of Jesus' best-known parables is of the prodigal son who squandered his inheritance. Ridiculed and abused, the son saw the misery of his life and decided to return to his father, who greeted him warmly. The prodigal's brother, however, was angry, because a great banquet was served in honor of the returnee, but the brother who had led an upright life all along was not receiving attention.

The father told the jealous son: "You've done well, but he was lost and now is found, so let us rejoice." We do not know how the jealous son responded to that good advice. For a long time the jealous son probably had been angry at his prodigal brother for abandoning the homestead, leaving him without company and assistance. It was probably hard for him to break out of an established pattern of thought.

Imagine, though, what the jealous son's feelings would have been had the prodigal not only taken the money and run, but boasted of the offense daily? What if the jealous son had received daily sneering letters from the prodigal? What if the prodigal son had constantly lied about his industrious brother, libeling and ridiculing him? How much greater the anger! And how much greater the need to pray for the prodigal's return, and to remind him constantly that he, despite sins, is still a member of the family.

American journalism is one of Christianity's prodigal sons. Until the mid-nineteenth century American journalism was Christian. But as the first part of this book will show, journalists influenced by anti-Christian humanism and pantheism abandoned their Christian heritage and ended up wallowing among the pigs. For many years it was difficult to see the analogy because the biblical prodigal son was soon starving. The prodigal press, on the other hand, managed to live lavishly for a century on the material and reputational capital its Christian heritage had accumulated. But in spirit, the living death is parallel.

The flight of the prodigal press has been hard on American Christians precisely because journalism has departed in spirit but not in physical presence. The prodigal frequently files reports full of hatred for Christianity. Many Christians have responded angrily. Just as church bashing is a favorite sport among some reporters, so media bashing is the pastime of many Christians. This book, however, points out ways for Christians to reclaim American journalism. We need to examine not just the abuses but the uses of sensationalism and crusading. We need to contribute our time and money. Most important, we need to pray for journalism and journalists.

Christians in the early twenty-first century should work hard on the reclamation project, because every year shows more clearly how journalism can have a positive as well as a negative impact on American society. Let's go back a way to two sensational stories from 1987, one involving Gary Hart and the other the televangelists Jim and Tammy Bakker.

U.S. Senator Gary Hart was a rising star in the Democratic Party and a front-runner for the Democratic nomination for president. His candidacy derailed when the *Miami Herald* and other newspapers published photos of him at a party with a young woman sitting on his lap. The accompanying story laid out the details of an adulterous affair. Some Christians criticized the press for breaking and then pushing the story of the presidential candidate who could not keep his pants on. The story was more than titillation, though. It provided essential voting information for Christians, and for some non-Christians. Biblically, we should not vote for adulterers (unless the incident happened long ago and has been repented). Adultery is a grievous sin against God as well as spouse.[1] It shows not only a lack of judgment but a lack of trustworthiness.[2]

Many Christians know this, but how do we apply these general principles to choosing leaders unless we learn about leaders' behavior? And how will we learn without journalism? Many Christians are queasy about looking at the underside of life. Biblically, however, truth must come out, even when it hurts. If Christians are to reclaim American journalism, we need to be hard-hitting, within biblical principles. This book discusses exactly how to do that.

The Jim and Tammy Faye Bakker scandal, and the subsequent fall of their PTL (Praise The Lord) Network, also showed the importance of journalism, in a different way. Just as presidential candidates used to be chosen by those who knew their personal habits and character traits, so congregant members could see their ministers up close and personal each Sunday. They would know if he was spending money unwisely or getting too close to an attractive member of the flock.

The political equation changed with the advent of mass primaries. Voters, making choices directly, became dependent on information provided by reporters covering campaigns. Religious relationships also changed as televangelism emerged. Contributors who wanted to know how their money was spent

1. Jeremiah and the other prophets repeatedly describe the "spiritual adultery" involved in Israel's worship of other gods. Similarly, physical adultery separates what God has covenantally united.

2. First Corinthians 7 notes that a husband's body belongs to his wife. If a husband steals from his wife, won't he steal from others?

had to depend on public relations reports rather than firsthand observation. Christians capable of doing investigative reporting backed off, not wanting to help atheistic antagonists of the ministries. As Joel Belz was starting up *WORLD*, he received tips from readers that something was amiss at PTL, but he did not have the capability to pursue the story. "I regret that," he said twenty-five years later. "I sometimes wonder if things might have turned out differently there if Christian journalists rather than secular journalists had broken that story." Christian journalists, Belz believes, might have approached the story in ways that could have led to restoration rather than destruction.

Because no Christian outlet investigated the story, contributors did not receive information needed to make informed choices. By the time the story attracted the attention of secular outlets, tens of millions of dollars had poured into PTL coffers. The Bakkers and the senior leadership at PTL were intoxicated on money and their celebrity status. They indulged in mansions, private jets, and luxury automobiles. The PTL Network ultimately collapsed in financial, sexual, and legal scandal. The *Charlotte Observer* ultimately won a Pulitzer Prize for its coverage of the Bakker scandal.

Many Christians learned the importance of looking before we pledge. Many saw the difference between invading privacy and puncturing hypocrisy. Those are positives. But the Bakker coverage had many negatives also.

First, it's important to remember what was happening when the scandal broke. Federal District Court Judge Brevard Hand had just ruled that some Alabama school textbooks were promoting a religion by advocating secular humanism, the belief that universal moral standards have no relevance to our lives. His was a serious decision on a serious subject. It was becoming harder for anti-Christian journalists to ridicule all Christian thought. Many tried. For example, the editor of the *Austin*

American-Statesman yelped about "book burning" and sneered at the judge who "made up a religion." But his sneers were not very convincing. Coverage of the Bakker scandal allowed journalists to return to familiar ground—Elmer Gantry revisited—at just the time when it looked as if they finally might have to deal with basic presuppositions.

Second, the PTL scandal diverted reporting resources from important stories. While Jim and Tammy were on the front page of *USA Today*, Christians in the Soviet Union continued a decades-old struggle that would soon contribute to the demise of the Soviet Union. As one Soviet Christian, Alexandr Ogordinokov, wrote after eight years in the Gulag, "Concentration camps are scattered over the vast expanse of Russia, behind tall fences of barbed wire and high-voltage cables . . . you are buried in the tomb-like twilight of solitary punishment cells; the oppressive silence of faceless days turns time itself into an instrument of torture. Your tongue cleaves to the roof of your mouth in a senseless babble of misery. Hunger gnaws your belly, the cold numbs your flesh and desperation courses through your blood."[3]

Major American media did not spotlight the reality of Christians suffering. They played with Tammy Bakker's furs and air-conditioned doghouses. The Bakker scandal showed Christians that activities of the church needed close coverage, but the front-paging of the story for months and months also showed bias. Which events receive coverage? Which do not, and why? Christians have been asking these questions more insistently over the past year.

In this book we examine the influence of worldviews on reporting. We analyze the meanings of objectivity, sensationalism, and crusading, and the impact of legal, ethical, and

3. Alexandr Ogordinokov quoted in Koenraad De Wolf, *Dissident for Life: Alexander Ogorodnikov and the Struggle for Religious Freedom in Russia* (Grand Rapids, MI: Eerdmans, 2013).

technological changes. We explain how to read a newspaper with discernment and how to look at the lives of journalists with sorrow and sometimes pity.

What we refrain from is indiscriminate media bashing, because the prodigal son deserves compassion, not condemnation. We have reported for and edited newspapers, and still love them. We like many reporters, most of the time. The object of this book is not to wail, but to suggest how we can be God's servants in helping to bring that prodigal press home.

PART 1

DEPARTURE

All the devils in hell and tempters on earth could do us no injury if there were no corruption in our own natures.
—*Charles Haddon Spurgeon*

I The Decline of American Journalism

A 1986 study by New York University Professor Paul Vitz found that the vast majority of elementary and high school textbooks go to great lengths to avoid reference to religion. Vitz found American history textbooks defining pilgrims as "people who make long trips" and fundamentalists as rural people who "follow the values or traditions of an earlier period." One textbook listed three hundred important events in American history, but only three of the three hundred had anything to do with religion. A world history textbook left out any mention of the Protestant Reformation. A literature textbook changed a sentence by Nobel Prize laureate Isaac Bashevis Singer from "Thank God" to "Thank goodness."[1]

Standard journalism history textbooks provide similar distortions in their accounts of early nineteenth-century newspapers. Two chapters in the most-used textbook, Emery and Emery's *The Press and America*, deal with the 1800–1833 era of American journalism without once mentioning the Christian worldview that then characterized many major American newspapers and magazines.[2] The textbook does not even mention the

1. Paul Vitz, *Religion and Traditional Values in Public Textbooks* (Washington, DC: National Institute of Education, 1986). For comments on Vitz's study, see *Newsweek*, July 28, 1986, 20; *Saturday Evening Post*, July-August 1986, 16; *Christianity Today*, January 17, 1986, 49; *Christianity Today*, March 7, 1986, 15.

2. Edwin Emery and Michael Emery, *The Press and America*, 5th ed. (Englewood Cliffs, NJ: Prentice-Hall, 1984), 109–38.

3

New York Christian Advocate, in 1830 the weekly with the largest circulation in the country, or the *Boston Recorder*, which had the second largest circulation in that city.[3]

Other textbooks still in use have similar blinders.[4] They ignore comments by early nineteenth-century press watchers who noted, "Of all the reading of the people three-fourths is religious . . . of all the issues of the press three-fourths are theological, ethical and devotional." They do not mention that New York City alone boasted fifty-two magazines and newspapers that called themselves Christian, or that from 1825 to 1845 over one hundred cities and towns had explicitly Christian newspapers.[5] The facts, though, are irrefutable, once they are dug up: in the early nineteenth century, American journalism often was Christian journalism.

In those days, many Christian newspapers covered everything from neighborhood disputes to foreign affairs. They did not restrict themselves to church activities. The *Boston Recorder*,

3. Roberta Moore, *Development of Protestant Journalism in the United States, 1743–1850* (unpublished doctoral dissertation, Syracuse University, 1968), 237.

4. Frank Luther Mott's *American Journalism*, rev. ed. (New York: Macmillan, 1950), has one paragraph on page 206 about the "religious newspapers" of the 1801–1833 period. According to Mott, about one hundred such publications, scattered across the country, covered both secular events and church activities: The newspapers were "a phenomenon of the times" and "often competed successfully with the secular papers." Mott noted that "many of these papers were conducted with great vigor and ability."

Mott did not go into detail, but his brief mention was more than these newspapers have received in other journalism history textbooks written in the twentieth century, such as James M. Lee, *History of American Journalism* (Boston: Houghton Mifflin, 1917); George H. Payne, *History of Journalism in the United States* (New York: Appleton-Century-Crofts, 1920); or Sidney Kobre, *Development of American Journalism* (Dubuque, IA: Wm. C. Brown Co., 1969). A history written in the late nineteenth century, Frederic Hudson, *Journalism in the United States from 1690 to 1872* (New York: Harper & Brothers, 1873), is also unsympathetic to the Christian press, but at least provides some information. A monograph by Waley Norton, *Religious Newspapers in the Old Northwest to 1861* (Athens, OH: Ohio University Press, 1977), and dissertations by Moore (noted above) and Kenberry (see note 5 below), provide useful records.

5. Howard Kenberry, *The Rise of Religious Journalism in the United States* (unpublished dissertation, University of Chicago, 1920), 35.

4

for example, included news of everyday accidents, crimes, and political campaigns. Its circulation success allowed one editor to conclude that the *Recorder* had gained "the attention of the public" and "stirred up the minds of Christians to duty."[6]

Recorder cofounder Nathaniel Willis was an experienced journalist. Born in 1780, he edited the *Eastern Argus*, a partisan newspaper in Maine, during the early years of the new century. In 1807, though, Willis's life changed. He went to hear what he thought would be a political speech by a minister, but the minister went back to biblical basics. Willis, in his own words, "was much interested, and became a constant hearer. The Holy Spirit led me to see . . . that the Bible is the Word of God—that Christ is the only Saviour, and that it is by grace we are saved, through faith."[7]

The new vision changed Willis's life. He began to moderate the severity of political advocacy in the *Argus*, and he excerpted from other papers articles on religious subjects. He wanted to make the *Argus* an explicitly Christian newspaper, but local politicians who had backed the newspaper were opposed. Willis gave up the *Argus* and moved to Boston. He opened up a print shop there and investigated the journalistic marketplace.

Some newspapers, Willis found, were largely political and commercial, others largely church public-relations organs specializing in ecclesiastical news. Willis closely analyzed three religious weeklies in particular and would not even count them as newspapers, for "a proper newspaper. . . contains secular news, foreign and domestic, and advertisements." With coeditor Sidney Morse, Willis then produced the first issue of the *Boston Recorder* on January 3, 1816. According to the Prospectus published that

6. *New York Observer,* June 23, 1849, 98.

7. *Puritan Recorder,* October 21, 1858; quoted in Hudson, *Journalism in the United States from 1690 to 1872,* 290. Willis had had no particular theological interests and did not attend church, "but spent my Sabbaths in roving about the fields and in reading newspapers."

day, the *Recorder* was to be a newspaper with "the earliest information of all such events as mankind usually deem important," rather than a set of abstract sermonettes.[8]

Willis stuck to his plan, and did not consider it lacking in piety. He knew that news stories could be written in a way showing the consequences of sin and the need for Christ. For example, an article in 1819 headlined "Shocking Homicide" reported that a man had killed his own son after being "for a long time troubled with irreligious fears, and a belief that his sins were too numerous to be pardoned."[9] An 1820 article criticized Admiral Stephen Decatur for fighting a duel for fear of being declared a coward: he forgot "that there is no honor, which is valuable and durable, save that which comes from God."

For Willis, in his own words, all kinds of stories provided "occasion to record many signal triumphs of divine grace over the obduracy of the human heart, and over the prejudices of the unenlightened mind." The *Recorder*, he wrote, was a record of "these quickening influences of the Holy Spirit."[10]

Christian-run newspapers in other cities had similar formats and success. The *Baltimore Chronicle*, in its international coverage, described the troubles of one king: "A bloody cloud now swims before his vision, distilling blood instead of rain; the agitated monarch sees nothing but mangled limbs and bleeding bodies. . . . If Divine Providence had intended to have produced a living instance of the worthlessness of human grandeur, could a more awful example have been afforded?" The *Portland Gazette*, for its local coverage, described how two persons were killed by lightning within a house, for want of a lightning rod. It then concluded, "By such events, as well

8. *Boston Recorder,* January 3, 1816, 1.

9. Ibid., September 11, 1819, 147. (The *Recorder* produced four-page issues but numbered its pages consecutively throughout the year.)

10. Ibid., December 23, 1817, 202; August 25, 1826, 136.

as by a multitude of electrical experiments, Providence is teaching us."[11]

Christian newspapers through the mid-nineteenth century attempted to provide a biblical worldview on all aspects of life. One Ohio newspaper declared in 1858 that the Christian newspaper should be a provider of not "merely religious intelligence, but a news paper, complete in every department of general news, yet upon a religious, instead of a political or literary basis." Another, the *Northwestern Christian Advocate*, proclaimed in 1860, "Let theology, law, medicine, politics, literature, art, science, commerce, trade, architecture, agriculture—in fine, all questions which concern and secure the welfare of a people—be freely discussed and treated, and this, too, for God, for Jesus Christ, and the advancement of the Redeemer's kingdom among men."[12]

Overall, many early Christian journalists showed an awareness of how the Bible uses bad news to show us the wages of sin and to prepare us for understanding the necessity of the Good News. The journalists knew that general statements about man's corruption were far less gripping than coverage with specific detail of the results of sin and misery.

A Great Christian Newspaper: *The New York Times*

Harvard, Yale, and other universities founded by Christians now preach an atheistic gospel. A similar story could be told of some of the great newspapers of the land, including the *New York*

11. Contents of the early publications could be almost as varied as those of newspapers. One early Christian magazine became a bit carried away in describing its variety: The *New England Magazine* contained, according to the editors, "Relations Wonderful, and Psalm, and Song, / Good Sense, Wit, Humour, Morals, all ding dong; / Poems and Speeches, Politicks, and News, / What Some will like, and other Some refuse; / Births, Deaths, and Dreams, and Apparitions, too . . . To Humour Him, and Her, and Me, and You." Kenberry, *The Rise of Religious Journalism in the United States*, 64.

12. *Presbyterian of the West*, December 30, 1858; *Northwestern Christian Advocate*, November 28, 1860; quoted in Norton, *Religious Newspapers in the Old Northwest to 1861*, 2.

Times, established in 1851 by Henry Raymond, a Bible-believing Presbyterian.[13] The *Times* became known for its accurate news coverage and for its exposure in 1871 of both political corruption (the "Tweed Ring") and abortion practices. Tales of the *Times'* political exposes may be found in journalism history textbooks.[14] The abortion story is ignored, but it had a far greater long-range impact, one that shows how significant Christian journalism could be.[15]

Abortion was officially illegal but nevertheless rampant in New York City from the 1840s through the 1860s. *Times* editorials complained that the "perpetration of infant murder . . . is rank and smells to heaven."[16] But little was done about it until the *Times* sent one of its reporters, Augustus St. Clair, to carry on an undercover investigation of Manhattan's abortion businesses. For several weeks St. Clair and "a lady friend" visited the most-advertised abortionists in New York, posing as a couple in need of professional services. The result was an August 23, 1871, story headlined "The Evil of the Age."

The story began on a solemn note: "Thousands of human beings are murdered before they have seen the light of this world, and thousands upon thousands more adults are irremediably robbed in constitution, health, and happiness." St. Clair then

13. For details on Raymond, see *New York Times*, June 19, 1869, 4 (obituary); June 22, 1 (funeral); June 28, 8 (eulogy); also see Francis Brown, *Raymond of the Times* (New York: Norton, 1951), and *Augustus Maverick, Henry J. Raymond and the New York Press for Thirty Years* (Hartford: Hale, 1870).

14. See Emery and Emery, *The Press and America*, 215. When Raymond died in 1869 he was succeeded by his long-time partner George Jones in the business management of the *Times* and, after two short-lived appointments, by Louis Jennings as editor; both Jones and Jennings were Christians. When Jones turned down a $5 million bribe offered him by Boss Tweed, he said the Devil never again would offer him so high a price.

15. One pro-abortion article cited in the U.S. Supreme Court's *Roe v. Wade* decision suggests that newspaper stories contributed to a long-lasting abortion setback. See Cyril C. Means, "The Law of New York Concerning Abortion and the State of the Foetus, 1664–1968: A Case of Cessation of Constitutionality," *New York Law Forum* (Fall 1968): 458–90.

16. *New York Times*, November 3, 1870, 4.

skillfully contrasted powerlessness and power. He described the back of one abortionist's office: "Human flesh, supposed to have been the remains of infants, was found in barrels of lime and acids, undergoing decomposition." He described the affluence of a typical abortionist: "The parlors are spacious, and contain all the decorations, upholstery, cabinetware, piano, book case, etc., that is found in a respectable home."

St. Clair also listed leading abortionists by name and noted their political connections: "You have no idea of the class of people that come to us," one abortionist said. "We have had Senators, Congressmen and all sorts of politicians, bring some of the first women in the land here." St. Clair concluded with a call for change: "The facts herein set forth are but a fraction of a greater mass that cannot be published with propriety. Certainly enough is here given to arouse the general public sentiment to the necessity of taking some decided and effectual action."[17]

When the *Times* laid out the basic facts, public interest evidently was aroused, but a specific incident still was needed to galvanize readers. Tragically for a young woman, providentially for the anti-abortion effort, an ideal story of horror arrived within the week. St. Clair published his expose on August 23. On August 27 a *Times* headline at the top of page 1 read: "A Terrible Mystery."

General facts of the story were miserable enough: the nude body of a young woman was found inside a trunk in a railway station baggage room. An autopsy showed that an abortion had led to her death. The *Times* provided evocative specific detail: "This woman, full five feet in height, had been crammed into a trunk two feet six inches long. . . . Seen even in this position and rigid in death, the young girl, for she could not have been more than eighteen, had a face of singular loveliness. But her chief beauty was her great profusion of golden hair, that hung in heavy

17. Ibid.

9

folds over her shoulders, partly shrouding the face. . . . There was some discoloration and decomposition about the pelvic region. It was apparent that here was a new victim of man's lust, and the life-destroying arts of those abortionists."

Details of the exciting "trunk murder" detective story were played out in the *Times* during the next several days, as police searched for the perpetrator. Meanwhile, the *Times* reminded readers every day that this particular incident showed what went on "in one of the many abortion dens that disgrace New York, and which the TIMES had just exposed as 'The Evil of the Age.' "[18] The police arrested one of the abortionists whose advertisements had been quoted in St. Clair's story, and the *Times* followed with an editorial, "Advertising Facilities for Murder." An editorial quoted St. Clair's article, discussed the death of the "golden-haired unfortunate," and asked whether "the lives of babes are of less account than a few ounces of precious metal, or a roll of greenbacks?"[19]

The *Times* also printed a superbly written follow-up by St. Clair. "A Terrible Story from Our Reporter's Note-Book" revealed how St. Clair, in his undercover research for the expose, had visited several weeks earlier the accused abortionist's Fifth Avenue office, with its "fine tapestry carpet" and "elegant mahogany desk." St. Clair described one of the patients he had seen: "She seemed to be about twenty years of age, a little more than five feet in height, of slender build, having blue eyes, and a clear, alabaster complexion. Long blonde curls, tinted with gold, drooped upon her shoulders, and her face wore an expression of embarrassment at the presence of strangers."[20]

18. Ibid., August 28, 29, 30, 1870, 8. A boy who had helped carry the trunk into the station tried to find a man and a mysterious lady who had delivered the trunk. Readers daily absorbed the strategy of the detective in charge, Inspector Walling, who "issued orders which practically put every policeman in the force upon the case."

19. Ibid., August 29, 1870 8; August 30, 4.

20. Ibid, August 30, 1870, 8.

St. Clair then noted the abortionist's reply when St. Clair asked what would happen to the aborted infant: "Don't worry about that, my dear Sir. I will take care of the result. A newspaper bundle, a basket, a pail, a resort to the sewer, or the river at night? Who is the wiser?" On his way out, St. Clair glimpsed once again the beautiful young woman he had seen on his way in. This time, as a fitting conclusion to his story, he drove the point home: "She was standing on the stairs, and it was the same face I saw afterward at the Morgue."[21]

The abortionist received a seven-year sentence. The *Times* insisted, though, that legal action by itself was not enough. Only a change of heart among New Yorkers would bury the abortion business for several generations. Providentially, New Yorkers had been "grievously shocked by the terrible deeds of the abortionists," the *Times* could report, and it was clear that abortion would no longer receive approval.[22] Abortion continued to be considered disgraceful until the 1960s, when a much-changed *New York Times* and other newspapers began pushing pro abortion positions.

A reading of the *New York Times* through the mid-1870s shows that editors and reporters wanted to glorify God by making a difference in this world. They did not believe it inevitable that sin should dominate New York City or any other city. They were willing to be controversial. One *Times* anti-abortion editorial stated, "It is useless to talk of such matters with bated breath, or to seek to cover such terrible realities with the veil of a false

21. Ibid. What would be called today a "free press vs. fair trial" issue does emerge here: With one of its own reporters giving a firsthand account, the *Times* sometimes seemed to be convicting the abortionist in the press.

22. Ibid., December 8, 1871, 2. The *Times* did recommend passage of a bill "far-reaching enough to catch hold of all who assist, directly or indirectly, in the destruction of infant life," and gave its recommendation one additional populist thrust: "The people demand it." The New York legislature of 1872 passed tough new anti-abortion laws, with easier rules of evidence and a maximum penalty of twenty years' imprisonment. Enforcement also was stepped up.

delicacy. . . . From a lethargy like this it is time to rouse ourselves. The evil that is tolerated is aggressive."

The editorial concluded that "the good . . . must be aggressive too."[23]

Sunset for Christian Journalism

Aggressive journalism by Christians disappeared soon after one of its major successes, for four particular reasons and two underlying causes.

First, looking at the *New York Times* specifically, one generation died or departed. Owners and editors who knew not Joseph emerged. The newspaper's slogans became "It Does Not Soil the Breakfast Cloth" and "All the News That's Fit to Print." Evil unfit for breakfast table discussion or considered unfit to print was ignored and thereby tolerated. Several generations later, it was embraced.[24]

Second, many Christian publications began to prefer "happy talk" journalism. They ran stories about individuals who seemed overwhelmingly decent, cooperative, responsible, and benevolent. Such coverage hardly left the impression that man is a fallen creature desperately in need of Christ. The refusal to cover evil also led to a certain dullness of copy, because without real villains there is little real drama. The *Central Christian Herald* once ran the following news report: "There is literally nothing stirring."[25]

Third, many Christian publications refused to meet the communication demands of an increasingly fast-paced marketplace. There is a place for both popular and elite publica-

23. Ibid., November 3, 1870, 4.

24. The *New York Times* continued to run anti-abortion stories through the remainder of the century. Chapter 12 has more discussion of the overall anti-abortion campaign.

25. *Central Christian Herald*, September 2, 1852; quoted in Norton, *Religious Newspapers in the Old Northwest to 1861*, 32.

tions, and there is always a need for careful scholarship, even when short attention spans become typical. Some Christian magazines, though, seemed to pride themselves on unnecessary verbiage. The classic statement of literary arrogance was offered by the editor of one very dull magazine, *Spirit of the Pilgrims*, when he announced that "extended and labored articles" were the best kind. Readers who "are uninterested in communications of this nature," the editor wrote, "may as well give up their subscription and proceed no farther with us." *Spirit of the Pilgrims* soon went out of business.[26]

Fourth, denominational infighting was on the rise. Some newspapers spent much of their space attacking their brethren. Other newspapers, noting that splits had resulted from differences on key issues such as slavery, thought that divisions could be resolved if Christian newspapers steered away from controversial issues.

Overall, however, the problem was not particular villains, but two underlying theological trends. One was anti-Christian, one operated within Christendom, but they worked together to provoke journalistic retreat.

The outside trend is obvious: during the last two-thirds of the nineteenth century, American society generally was casting aside the Christian principles on which it had been founded. This shift affected every area of American life.

The *Boston Recorder*, located in the New England cockpit of theological liberalism, was hit very early by the great slide. It held its own against Unitarianism, which had captured Harvard College. *Recorder* editorials frequently explained the fallacy of believing in man's natural goodness, and complemented those editorials with stories showing the outworkings of original sin.[27]

---

26. Quoted in Kenberry, *The Rise of Religious Journalism in the United States*, 158.
27. See 208 of each *Recorder* volume during the 1820s for a list of such articles. See also *Recorder*, January 27, 1837, 14.

But in the mid-1830s, a new attack emerged from a peculiar merger of materialism and pantheism.

The threat had grown for a long time. Rousseau, Kant, and other purveyors of intellectual romanticism—the idea that man's reason did not have to operate within God's revelation, but could actually create truth out of its own resources—had long been read at Harvard and absorbed by Unitarian ministers. But Harvard's alternative to Christianity seemed cold until 1836. In that year Ralph Waldo Emerson's essay "Nature" appeared, and the Transcendental Club, composed of young Unitarian preachers, began meeting at the parsonage of George Ripley, who later became an editor of the *New York Tribune*.

Emerson laid out the Transcendentalist challenge in "Nature," and more precisely in his 1838 speech at the Harvard Divinity School. Christianity, he said, speaks "with noxious exaggeration about the person of Jesus," instead of emphasizing "the moral nature of man, where the sublime is." Humanity, Emerson proclaimed, "is drinking forever the soul of God" and becoming Godlike itself. Speak no further of man's sin and his responsibility before God, Emerson suggested: man is God, or at least part of God, because a little bit of godstuff is sprinkled everywhere.[28]

If God is everywhere in Emerson's sense, though, God is nowhere. Theoretical pantheism could merge nicely with practical materialism. Transcendental thinking was spread in magazines such as *Dial* and then popularized through non-Christian newspapers and the new public school systems set up by Unitarian Horace Mann and his disciples. There was no need to report on "God's providence" if news events arose from a combination of natural chance and man's godlike skill. The movement away from Christianity was heightened after midcentury when

28. Emerson's address is published in many books, including Volume 5 of the *Harvard Classics*, ed. Charles Eliot (New York: Collier, 1937), 25–42.

Charles Darwin provided a convenient way to satisfy the long-felt desire of haughty hearts.[29]

Following the traumatic Civil War, even editors of some Christian publications succumbed to intellectual trendiness. For example, editor Lyman Abbott of the *Christian Union*, a large-circulation weekly newspaper of the 1870s, decided that the Bible was fable rather than fact. He became known for attacking God's sovereignty in the name of Darwin. With the support of others similarly swayed, Abbott eventually took Christianity out of the magazine's title as well as its pages, with the name becoming *Outlook* in 1893. By that time, other anti-Christian doctrines—Marxism and a general emphasis on "science" as mankind's savior—had kicked in also, or soon would.[30]

And yet, just as those trends were gaining power, a counter influence was developing. The period of great advances for anti-Christian thought also was a great era of revivals. During the last two-thirds of the nineteenth century, God used great evangelists such as Charles Finney and Dwight Moody to expound the gospel of grace to millions. Many were saved through their preaching. Many also learned, as Proverbs 1:7 notes, that "the fear of the LORD is the beginning of knowledge" and wisdom. They thus stayed clear of belief in evolutionary or Marxist scriptures.[31]

29. This chapter has room to mention only in passing the major theological and social developments. It does not attempt to be anything more than a quick overview. For general discussions of the period, see Perry Miller, *The Life of the Mind in America: From the Revolution to the Civil War* (New York: Harcourt, Brace and World, 1965), and Sydney E. Ahlstrom, *A Religious History of the American People* (New Haven: Yale University Press, 1972). For a discussion of Unitarianism and the public schools, see Samuel Blumenfeld, *Is Public Education Necessary?* (Boise: Paradigm, 1985). For a discussion of the impact of evolutionism, see appendices to Gary North, *The Dominion Covenant* (Tyler, TX: Institute for Christian Economics, 1982), 245–454.

30. Abbott's books include *The Evolution of Christianity* (Boston: Houghton Mifflin, 1900); *The Other Room* (New York: Grosset, Dunlap, 1903); *Christianity and Social Problems* (New York: Houghton Mifflin, 1896); and *Reminiscences* (Boston: Houghton Mifflin, 1915).

31. This discussion of Christian trends is, again, just a quick overview. For further information and perspective, see George Marsden, *The Evangelical Mind and the New*

Revivalism, though, did not particularly help those Christian newspapers that were endeavoring to cover every aspect of God's creation and perhaps "stir up the mind of Christians to duty." The great revivalists' focus on evangelism tended to be specifically individualistic. Worldview was not stressed. Furthermore, many Christians began to believe that the general culture inevitably would become worse and worse. They thought that little could be done to stay the downward drift. Christian publications should cover church news, they thought, and ignore the rest of the world.[32] The anti-Christian trend and separatistic Christian reaction combined to end the Christian presence in newsrooms. Journalists who embraced materialism and/or pantheism advanced in newspaper and magazine work. Christians who embraced separatistic revivalism retreated. Some Christian newspapers may have died after being overrun, but many evacuated the social realm without ever engaging the invading forces.

The general result of these two underlying movements—revivalism and separatism within the church, and an increasing materialism and pantheism without—was neglect of the Reformational idea of Christ as Lord of all of life. Relations of ministry and laity, and of sabbatical and general church activities, also were affected. Calvin and other leaders of the Protestant Reformation had argued that good work outside the pulpit glorified

---

School Presbyterian Experience (New Haven: Yale University Press, 1970); Timothy L. Smith, *Revivalism and Social Reform in Mid-Nineteenth-Century America* (Nashville: Abingdon Press, 1957); James F. Findlay Jr., *Dwight L. Moody: American Evangelist, 1837–1899* (Chicago: University of Chicago Press, 1969); John Woodbridge, Mark Noll, and Nathan Hatch, *The Gospel in America* (Grand Rapids: Zondervan, 1979).

32. As historian George Marsden has noted in *Fundamentalism and American Culture* (London: Oxford University Press, 1980), the 1860–1900 period brought with it "a transition from a basically 'Calvinistic' tradition, which saw politics as a significant means to advance the kingdom, to a 'pietistic' view of political action as no more than a means to restrain evil." This movement led to what Marsden calls the "Great Reversal" early in the twentieth century, with social concerns becoming suspect among revivalist evangelicals. Meanwhile, the older Reformed concern for social action was transmuted into a "social gospel" clung to by many who no longer held to the biblical gospel.

God as much as the activities of the ministry proper.[33] But as views of inevitable cultural decay began to grip nineteenth-century American Protestantism, some editors began to consider journalism inferior to preaching. The editor of one Ohio newspaper said that "the work of a Christian minister" was far more important than the work of an editor.[34]

As Christian publications became less significant, selection of editors became more haphazard. Often those who could, preached, while those who could not, edited—and the latter knew that they were considered second-class Christians. One minister thrown into an editor's chair in Cincinnati wrote: "I had never seen a newspaper made up. . . . I was stunned by the cry of 'copy!' 'copy!' " That newspaper ceased publication when a follow-up editor took a vacation and never came back. The editor of the *Southern Christian Advocate* proclaimed that it was better to "wander through the earth on foot, preaching Christianity, than to be the editor of a religious newspaper."[35]

33. See Abraham Kuyper, *Lectures on Calvinism* (1899; repr. Grand Rapids, MI: Eerdmans, 1983). Also see Henry Van Til, *The Calvinistic Concept of Culture* (Grand Rapids: Baker, 1959), and John T. McNeill, *The History and Character of Calvinism* (London: Oxford University Press, 1954). Primarily, see John Calvin, *Institutes of the Christian Religion*, 1559 ed., trans. Ford Lewis Battles, ed. John T. McNeill (Philadelphia: The Westminster Press, 1960).

34. Norton, *Religious Newspapers in the Old Northwest to 1861*, 38.

35. Just as the *Boston Recorder* had been one of the first to see the entire society as a journalistic mission field, so it was one of the first to drop out under the twin pressures of Boston transcendentalism and the tendency to turn inward. Circulation during the 1840s was stagnant at a time when non-Christian newspapers were soaring. A *Recorder* editorial in 1848 suggesting "encouraging prospects" for the newspaper was belied by both appearance and context. Type size was smaller, typography was muddy, and page size had decreased. Those pages were filled with monthly, quarterly, and annual reports of various church groups, indicating clearly that the *Recorder* had died as a newspaper and had become a public relations organ. In 1849 the *Recorder* officially merged with the *Puritan*, a ten-year-old newspaper. Examination of one advertisement in the last issue of the *Recorder*, though, makes the agreement seem more like a subscription list buyout than a merger. The little notice, placed by the *Recorder* itself, offered "the type and other printing materials which are now used in this office—the whole comprising all the fixtures of a weekly newspaper establishment." *Recorder*, January 7, 1848, 2; May 4, 1849, 71.

Sometimes it even seemed that a sense of "Whew! Glad I'm saved!" had replaced a strong sense of God's sovereignty over all areas of human life. The theological vision of social defeatism and separatism had some immediate practical consequences. With many Christian journalists hiding their light under a bushel, the newspaper field was wide open for the triumph of "yellow journalism" at the end of the nineteenth century, and the expulsion of God from the front page early in the twentieth.[36] By 1925, Christians often were voiceless, except in publications that largely preached to the choir.

The almost total dominance of major newspapers by non-Christians showed up in the way they covered news stories generally, and major news stories with obvious theological dimensions in particular. One of the most striking involved coverage of a 1925 trial that divided believers in the biblical account of creation from those who had made their peace with materialism, pantheism, or some combination of the two.[37]

Journalistic Monkeys

Two faiths were in conflict at that Dayton, Tennessee, "monkey trial." The *New York Times*, greatly changed from the 1870s, editorialized for "faith, even of a grain of mustard seed, in the

36. An interesting test arose in 1899 and 1900, when international attention was focused on the battle in South Africa between the Boers and the British. Race was not an issue at the time, since neither side spoke much of the black inhabitants; the issue was social Darwinist "progress," and to the *New York Times* the Boers seemed least likely to succeed, due to their fundamentalist religious beliefs. "Poor, hidebound, Bible reading, otherwise illiterate Boers," the *New York Times* sniffed. The Boers' religion, according to the *Times*, makes them a "very stubborn people . . . in a state of arrested development. They are not much different from the Dutch of this island two centuries ago. That is to say, they are simple minded, Bible-reading, God-fearing people" with an "idiotic-heroic attitude" (August 24, 1899, 6; August 10, 1899, 6).

37. *New York Times*, July 26, 1925, Section 2, 4. Leslie H. Allen, ed., *Bryan and Darrow at Dayton: The Record and Documents of the Bible-Evolution Trial* (New York: Russell & Russell, 1925), 1, conveniently assembles materials against which press reports may be checked.

evolution of life. . . ." Realizing that only two ways led upward from sin and misery—God's grace or man's evolution—a *Times* editorial stated that evolution offered the most hope: "If man has evolved, it is inconceivable that the process should stop and leave him in his present imperfect state. Specific creation has no such promise for man."[38] That faith ran up against Christian faith in God's sovereignty and the hope offered by Christ's sacrifice.

The events leading up to perhaps the most famous trial of the twentieth century began when Tennessee legislators passed a law forbidding the teaching of evolution as scientific truth. The battle was joined when one young Dayton teacher, John T. Scopes, responded to an American Civil Liberties Union plea for someone to agree to be the defendant in a test case, with the ACLU paying all legal expenses. Clarence Darrow, the most famous lawyer of the era, and an atheist, headed the defense. William Jennings Bryan, thrice-defeated Democratic presidential candidate, former Secretary of State, and a fundamentalist Christian, became point man for the prosecution.

The issue and the superstars brought out the journalists. More than one hundred reporters came to the trial. They wired 165,000 words daily to their newspapers during the twelve days of extensive coverage in July 1925. In theory, trial coverage could have been an opportunity to illuminate the theological debate that lay behind the creation versus evolution issue. But in practice, with few if any Christians among those reporters, the position established early on by columnist H. L. Mencken went largely

38. The importance of the Dayton trial, for both prosecution and defense, lay in the chance to debate the issues of the case. The judicial proceedings themselves were not of great interest. The case was open-and-shut, deliberately designed for conviction on obvious lawbreaking so that the decision could be appealed to the U.S. Supreme Court for a ruling on the act's constitutionality. (Ironically, although Scopes was convicted, as planned by the ACLU, and although the anti-evolution law itself was upheld by the Tennessee Supreme Court, the Tennessee Supreme Court also overturned the conviction on a technicality involving the imposition of a $100 fine without jury approval.)

unchallenged: "On the one side was bigotry, ignorance, hatred, superstition, every sort of blackness that the human mind is capable of. On the other side was sense."[39]

Journalists from major city newspapers saw the story as one of evolutionist intelligence versus creationist stupidity. Nunnally Johnson, who covered the trial for the *Brooklyn Eagle* and then became a noted Hollywood screenwriter, remembered years later, "For the newspapermen it was a lark on a monstrous scale. . . . Being admirably cultivated fellows, they were all of course evolutionists and looked down on the local fundamentalists." Such ridicule was not merely a function of geography or politics. Both liberal and conservative newspapers lambasted the creationists. Journalists constantly attacked the theology of the creationists, perhaps because it was something their cultures had only recently "outgrown."[40]

39. *Baltimore Sun*, July 9, 1925, 1. Mencken attacked the Dayton creationists (before he had set foot in the town) as "local primates . . . yokels . . . morons . . . half-wits." Mencken put aside his typical amusement with life to ride Paul Revere-like through the land with dire warnings about the trial: "Let no one mistake it for comedy, farcical though it may be in all its details. It serves notice on the country that Neanderthal man is organizing in these forlorn backwaters of the land, led a by a fanatic, rid of sense and devoid of conscience" (*Baltimore Sun*, July 18, 1925, 1).

Mencken's intolerance was parallel to that of many pro-evolution spokesmen. Columbia University dean Henry H. Rusby demanded that universities not recognize degrees from universities that did not accept evolution. A leading liberal minister, Charles Francis Potter, argued that "educated and enlightened men ought not to rest until the possibility of such dense mental darkness is removed." The *New York Times* then editorialized against "the mental and moral infection which has been let loose upon the land" (*New York Times*, July 12, 1925, section 1, 2; *Arkansas Gazette*, June 16, 1925, 2). Fundamentalists had some justification for believing that they were being told not "live and let live," but "your diseased religion does not deserve to exist."

40. Acid-tongued Westbrook Pegler, who covered the trial briefly, admired Mencken and imitated his coverage, but noted years later concerning the creationists, "They were intelligent people, including a fair proportion of college graduates. Nevertheless, the whole Blue Ridge country was ridiculed on religious grounds by an enormous claque of supercilious big town reporters." Such ridicule was not primarily a function of politics. It underlay the politics of liberal and conservative newspapers. The liberal *New York Times* editorialized that the creationist position presented a "breakdown of the reasoning powers. It is seeming evidence that the human mind can go into deliquescence without falling into stark lunacy" (July 13, 1925, 16). The conservative

The *New York Times* even noted at one point "a certain unexpectedness in the behavior and talk of the Dayton people. The unexpectedness comes from the absence in these Dayton people of any notable dissimilarity from people elsewhere except in their belated clinging to a method of Scriptural interpretation that not long ago was more than common in both North and South." The *Times* writer in those two sentences understood that fundamentalist beliefs were far from bizarre. In fact, the newer method of scriptural interpretation had been regarded as bizarre in Times Square as well as Tennessee only a short time before.[41]

The Christian exile from mainline journalism—the absence of salt—led to poor reporting. The evolutionists, without anyone to check them, wrote that Christians were trying to make one pro-evolution book "a book of evil tidings, to be studied in secret."[42] This was nonsense. Hundreds of pro-evolution writings were on sale in Dayton. Even a drugstore had a stack of materials representing all positions. John Butler, the legislator who introduced the anti-evolution bill, had a copy of Darwin's *The Origin of the Species* for his teenage children to read. He told reporters, "I am not opposed to teaching of evolution, but I don't think it ought to be taught in state-supported schools."[43]

The key issue, clearly, was not free speech, but parental control over school curricula. Even in Tennessee, Christian parents were already beginning to sense that their beliefs were being excluded from schools they were funding. William Jennings Bryan spoke for them when he said he "never advocated teaching the Bible in public schools," but believed "school children should . . . hear of Bible characters as well as other characters. In other words, there is no reason why

Chicago Tribune sneered at fundamentalists looking for "horns and forked tails and cloven hoofs" (July 19, 1925, 5).

41. *New York Times*, July 20, 1925, 14.

42. *Arkansas Gazette*, July 18, 1925, 5.

43. *Baltimore Sun*, July 10, 1925, 1. Also see *Atlanta Constitution*, July 9, 1925, 10.

the reading of the Bible should be excluded while the reading of books about other characters in history, like Confucius, should be permitted."[44]

Tennessee legislators saw their anti-evolution bill not as a way of putting Christian religion into the schools, but of forbidding proselytizing for what they saw as a trendy but unproved evolutionary faith. Tennessee Governor Peay opposed the uncritical acceptance of evolutionary material "that no science has established."[45] One anti-evolutionary organization called itself the Defenders of True Science versus Speculation, contending that evolution "is a theory not yet approved by science," particularly since species-transitional fossils ("missing links") had not been found. "Demonstrated truth," Bryan insisted, "has no terrors for Christianity."[46]

Journalists, instead of explaining that, wrote leads such as "Tennessee today maintained its quarantine against learning." The battle was "rock-ribbed Tennessee" versus "unfettered investigation by the human mind and the liberty of opinion of which the Constitution makers preached." Reporters regularly attacked Christian faith and "this superheated religious atmosphere, this pathetic search for the 'eternal truth.' "[47]

One journalist described Scopes, the teacher-defendant, as an imprisoned martyr, "the witch who is to be burned by Dayton." (Actually, Scopes did not spend a second in jail and received regular dinner invitations from Dayton Christians.) If the creationists win, another wrote, "The dunce cap will be the crown of office, and the slopstick will be the sceptre of authority." Residents of Dayton were "the treewise monkeys" who "see

44. *Arkansas Gazette*, July 12, 1. Also see *Arkansas Gazette*, June 23, 1925, 1, and June 28, 1925, 1; *Washington Post*, July 16, 1925, 6.

45. *Arkansas Gazette*, June 27, 1925, 1.

46. *Atlanta Constitution*, July 2, 1925, 1; July 8, 1925, 22.

47. *New York American*, July 18, 1925, 1; July 14, 1925, 1; *Arkansas Gazette* (New York Times/Chicago Tribune news service), July 16, 1925, 3.

no logic, speak no logic and hear no logic." When William Jennings Bryan Jr., an attorney, arrived for the trial, a columnist wrote, "Junior is bound to be a chip off the old blockhead. . . . Like father, like son, and we don't like either."[48]

Dayton jurors, who following the trial gave thoughtful accounts of the proceedings, were described in one New York headline: "Intelligence of Most of Lowest Grade." It seemed that "All twelve are Protestant churchgoers."[49]

Reporters did not even cover accurately the debates between creationists and evolutionists. For instance, when Bryan debated Darrow's associate Dudley Malone on July 16, the court transcript shows strong and intelligent orations by both sides. Bryan, within Christian presuppositions, made a sophisticated and coherent argument. He stressed the evolutionary theory's lack of scientific proof and emphasized its inability to answer questions about how life began, how man began, how one species actually changes into another, and so on. He pointed out the irreconcilability of Darwinian doctrines of extra-species evolution with the biblical account of creation, original sin, and the reasons for Christ's coming.[50]

Malone stated the evolutionist position in a similarly cohesive way. Both sides apparently did well. But journalists wrote that Bryan's speech "was a grotesque performance and downright touching in its imbecility."[51] Reporters often salted their stories with sarcastic biblical allusions: "Dayton began to read a new book of revelations today. The wrath of Bryan fell at last. With whips of scorn . . . he sought to drive science from the temples of God and failed."[52] According to the *Chicago Tribune*, the debate proved that "the truth as

48. *New York American*, July 13, 1925, 1; July 15, 1925, 4; July 16, 1925, 2; July 17, 1925, 2.
49. *New York American*, July 12, 1925, 1; see also *Arkansas Gazette*, July 11, 1.
50. See Allen, ed., *Bryan and Darrow at Dayton*.
51. *Baltimore Sun*, July 17, 1925, 1.
52. *Arkansas Gazette*, July 12, 1925, 1; July 13, 1925, 1; July 17, 1925, 3.

applied to man's origin was not locked in a book in the days of Moses."[53]

Overall, most major newspaper reporters produced so many unobservant stories that it often seemed as if they were closing their eyes and not even seeing the trial at all. The ultimate in this came when one New York scribe, under the headline "Scopes Is Seen as New Galileo at Inquisition," wrote that the "sultry court-room in Dayton, during a pause in the argument, became hazy and there evolved from the mists of past ages a new scene. The Tennessee judge disappeared and I racked my brain to recognize the robed dignitary on the bench. Yes, it was the grand inquisitor, the head of the inquisition at Rome. . . . I saw the Tennessee Fundamentalist public become a medieval mob thirsty for heretical blood. . . . [It was] 1616. The great Galileo was on trial."[54]

It seemed that most reporters in Dayton, even when they tried to be fair—some had no such intention—could not help seeing the atheistic side as plausible and the Christian view as "nonsensical." The life and beliefs of one of the best of the Scopes trial reporters, Raymond Clapper, shows the pattern. In 1912, ready to enter college, he was leading Presbyterian church meetings in Kansas. But after four years at the University of Kansas, he chose "a more reasonable belief." By 1923 Clapper and his wife had "discarded the orthodox teachings of our youth. We could not believe the Old Testament prophets, whose teachings no doubt fitted well the savage age in which they lived but suited

53. *Chicago Tribune.* See also *Arkansas Gazette*, July 14, 1925, 5.

54. *New York American*, July 14, 1925, 1. One more bizarre twist to the trial deserves mentioning. The last Bryan-Darrow confrontation arose unexpectedly on the final day of the trial. Many reporters were off swimming or carousing, with the result that other reporters, after telegraphing their own stories, hastily rewrote parts and sent them to the missing reporters' newspapers in order to cover for their friends. Several reporters asked Scopes himself to write parts of the new articles; so journalistic coverage of the trial concluded with a bizarre touch: the defendant reporting on his own case under someone else's byline. See John T. Scopes and James Presley, *Center of the Storm: Memoirs of John T. Scopes* (New York: Holt, Rinehart and Winston, 1967), 183.

our world no better than the Greek oracles. The story of Christ we thought was moving and beautiful but we could not accept the virgin birth or the resurrection."[55]

Before Clapper arrived in Dayton to cover the trial, his mind already was made up. He believed "the whole case of fundamentalism [was] ridiculous." It was no surprise, then, when Clapper's stories argued that "fundamentalist justice has plugged up the ears of this Tennessee mountain jury." Olive Clapper, his wife, argued that "unbelievable as the trial was to intelligent people, it did have value because the end result was greater enlightenment of people on the subject of evolution." Clapper had done his best to provide that enlightenment.[56] The Clapper story could be repeated many times. Journalists who were or had become opposed to the Bible wanted to teach readers the anti-Christian "truth" as they saw it. There was no one to counterbalance their emphases, because Christians no longer had much of a presence in American journalism. Yes, there were denominational magazines and church newsletters, but coverage of major events such as the Scopes trial was in the hands of those who might be ever watching but never seeing.[57]

Mainline news coverage in the United States is still in those hands, as the next chapter will indicate.

55. Olive Clapper, *One Lucky Woman* (Garden City, NY: Doubleday, 1961), 34, 51, 109.
56. Ibid., 99.
57. The *Atlanta Constitution* editorialized about the trial coverage's potential effect: "Thousands of columns of newspaper debate have been published under Dayton date lines in the past two weeks, and from it all the cause of the religion of Jesus Christ has not been helped, but the world has been broadcast with the seeds of doubt and skepticism, and only the future can tell what the harvest will be . . . among the millions of people who congest the bumper ground between science and the Bible there may be thousands who will now find themselves drifting into the easy-going channels of agnosticism" (July 22, 1925, 6).

2 Spiking the Spiritual

Amcrican journalists and their critics have engaged in a lively liberal versus conservative debate over the past two decades. The number of books and articles about the tilt to the left at mainline media institutions has multiplied.[1] But a far more crucial type of bias has been ignored almost entirely.

As noted in chapter 1, much of American journalism until the mid-nineteenth century emphasized God's sovereignty and man's responsibility. Kings who disobeyed God were exposed as sinful. Duelists were without honor because they thought esteem among men more important than following God's commands. Lightning storms taught spiritual lessons. Lack of repentance had murderous consequences. One minister said he enjoyed opening up the newspaper to see what God had done that day.[2]

1. Some of the best books with a conservative perspective: Russ Braley, *Bad News: The Foreign Policy of the* New York Times (Chicago: Regnery, 1984); Tom Kelly, *The Imperial Post* (New York: William Morrow, 1983); James Tyson, *Target America* (Chicago: Regnery, 1981); Philip Lawler, *The Alternative Influence* (Lanham, MD: University Press of America, 1984); Herman Dinsmore, *All the News That Fits* (New Rochelle: Arlington House, 1969); Leopold Tyrmand, *The Media Shangri-La* (Rockford, IL: Rockford College Institute, 1975); Jim Kuypers, *Press Bias and Politics: How the Media Frame Controversial Issues* (Westport, CT: Praeger, 2002); Bernard Goldberg, *Bias* (New York: Harper Perennial, 2003). Many book chapters—for instance, "The Media, Shield of the Utopians," in Rael Jean Isaac and Erich Isaac, *The Coercive Utopians* (Chicago: Regnery, 1984)—provide valuable perspective, as do essays by Irving Kristol, Paul Weaver, and others in back issues of *Public Interest*. In 1987 Reed Irvine's Accuracy in Media newsletter and Tom Bethell's monthly columns in *American Spectator* continued to provide useful and provocative criticism.

2. *Boston Recorder,* July 10, 1819, 116; March 15, 1823, 41; and other issues from the two decades beginning in 1816.

Non-Christian journalists who came to dominate newspapers following the departure of Christians tended to put out a very different kind of product. These editors did not explicitly ban God from the front page. Instead, they redefined "reality" to exclude the spiritual realm. For earlier editors, material and spiritual aspects of the world were both important. They knew that comprehensive news stories and news analysis require reporting of the workings of Providence, as best we can understand them. But many editors of the past century have tried to publish God's obituary.

The Bible provides excellent examples of complete news coverage, coverage that takes into account both material and spiritual. News reports circulated immediately after the parting of the Red Sea (Ex. 15) or the defeat of the Canaanites (Judg. 8) noted the interaction of spiritual and material forces. The book of Job's report of a sensational disaster story—family wiped out, house smashed by tornado, herds stolen, and so on—is introduced by a dialogue in heaven between God and Satan that is essential to an understanding of the drama below. One realm is no more "real" than the other. Both heaven and earth are fact.

Earthly reporters, of course, cannot know exactly what is going on in heaven. Inspired biblical reporting is greater than anything we can produce. But Christians do know there is a spiritual realm as well as an earthly one, and activities in the spiritual realm do influence the origin and outcome of news stories on earth. Christians know four spiritual facts that are essential to understanding earthly news events:

- God is sovereign, so events do not happen by chance. Obedience to God brings blessings. Disobedience brings curses. The blessings and curses may not always be apparent immediately.

- Satan is active in the world, intent on doing evil. Since events on earth are subsets of a larger battle between God and Satan, we may not know why certain events occur.

- Because of the ravages of sin, man without God's grace is prone to do evil. Yet, the redemption brought about by Christ's sacrifice is real. It gives Christians not only eternal salvation, but the power to fight Satan's attempts to rule this world.

- God answers prayers. He does so not by making us feel better psychologically, but by actually transforming earthly situations, not always in the way we expect.

Few reporters now accept this spiritual reality as a necessary backdrop to stories, because most reporters define fact to include only the material. The result has been incomplete reporting. If, for example, we apply only the last of the spiritual facts listed above—God answers prayer—there emerges a different way of covering one of the major stories of 1986, the overthrow of Ferdinand Marcos in the Philippines.

The *New York Times*, ignoring its Christian origins once again, covered the material facts. But an article in the *Evangelical Beacon* by Robert Carey told a much deeper story: "Christians of all persuasions had been uniting in fervent prayer before, during and after the election. . . . Many churches held all-night prayer meetings. Others met for special times of prayer in homes or churches. . . . There is, I believe, no way to explain the events we have witnessed apart from answered prayer."

There was, of course, another means of explanation, that used by the *Times*: count the tanks and guns, and estimate popular support for each side. But Carey in his report asked a series of hard questions:

- "What accounted for the fact that the military forces did not overrun the crowds? They had sufficient tear gas and water cannons to disperse the people."

- "What kept hundreds of thousands of people from becoming a wild, uncontrolled mob? What held their emotions in check?"

- "What enabled President Marcos to exercise restraint and keep cool when his top military man called for action to attack and neutralize the rebel forces?"

- "What enabled the crowds to show kindness and offer food and drink to their 'enemies' in the government forces?"[3]

Carey concluded, "As I lay in bed listening to the radio through my headset during the wee hours of the morning, I heard an evangelical leader asking people to get up and wake their families and pray during a particularly crucial period. On two such occasions I woke [my wife] and we prayed together for God to control the situation. The same thing was taking place in thousands of households across Manila and throughout the Philippines. . . . And God answered prayer."[4]

Carey's reporting was moving, and the outcome of these events defy materialistic explanation. The country avoided a civil war. In what became known as the People Power Revolution, Corazon Aquino became president and set in motion a series of reforms that transformed the country. The country ratified a constitution in 1987. The constitution restored the presidency and established a bicameral congress. The country still struggles to erase the consequences of decades of dictatorship and corruption, but it is on a very different path than the one it was on in 1986, when civil war was a real and present threat.

3. *Evangelical Beacon*, April 1986, 20.
4. Ibid.

The Bible tells us that events happen not just because of individual or national sin or faith, but for God's glory. We now know that those who spiked the spiritual by refusing to recognize the mystery of the Philippine crisis—that something outside of what we perceive as the usual chain of events happened there—missed a major story.[5]

Carey's story, then, was different from that of the *New York Times*: different not only in interpretation of events but different in selection of details. A former *Times* editor, Lester Markel, described his newspaper's reporting and editing process by explaining that

> the reporter, the most objective reporter, collects fifty facts. Out of the fifty facts he selects twelve to include in his story (there is such a thing as space limitation). Thus he discards thirty-eight. This is Judgment Number One.
>
> Then the reporter or editor decides which of the facts shall be the first paragraph of the story, thus emphasizing one fact above the other eleven. This is Judgment Number Two. Then the editor decides whether the story shall be placed on Page One or Page Twelve; on Page One it will command many times the attention it would on Page Twelve. This is Judgment Number Three. This so-called factual presentation is thus subjected to three judgments, all of them most humanly and most ungodly made.[6]

Markel's description of the "ungodly" process is generalizable. Reporters and editors, like all of us, are always making choices. *New York Times* reporters in the Philippines, if they were pounding the pavements or even listening to local radio, had to be aware of what Filipinos were calling "prayer power," but

5. Ibid. Our only totally reliable source of information and perspective is God's revealed will. Since Christians have been fooled before about international developments and leaders, it is vital not to leap to conclusions.

6. Quoted in William Rivers, *The Opinionmakers* (Boston: Beacon Press, 1965), 43.

they evidently saw that set of activities as relatively insignificant. Robert Carey was clearly aware of the military and public opinion configurations, but he considered those facts to be of secondary importance.

Many major American journalists prefer, for three reasons, the materialistic accounts of the *Times* to the spiritual/material accounts of Carey.

First, many would say that the *Times* is objective, but the Bible points out that all descriptions of human activities are based on certain convictions as to the nature of the universe. Readers of every news story are receiving information but are also being taught, subtly or explicitly, a particular worldview, whether it is theistic, pantheistic, materialistic, or whatever.

In philosophical terms, newspapers offer not only phenomena, but noumena: not only facts learned from study, but an infrastructure that gives meaning to the facts. The *Detroit Free Press* offered its readers a typical newspaper report on urban crime. Introductory facts and anecdotes were immediately followed by a list of "things that spur killings . . . stress, joblessness, poverty, guns, and subcultures of violence." Sin went unmentioned.[7]

The key line of defense for most journalists would be the second: that the *New York Times*, in describing material, was describing fact. Anyone, regardless of his theology, can see or touch the tanks and guns. Therefore the tanks and guns were really there, while the spiritual world cannot be seen or touched by many people, so it might not be there.

And yet, without diving too deeply into the philosophical black hole of epistemology (how we know things), we could say that the tanks and guns were not dependent for their existence

7. *Detroit Free Press*, June 15, 1986, B1. For an excellent discussion of presuppositionalism, see Cornelius Van Til, *The Defense of the Faith* (Philadelphia: Presbyterian and Reformed Publishing Co., 1955).

on the ability of reporters to see or touch them. If all reporters were blind and deprived of their other senses as well—in which case, obviously, they would be inadequate reporters—the tanks and guns would still have been there.

The Bible makes a similar point about spiritual things. Paul writes in Romans 1:20, "For his invisible attributes, namely, his eternal power and divine nature, have been clearly perceived, ever since the creation of the world, in the things that have been made." That some do not see has no more to do with the factuality of the matter than the absence of sight or touch in some has to do with the factuality of tanks.

Psalm 19:1–4 discusses this crucial point more poetically: "The heavens declare the glory of God, the sky above proclaims his handiwork. Day to day pours out speech, and night to night reveals knowledge. There is no speech, nor are there words, whose voice is not heard. Their voice goes out through all the earth, and their words to the end of the world." Many reporters do not acknowledge God's glory. They develop convoluted interpretations to avoid admitting that creation is his. But, as Romans 1:20 notes, they are without excuse.

Just because reporters do not see spiritual things, or admit to seeing spiritual things, does not mean that spirit is not fact. John Newton, a slave trader who became a Christian, wrote of differential sight two centuries ago: "Amazing grace, how sweet the sound, that saved a wretch like me. I once was lost, but now am found, was blind, but now I see."[8]

Reporters might say that everyone with normal senses can experience tanks, but not everyone with normal senses can experience spirit—yet what makes us think our senses are normal? The Bible says they are abnormal apart from God's grace, since man's fall from the garden of Eden onward has cut us off from natural perception of the spiritual. The Bible also tells us that

8. "Amazing Grace," 1779.

33

man's decision to suppress the truth by ignoring the spiritual is a conscious, deliberate result of sin and guilt.

The third, fall-back defense of journalists who defend the reporting of material fact and the spiking of the spiritual is journalistic tradition, backed up by their own personal sense that the tradition is right. Reporters are right to assert that tradition is now on the antispiritual side. Let's look at a few examples of the ways in which materialist reporters have missed stories of man's sin and redemption, God's sovereignty, and Satan's activities.

Ignoring Facts of Sin and Redemption

Whittaker Chambers and Alger Hiss were the two major figures in a big story of the late 1940s.[9] Chambers was a former Communist Party member and spy who had become a Christian. He gave investigators solid evidence (unlike most of that produced by Joseph McCarthy during the 1950s) of Soviet espionage in the State Department. Alger Hiss was a former State Department official with favorable recommendations in his file from presidents, Supreme Court justices, and dozens of other leaders. Chambers charged that Hiss had been a spy, and produced microfilm and other evidence to back up his accusations.

9. Whittaker Chambers, a senior editor of *Time*, testified that he had been a courier during the 1930s between Soviet officials and several Roosevelt Administration officials who had agreed, for ideological reasons, to copy secret documents and have them delivered to the Soviets. One Administration official, Julian Wadleigh, confessed his role. Others had died or, when called to testify, took the Fifth Amendment.

One of the accused, Alger Hiss, denied having been a Communist Party member, initially denied ever knowing Chambers, and later admitted an acquaintance but denied any participation in espionage. Hiss's alleged complicity was front-page news because he had been a highly placed State Department official during the 1930s and most of the 1940s, and had then left the State Department to accept a prestigious position as head of the Carnegie Endowment for World Peace.

Hiss stayed on the front pages for the next year and a half because he continued to deny any involvement with the Soviets, even as Chambers produced copies of secret State Department documents with Hiss's initials on them, and so on. Eventually a jury found Hiss guilty of perjury.

Washington Post reporters, for two reasons, refused to believe Chambers' charges, even when the evidence became overwhelming. One reason apparently was economic: Chambers was casting doubts on not only the integrity of Hiss but the management of the federal bureaucracy generally. The growth of that bureaucracy, Washington's major industry, was crucial to the *Post*'s economic future. The *Post* regularly sprang to the defense of that industry just as newspapers in other cities tended to protect their own.[10]

The second reason, judging from *Post* articles, was theological. Reporters evidently did not understand that the ravages of sin had turned Hiss into a traitor. Nor did they see that the grace of redemption propelled Chambers to leave a comfortable job to become a witness against communism.[11]

Chambers tried to teach the reporters. He told them of the true evil of communism (not just mistake, or misfortune, or trying too hard to make progressive changes, but satanic evil). He described the true grace of God (not just existing in some abstract form, but actively changing men's hearts and creating

10. For examples of reporter's bias, see John Chabot Smith, *Alger Hiss: The True Story* (New York: Holt, Rinehart and Winston, 1976), 293, and Chalmers Roberts, *The* Washington Post: *The First 100 Years* (Boston: Houghton Mifflin, 1977), 277. This relationship between the growth of government bureaucracy and the economic health of the city's newspaper shows up in cities all across America. In most big cities in the United States, the local government (including the school system) is the largest employer. Local governments, who must purchase legal advertisements and often have advertising budgets for their programs, are also often among a newspaper's largest advertisers. In state capital cities, the alignment of economic interests of newspapers and the bureaucracies they cover is even more profound. This phenomenon helps explain why most big-city dailies favor government solutions to problems, why most big-city mayors are Democrats, and why most urban core counties in the U.S. vote Democrat even if they are in a deeply Republican state.

11. Whittaker Chambers, *Witness* (New York: Random House, 1952), 9. See also *Washington Post*, July 7, 1949, 1, 11; November 24, 1949, 6. Other Christians with well-publicized records of misconduct who have been "born again" since then—for example, Charles Colson and Eldridge Cleaver—have had to run a similar media gauntlet. While it is important to test over time the firmness of faith among new believers, utter hostility among journalists shows an unwillingness to admit that new life is possible.

the opportunity for new lives). His first statement to the press, shortly before appearing at a Congressional hearing, was that he had left the Communist Party because "it was an evil." He continued to use such blunt words throughout his public agony.[12]

Chambers consistently stressed religious presuppositions. He criticized "the great alternative faith of mankind," the Communist vision of "Man without God . . . man's mind displacing God as the creative intelligence of the world." Chambers argued that many non-Communists also had the modern "vision of man, once more the central figure of the Creation, not because God made man in His image, but because man's mind makes him the most intelligent of the animals." Chambers testified that he had been consumed by that sinful vision also, until God had changed his heart through free grace. Sin and grace—Chambers' story was impossible to understand unless reporters took those concepts seriously.[13]

Articles from both liberal and conservative newspapers, though, indicated that many journalists did not consider sin and grace to be facts of human life. It made no sense that officials with impressive resumes should become traitors—but it made perfect sense, given an awareness of original sin. (Biblically, scribes and Pharisees often are traitors.) It made no sense that a liar such as Chambers should now be trusted—but it made perfect sense if there is a God who so transforms hearts that those who once loved lying now find false witness abhorrent.

This spiritual and ideological blindness was so great that Alger Hiss, despite his conviction, could maintain his innocence

12. Chambers, *Witness*, 9. More details of the Chambers story will be provided in chapter 8.

13. Ibid. Alexander Solzhenitsyn addresses the battle against communism much as Chambers did. Solzhenitsyn received considerable American media attention when he first arrived in this country—he was a novelty and his message seemed political—but he became a nonperson in the press, in part because many journalists will not grapple with his theological critique.

and often get a sympathetic hearing in the press. Hiss died in 1996, generating new interest and new discoveries from the archives of former Soviet bloc countries. Finally, in 2001, the *New York Times* reported "growing consensus that Hiss, indeed, had most likely been a Soviet agent."[14]

Minimizing the Spiritual Dimensions

Newspaper coverage of two major stories of 1962—the public school prayer debate in June and the beginning of the modern abortion controversy in July—showed how unimportant spiritual dimensions had become to many journalists.

The U.S. Supreme Court's contention in June 1962 that prayer in public schools is unconstitutional was heatedly denounced by many Christians. Major newspapers downplayed the controversy, though. The *New York Times* complained about "farfetched attacks" by opponents of the decision. The *New York Herald-Tribune* suggested that "we accept the ruling with respect, and calm." Other newspapers that waxed fervent even about small political issues editorialized that the prayer question was unimportant, or almost entirely ignored it.[15]

Another need for some spiritual discernment arose the following month (July 1962) when "Miss Sherri," star of the Phoenix version of "Romper Room" (a nationally syndicated children's program that ran from 1953–1994), decided to have an abortion. Sherri Finkbine was the "pretty mother of four healthy children" and the wife of a high school history teacher who also gave swimming lessons in the family pool behind the house. She was an attractive woman with high professional status who decided

14. James Barron, "Online, The Hiss Defense Doesn't Rest," *New York Times*, August 16, 2001.

15. See, for example, *Washington Post*, June 27, 1962, 6, and June 28, 1962, 1, 22; *Los Angeles Times*, June 26, 1962, 1; June 27, 1962, 21; June 28, 1962, 13; *Chicago Tribune*, June 26, 1962, 1, 2; June 27, 1962, 1, 12; *Atlanta Constitution*, June 28, 1962, 1.

to have an abortion because the child she had been bearing for two months faced the possibility of birth with substantial birth defects.[16]

Concerned journalists could have covered the story in this way: "She has a pleasant home, adequate finances, and a supportive husband, but plans to kill her baby." Or this way: "Woman insists on abortion even though there is only a 20 percent chance of deformity in the child she carries." Newspapers could have run features on babies with birth defects who were nevertheless thriving. But with isolated exceptions—one Catholic newspaper editorialized, "Brush away the sentimental slush of a thousand sob-sisters and the cold fact remains that this woman wants to kill the child now living within her"—reporters rallied behind the visible and even changed typical vocabulary in order to ignore the hidden.[17]

Some examples: The *Los Angeles Times* defended Miss Sherri, a "tanned brunet wearing a sleeveless dress of white linen," and instead of using the word "abortion," headlined her desire for "Baby Surgery." A columnist wrote of Finkbine's desire to avoid the possibility of "mothering" a drug-deformed child. The *New York Journal-American* described an operation to "lose the baby," and the *New York Times* reported, "Couple May Go Abroad for Surgery to Prevent a Malformed Baby." Eventually, reporters dropped use of the word "baby" entirely, and substituted the medical term "fetus."[18]

Reporters were not trying to be daring. Nor were they thoughtfully attempting to transform editorial interpretation by changing abortion terminology that had been dominant for almost a century. Reporters were only doing what came natu-

16. More details of this story will be provided in chapter 8.

17. *The Tablet*, August 4, 1962; clipping from *Journal-American* archives, Humanities Research Center, The University of Texas at Austin.

18. *Los Angeles Times*, August 4, 1962, 1; *New York Journal-American*, August 18, 1962, archives clipping; *New York Times*, August 1, 1962, 19; *New York Times*, August 19, 1962, 12.

rally, telling a story about likable folks in trouble. But in doing so they ignored key questions.[19]

Misunderstanding Basic Questions

By the 1970s, many reporters seemed unable to understand even basic Christian concepts. Ignorance of fundamental definitions of sin was evident on Easter Sunday 1973, when embattled President Richard Nixon went to church in Key Biscayne, Florida. Minister John Huffman noted in his sermon, "I don't like to talk about sin. But let's face it. It's a fact of society and a fact of your and my life. We can sweep it under the rug and dismiss it . . . or you can walk out of here transformed individuals by the power of Jesus Christ."[20]

One member of the White House press corps, doing his job, asked Huffman after the service, "Was this aimed at the President?" Huffman said, "No." A reporter asked, "Was it a Watergate sermon?" Huffman said, "No, it was not a Watergate sermon." The reporter then asked, "Well, then, apparently you are saying that nothing in your sermon had any relation to the President?" Huffman replied, "Absolutely not. I wouldn't say

19. For glimpses of the immediate impact of Finkbine coverage, see *New York Post*, August 20, 1962, 1; George H. Gallup, *The Gallup Poll: Public Opinion, 1935-1971* (New York: Random House, 1972), 1984; Garrett Hardin, *Stalking the Wild Taboo* (Los Altos, CA: William Kaufmann, 1973), 4, 11. In 1992 the incident became a (pro-abortion) made-for-TV movie starring Sissy Spacek. Fifty years after the incident, Planned Parenthood of Arizona published online its account of the importance of Sherri Finkbine's story on attempts to legalize abortion in this country. A portion follows: "Finkbine's story is seen now as a pivotal moment in the history of abortion laws in the United States. In her book *The Pig Farmer's Daughter and Other Tales of American Justice: Episodes of Racism and Sexism in the Courts from 1865 to the Present*, Dr. Mary Frances Berry wrote that Finkbine's story 'helped change public opinion [on abortion]. Fifty-two percent of respondents in a Gallup poll thought she had done the right thing.' " Berry adds that by 1965, "most Americans, 77 percent, wanted abortion legalized 'where the health of the mother is in danger' "; in that same year, the *New York Times* called for reform of abortion laws (http://blog.advocatesaz.org/2012/08/15/sherri-finkbines-abortion-its-meaning-50-years-later/).

20. Forrest Boyd tells this story in his *Instant Analysis* (Atlanta: John Knox Press, 1974), 79–86.

that at all, because if I single out anyone in the congregation and say a sermon had nothing to do with them, that person might as well not come to church."

The press corps persisted. Another reporter asked, "Well, then, you're saying that you were preaching to the President." Huffman replied, "No, I did not say I was preaching to the President as far as singling anyone out." A reporter demanded, "Well, what are you saying?" Huffman responded, "I'm saying simply this: that I preach the gospel of Jesus Christ. I try to preach it as clearly as possible, as faithfully to the Scripture as possible, and I start with myself, and I am a sinner. I need to repent and every one of us in the room is under the same conditions and whatever the President wants to make of what was said this morning is between him and the Lord."

Many reporters evidently refused to accept this basic concept of original sin, and persisted in thinking of the sermon in terms of a particular sin. News stories the next morning were predictable: Huffman had warned Nixon he should quit pretending to be a Christian, Nixon should repent of his Watergate sins, Nixon had been chastised, and so on.[21]

In one sense, such stories were predictable. It was open season on Nixon, and he had brought that particular volley on himself. But the story behind those stories is threefold: sometimes a lack of understanding of basic Christian concepts; sometimes a refusal to believe that intelligent people actually take those beliefs seriously; and, probably most often, deliberate suppression of truth about God and self. As sociologist Robert Bellah said, journalists think Christianity is "somehow slightly embarrassing, a holdover from the Dark Ages . . . something only ignorant and backward people really believe in."[22]

21. Ibid.

22. Quoted in *Los Angeles Times*, December 28, 1983; *Times* article by David Shaw reprinted in Ray Hiebert and Carol Reuss, eds., *Impact of Mass Media: Current Issues*

Many Washington correspondents, living in a politicized world, see error or plot in politics and economics, but will not accept its origin in the original sin within individuals. They consciously avoid admission of sin's power, for such admission would condemn themselves. Journalists, like all of us, have trouble answering Jesus' question: "Why do you see the speck that is in your brother's eye, but do not notice the log that is in your own eye?" (Luke 6:41).

Refusal to Acknowledge Warnings

Pharisees in New Testament times liked to believe that everyone on this earth received what they deserved. Those who were healthy and materially prosperous could assume that their spiritual health also was good. But Scripture teaches that "all have sinned and fall short of the glory of God" (Rom. 3:23). Jesus made this point plainly in comments concerning Galileans whom Pilate had treated brutally: "Do you think that these Galileans were worse sinners than all the other Galileans because they suffered this way? No, I tell you; but unless you repent, you will all likewise perish. Or those eighteen on whom the tower in Siloam fell and killed them: do you think that they were worse offenders than all the others who lived in Jerusalem? No, I tell you; but unless you repent, you will all likewise perish" (Luke 13:2–7).

Modern journalists, like the Pharisees, have trouble with tragedy. One of the consequences of "spiking the spiritual" is an inability to see tragic events in their true light, as warnings to refrain from destructive behavior and—if the warnings go unheeded—invitations to repentance. When we spike the spiritual, we often miss God's warnings and invitations.

(New York: Longman, 1985), 434. Actually, many reporters probably understood all too well what Huffman was saying—but they did not want to apply it to themselves.

Nowhere did we see this phenomenon more plainly than in media coverage of the AIDS crisis. We will likely never know for sure how the AIDS epidemic began. The best science we now have suggests that the virus causing AIDS lived in animals for thousands of years but jumped to humans, and subsequently mutated into a deadly virus in the early twentieth century. We do know how this virus spread from person to person and quickly became a worldwide pandemic that by the end of 2009 had killed more than thirty million people. The cause was promiscuous sexual activity. More specifically, homosexual activity.

The facts could not be more clear about this point. The first two confirmed victims in New York City, in 1979, were homosexual men. By 1982, the Centers for Disease Control had confirmed 355 cases, with 198 of these cases, well over half, coming from two cities: New York and San Francisco. Four out of five victims were gay or bisexual men. Forty of these cases, or more than 10 percent of them, can be traced to a single homosexual, Gaetan Dugas, a Canadian flight attendant who admitted to having sex with at least 2,500 men before dying of AIDS-related complications in 1984.

The AIDS epidemic provided an opportunity for widespread repentance. In some places in the world, that repentance occurred. Ugandan pastor Jackson Senyonga wrote in 2003 that by the early 1990s AIDS had become so common in his country that the World Health Organization predicted Uganda's economy "would collapse by 1999 or 2000 because there would be only widows and orphans left. So people sought the Lord and prayed. Today, thanks to prayer, education, and abstinence campaigns, AIDS has dropped to five percent."[23] By 2011, the AIDS rate in Uganda had fallen further, to less than 4 percent.

Such responses were rare, and we should not be surprised. Paul says in Romans 1:18–32 that when men fail to thank and

---

23. *Pray!* (July/August 2003), subsequently reprinted on *Christianity Today*'s website.

glorify God, their thinking becomes futile, and "their foolish hearts were darkened." God, in essence, turns us over to our own devices. Our futile thoughts and foolish hearts turn into destructive behavior. Some men abandon "natural relations with women," are "consumed with passion for one another," and commit "shameless acts with [other] men." They receive "in themselves the due penalty" for their perversion, and go on to sin in non-sexual ways as well. Other men and women sin in other ways and should not point fingers at homosexuals, declaring themselves "righteous" and gays or lesbians as sub-humans.

Christian publications should remind readers that we all deserve God's judgment and should pray for his mercy, "for all have sinned and fall short of the glory of God, and are justified by his grace as a gift, through the redemption that is in Christ Jesus" (Rom. 3:23–24). Some denominations draw a line and refuse to accept homosexuals as leaders or members, but they are often in a difficult position because they did not draw the line much earlier, at our tendency to worship God's creatures and creation rather than God himself. Such denominations (and individuals) become self-righteous by telling themselves they are "standing for truth" when it comes to homosexuality, while not accepting the greater truth that they are guilty of pride, greed, and a wide range of sins God finds equally worthy of his judgment.[24]

We should not be surprised that materialist reporters did not take seriously the belief that AIDS was a God-sent warning. Both the media and the homosexual community downplayed the relationship between AIDS and promiscuous sex, and thereby ignored the hope for redemption. Randy Shilts, a homosexual journalist who wrote a groundbreaking history of AIDS (and

24. Many Christians have shown God's love through compassion toward those who are ill. AIDS patients should also be helped in their time of greatest need. Homosexuality itself should not be condoned, though.

ultimately died of the disease), said love of money was one of the roots of this evil: so-called "gay bathhouses," where anonymous sexual activity was rampant, had become a $100-million-a-year industry.[25] Bathhouse owners became wealthy, and they were often heavy advertisers in gay publications, so criticism from these publications, while not nonexistent, was muted.

Some journalists created general fear by blurring the relationship between homosexual behavior and AIDS. On May 6, 1983, the Associated Press, citing a study from the American Medical Association, suggested family members could transmit the disease to each other by "routine personal contact."[26] Others downplayed risk and the consequences of immoral behavior by suggesting that "liberated" lifestyles popularized in the 1960s could continue, with "safe sex" modifications. Homosexuals could continue their practices as long as they chose partners carefully and used condoms. Heterosexuals could continue in adultery, although it might be wise to have a one-night stand on the second night rather than the first. Other subsets of the one real sin—disobedience to God—could continue.

Journalists who refused even to consider a spiritual/material interface further weakened their stories by not acknowledging what is right in front of their eyes. For example, a *Newsweek* article gave accounts of AIDS patients, all of whom (with one exception) were heterosexuals. This was an obvious attempt to give a false impression of reality. A more subtle newspaper article, "Gays Rally for Right and Respect," reported a homosexual march as if it were an Easter parade, with the emphasis on "diversity" and "family."[27] Missing were accounts of groups

25. Randy Shilts, *And the Band Played On Politics, People and the AIDS Epidemic* (New York: St. Martin's Press, 1987).

26. Cited in ibid., 300.

27. *Detroit Free Press*, June 16, 1985, 3A: "The most striking thing about the 1986 Michigan Lesbian Gay Pride Parade and rally was diversity. There were men and women of all ages, and some people brought their kids. Some men said they were gay dads;

such as Dykes on Bikes, the pederastic North American Man-Boy Love Association, or the Society of Venus (a group that promotes sadomasochism as safe sex). Some conservative publications, though, also erred by making it seem that all homosexuals used whips and chains, or were pederasts.

Rarely did anyone use specific detail biblically to show us the nature of sin and drive home our need to repent. Amnon's rape of Tamar, Canaan looking on his father's nudity, Lot's sexual relations with his daughters—all make for vivid reading. The Bible is not shy about showing the ugly deeds of man, but the goal is always to show us our need for Christ. The cover-ups favored by liberal materialists, and the secular conservative focus on behavior only and not the belief that underlies behavior, are no favor to readers, and no service to the cause of printing the truth.[28]

Ridiculing Those with Spiritual Vision

Lack of understanding, along with outright anti-Christian prejudice, leads to journalistic amazement or horror at the supposed self-deception of those who do see a spiritual realm. Materialist reporters have been blind persons thinking that those with sight are obstinate for not employing the blind as guides. For example, the *New York Times* typically attacks theological conservatives as "inflexible" persons who want to "set a tone of anti-intellectualism" and "start exorcising the demon they call liberalism."[29]

---

a couple of women said they were Lesbian moms. At least four parents showed up to support their gay sons. They were doctors and lawyers, waiters and writers." In one sense, this *Detroit Free Press* article was neutral. Nowhere did it state explicitly that homosexuality was right. But the reporter, in providing positive coverage similar to that given Easter parades, and in making homosexuality seem natural and normal, supported the objective of the parade sponsors: "To show the state that gay men and women are a visible group that should enjoy full civil rights."

28. Chapter 11 discusses the question of how far to go in providing gruesome detail about sin.

29. *Detroit Free Press*, June 13, 1985, 4A.

The scorn particularly comes out, now as in the 1920s, when the topic of evolution versus creation is debated. In 1986, Tennessee Christian parents asked their school district either to create alternative classes with alternative books for the children, or to pay for their private school tuition. They said there should be some choice in public education, not just the foisting on their children of anti-Christian books. They said that if public schools cannot provide choice, parents should not be penalized financially for finding alternatives.

The case, referred to as "Scopes II," brought up important questions. Are the public schools infringing on the right to free exercise of religion? Can we move toward a pluralistic public school system? But many newspapers missed the real issues once again, as they did during Scopes I. Instead, the lead on one story in the *Austin American-Statesman* was, "In the peaceful hills of the Tennessee Bible Belt, Dorothy and Toto and the Good Witch are on trial this week."[30] The reporter did not understand or did not want to deal with the real, serious issue of the case, so he resurrected the strategy of six decades ago: poke fun at Bible thumpers.

More recently, the Intelligent Design (ID) movement has experienced the kind of scorn previously reserved for creationists. Perhaps the most public pillorying of ID came following a 2004 decision by the Dover (Pennsylvania) Area School Board to include Intelligent Design in its science curriculum. Several parents took the school board to court, and in December 2005, U.S. District Judge John E. Jones said, "We find that the secular purposes claimed by the board amount to a pretext for the board's real purpose, which was to promote religion in the public school classroom."[31]

30. Concerned Women for America, 1015 Fifteenth St. N.W., Suite 1100, Washington, DC 20005, an organization that provided legal help to the Tennessee parents, has a record of press coverage.

31. *Tammy Kitzmiller, et al. v. Dover Area School District, et al.* (400 F. Supp. 2d 707, Docket no. 4cv2688).

The media overwhelmingly sided with the evolutionists and the judge's ruling against Intelligent Design. This editorial from the *Philadelphia Inquirer* was typical: "The long-awaited ruling on the Dover 'intelligent design' trial came yesterday, and the results were bad for ID—and good for democracy. They were good for those who read the Bible, those who read Darwin, and those who never read anything. This was a triumph for the Constitution, so it is one we all can share."[32]

But Richard Thompson, president and chief counsel of the Thomas More Law Center in Ann Arbor, Michigan, saw it differently. He represented the school district and said: "What this really looks like is an *ad hominem* attack on scientists who happen to believe in God."[33]

Beyond the Liberal-Conservative Debate

Again and again over the past half-century, the same story emerges: spike the spiritual. By seeing the consistent downgrading of the biblical worldview of spiritual/material interface, we can go beyond the liberal versus conservative media debates of the past two decades. That debate is an important one, but some conservative reporters are as materialistic in philosophy as their liberal counterparts. Non-Christians on both sides tend to give only half the facts.

Often this tendency is not conscious. As John Corry of the *New York Times* acknowledged, "There are fewer rules of pure journalism here than journalists pretend, even to themselves. Journalists, especially big-time journalists, deal in attitudes and ideas as much as events." Those attitudes and ideas lead to the formation of a journalistic version of what sociologists call "plausibility structures," a system of belief for determining what

32. Unsigned editorial, *Philadelphia Inquirer*, December 21, 2005.
33. *Los Angeles Times*, December 22, 2005.

makes sense and what does not. Busy reporters often do not have time to think things through. As one Washington hand noted, "If I got to think about a story at all, it was in the few steps running from a Senate hearing room to the phone booth." Journalists, under such pressure, tend to make snap choices of emphasis based on their basic ideas of what is important and what is not.[34]

Some would say that personal beliefs are unimportant because "professionalism" takes over, but a few journalists with a good sense of self are also aware of the effect of "selective perception." William Rivers, a reporter turned professor, wrote frequently about the effect of attitudes on the ability of even well-trained reporters to spot a story. In describing one story he wrote, Rivers noted, "My prejudices did the work and I was unaware of it until, much later, I read about the phenomenon known as 'selective perception.'" As *Time*'s former chairman of the board, Andrew Heiskell, observed, "All writers slant what they write no matter how hard they try."[35]

The slant is obvious at times. *Washington Post* foreign editor Karen de Young, in explaining her positive coverage of the Sandinistas during their seizure of power, noted that "most journalists now, most Western journalists at least, are very eager to seek out guerrilla groups, leftist groups, because you assume they must be the good guys." Fox News commentator Geraldo Rivera, reporting from Panama for ABC during the 1970s, had a problem. The U.S. Senate was about to vote on U.S. relinquishing of the Panama Canal, and violence engaged in by the Panamanian National Guard showed that the government of Panama was not exactly a trustworthy guardian of the Canal. Rivera admitted later, "We downplayed the whole incident. That was the day I decided that I had to be very careful about what was

34. John Corry, *TV News and the Dominant Culture* (Washington: Media Institute, 1986).

35. Rivers, *The Opinionmakers*, 10, 126.

48

said, because I could defeat the very thing [passage of the treaty] that I wanted to achieve."[36]

More recent examples abound. The Center for Media and Public Affairs at George Mason University looked at 585 network news stories between August 23 and September 30, 2008, a critical time in the 2008 election cycle. It discovered that 65 percent of the stories were positive toward Barack Obama, while only 36 percent were positive toward John McCain. The bias was so pronounced that Robert Lichter, the author of the study, called it "Obama-mania." "For whatever reason, the media are portraying Barack Obama as a better choice for president than John McCain," Lichter concluded.[37]

Lichter may have been reluctant to attribute a reason for the bias, but we are not. Most reporters want to display the world as they see it, with the goal of bringing us around to how they think the world works. But instead of seeing patterns in events—events as either causes or consequences, with both prudential and moral lessons to teach—journalists with materialist worldviews simply see the random effects of time plus chance. When readers and viewers complain about the patternlessness of it all, journalists in turn tend to complain about readers and viewers demanding more than they feel they can offer.

36. *Accuracy in Media Report*, May 1980, No. 2; July 1979, No. 1; quoted in Isaac and Isaac, *The Coercive Utopians*, 262, 270. The power of the press to tilt, for better or for worse, was obvious both to new arrivals and to experienced journalists. Alexander Solzhenitsyn came, saw, and commented that the press is "more powerful than the legislature, the executive, and the judiciary." A *Washington Post* editor boasted that, in the capitol, the practice of "not only getting it from the horse's mouth but being inside his mouth" is "almost a way of life." Former reporter William Rivers noted that journalists "sometimes are the prime promoters or offstage prompters of the Congressional hearings, legislative battles and other events they are chronicling, theoretically with detachment." For additional discussion of this topic, see William Rivers, *The Other Government: Power and the Washington Media* (New York: Universe, 1982).

37. David Bauder, "Study: Media coverage has favored Obama campaign," *USA Today*, November 1, 2008.

The end result of this spiking of the spiritual is what we call Wheel of Fortune journalism, named for television's most popular game show. The game takes some skill, but winners are generally those who avoid a bad spin of the wheel. Chance apparently rules, and the audience tunes in regularly. On November 6, 2012, election night, *Wheel of Fortune*'s average rating for the week beat all the network's election night coverage but one: NBC. One network executive said, "You try to do everything right journalistically. . . and then the most successful game show in the history of the land comes along and cuts your head off." Another executive said, "It's dumb luck."

But is it dumb luck? Or does *Wheel*'s success reveal something about the failure of typical news shows? News shows tend to have standard stories of people murdered, houses destroyed by fire, and so on. There is no explanation, and the game goes on. Some are winners, most are losers. That description of a news show sounds like *Wheel of Fortune*. The main difference is that *Wheel of Fortune* has flashing lights and more glamour: same product, better package. Why shouldn't viewers prefer it?

Typical newspaper stories also show the tendency to ascribe events to chance. A *Houston Post* article related that a twenty-year-old woman "was killed because her hand accidentally snagged on a purse that had been grabbed by a man" who demanded money and shot her when she seemed to be resisting.[38] The *Post*'s cause of death, explicitly, was bad luck on the wheel of fortune. Yet, what about the sin of a murderer on drugs who had become so corrupt

38. Wheel of Fortune journalism often involves playing lawbreaking for laughs. A typical story of this kind began, "Something went wrong for a 26-year-old Austin man suspected of processing methamphetamine Monday afternoon at a Barton Hills apartment. His laboratory blew up." That story notes that the man suffered minor burns and was arrested, but not until the ninth and last paragraph of the story were readers told that the man was on probation for a previous conviction of manufacturing methamphetamine. Only then would readers see that the explosion was not a question of bad luck or chance, but repeated lawbreaking (*Austin American-Statesman*, July 29, 1986, 1).

that he was willing to kill? What about the sin of cultural leaders who tolerate and even encourage drug use? What about the activity of the murder victim who was sitting in a park at 3:30 A.M. after an evening of drinking? (She was certainly not to blame for what happened, but foolish actions do have consequences.)

Instead of probing, typical materialist explanations trivialize. One Wednesday, a fourteen-year-old student received on his report card an *F* for French. The next day he went to school, attended his classes, and at about 1:00 P.M. went to his French class. He waited outside the door for the previous class to be dismissed. The bell rang. The teacher opened the door. The student calmly shot her dead and wounded three others.

In the irony of God's providence, the student had mistakenly killed a substitute teacher. An NBC reporter explained that the student was "upset" over the *F*. A mild word, *upset*, to describe lack of self-control leading from anger to murder. A bland word, *upset*, to leave us shaking our heads over the wheel of fortune and saying, "How could a nice young man do such a thing?"

A prodigal press that intentionally spikes the spiritual hides from us deeper causes of the deaths of the twenty-year-old woman and the substitute French teacher: hidden from us, for example, are the war of Satan against God and Satan's use of corrupting sin. A Christian worldview teaches that every skirmish does have some significance in that war. Even without speculating about the heavenlies, a reporter looking for patterns in life and death, rather than assuming the operation of chance, can produce far richer stories than those developed by spiking the spiritual.

According to materialist reporters, though, life is a process of chance. Spin the wheel and see what number comes up. Most readers and viewers are so used to this method of presentation that it is difficult to imagine the news being done in any other way. Yet, what a weak and superficial journalism we have when materialism rules! What a profligate wasting of a proud heritage!

3 | Not without Personal Cost

C hapter 1 discussed the decline of Christian journalism. Chapter 2 argued that journalism without an awareness of the spiritual realm makes for incomplete journalism. This chapter will suggest that the lack of spiritual awareness also makes for incomplete journalists. Journalism history's pantheon is filled with statues of great crusaders, but crusades based on false ideology invariably come up short.

Some journalists were honest enough and smart enough to see their failures, with enormous personal repercussions later in life. The most innovative journalists, though, often were the most arrogant, slow to recognize that their leaps forward were taking them in circles. We cannot scientifically measure the sin and misery of many of these great lives, nor can we prove that writers without God fall into a pattern. But to get an impression of the personal costs involved in seeing self as God, let's briefly chronicle the lives of eight of the greats during the 1840–1940 period. That is recent enough so that their influence is still felt, long enough ago so that gossip has receded.[1]

1. Examining the personal lives and careers of non-Christian journalists helps us to remember that the struggle from a Christian perspective is not Christians versus non-Christians, us versus them. Many non-Christian journalists are broken inside, looking for love in all the wrong places; they need compassion as well as correction. Jesus did warn, though, that his enemies would hate Christians also. Although the battle is not us versus them, from the non-Christian perspective it may be them versus us.

Greeley

First of the key journalists during our period (and famous for the phrase, "Go west, young man") was Horace Greeley, editor of the *New York Tribune* from 1841 to 1872. He was a hands-on manager who demanded strong local reporting: "Do not let a new church be organized, a mill set in motion, a store opened, nor anything of interest to a dozen families occur, without having the fact daily, though briefly, chronicled in your columns." Reporters loved him, as "he steered the *Tribune* with relaxed, easy reins, and enjoyed giving his men their head." With a background as a printer, he also had an excellent sense of typography.[2]

But Greeley's theology was Unitarian. He thought man naturally good and able to "enoble" himself. Greeley did not understand original sin, and so he thought that man's corruption came from outside, from corrupt institutions. Believing all would be well if only major institutions were transformed, he began crusading for societal change.[3]

First, Greeley saw private property as the corrupting force, for economic competition made man evil. So Greeley backed, with profits gained from the *Tribune*'s competitive success, the

2. William Harlan Hale, *Horace Greeley: Voice of the People* (New York: Harper and Brothers, 1950), 83. See also A. Oakley Hall, *Horace Greeley Decently Dissected* (New York: Ross and Tousey, 1862); L. D. Ingersoll, *The Life of Horace Greeley, Founder of the* New York Tribune (Chicago: Union Publishing Co., 1873); Henry Luther Stoddard, *Horace Greeley: Printer, Editor, Crusader* (New York: Putnam's, 1946); Glyndon G. Van Deusen, *Horace Greeley, Nineteenth-Century Crusader* (Philadelphia: University of Pennsylvania Press, 1953); and Greeley's autobiography, *Recollections of a Busy Life* (New York: J. B. Ford and Co., 1868). Greeley's three decades of editorials in the *Tribune* are the best source for an in-depth study.

3. Greeley, *Recollections*, 68–74. Greeley learned from early nineteenth-century Unitarian leaders such as William Ellery Channing, who argued that "avarice was the chief obstacle to human progress. . . . The only way to eliminate it was to establish a community of property." Channing's view typified the materialistic approach to the problem of evil. Evil was created by the way society was organized, not by anything innately evil in man: to eliminate evil, change society.

founding of some forty communes during the 1840s. All of them failed. Then he moved on to other causes: agrarianism, anti-rent-ism, "free love," always something new, always something that sup-posedly would lead to a man-made utopia just around the corner.[4]

When each idea failed, Greeley often blamed those he had previously backed for their inability to implement the impos-sible. He eventually inspired a poem by William Grayson in 1856:

"There Greeley, grieving at a brother's woe, / Spits with impar-tial spite on friend and foe . . . / To each fanatical delusion prone, / He damns all creeds and parties but his own; / And faction's fiercest rabble always find / A kindred nature in the *Tribune*'s mind; / Ready each furious impulse to obey, / He raves and ravens like a beast of prey."[5]

None of the causes panned out, but Greeley kept trying something new. So did his wife, Mary Greeley. At one time she violently opposed the killing of animals for any reason. She met writer Margaret Fuller on the street one day, touched Fuller's kid gloves and screamed, "Skin of a beast, skin of a beast." Mary was wearing silk, and Margaret Fuller had the presence of mind to yell, "Entrails of a worm, entrails of a worm."[6]

4. Greeley received great individual renown for his work in promoting communes. At one banquet Albert Brisbane, theoretician of the communalists, toasted him for having "done for us what we never could have done. He has created the cause on this continent. He has done the work of a century. Well, then, I will give a toast: 'One Continent, One Man!'" (Hale, *Horace Greeley*, 105). Greeley gave Brisbane a column in the *Tribune*. Brisbane blamed the failure of the communes on the existence of a noncommunal society outside their boundaries. Many communalists, Brisbane wrote, "began to picture the broader, more independent fields of action in the great competitive life of the individual in civilization. This shows clearly that unless associative life is completely organized, so that all the sentiments and faculties of the soul find their normal development and action therein, it cannot stand . . . there must either be the complex harmony of a perfect organization, with a high order of spiritual activity, or man must remain in his little isolated, individual state" (ibid.). Brisbane, essentially, was saying he needed totalitarianism to succeed. Enter the Gulag.

5. Hale, *Horace Greeley*, xvi.

6. Van Deusen, *Horace Greeley*, 148.

Horace and Mary Greeley believed that children are without sin. The prime parental goal was to keep them from corruption. Their son Arthur (Pickie), born in 1844, spent most of his first five summers in various communes. At age five his hair had never been cut, lest that constrict his freedom, and he still wore baby clothes, to give him freedom of movement. He was to be a beautiful combination of intellect and nature, equipped with "choice" thoughts and language. But one day Pickie, age five, stood up before a commune meeting and complained that his mother was "so particular, particular, particular, particular." When she reminded him that he had been saved from corruption, he began shrieking at her, "Don't you dare shut me up in a room. . . . I want fun." The Greeleys did not change Pickie's regime, but he died shortly after during a cholera epidemic.[7]

Greeley's causes were no more successful than his utopian ideas of child-raising. When he tired of marriage and proposed "social enjoyment" and "individual sovereignty," opponents said he was proposing "only a brothel on a new plan."[8] He ran for president in 1872 and was politically crushed. Following the election, he reflected on his life and saw it as a waste, a sacrifice to foolish crusades. In one of his last statements before death took him on November 29, 1872, Greeley wrote, "I stand naked before my God, the most utterly, hopelessly wretched and undone of all who ever lived. I have done more harm and wrong than any man who ever saw the light of day. And yet I take God to witness that I have never intended to injure or harm anyone. But this is no excuse."[9]

Storey

Greeley was the father of modern journalistic crusading. Wilbur Storey of the *Detroit Free Press* and the *Chicago Times* is

7. As Greeley's family situation deteriorated, he became even a more driven man at work.

8. *Detroit Free Press*, October 20, 1855, 2.

9. Van Deusen, *Horace Greeley*, 423.

the father of modern journalistic sensationalism. Storey, an innovative editor from 1855 through 1884, anticipated the racy details of New York "yellow journalism" by running headlines such as "How to Get Rid of a Faithless Wife," "Suicide by Swallowing a Red-Hot Poker," "Fountain of Blood in a Cavern," and "Saved by His Wife's Corpse."[10]

Storey became particularly known for decked headlines such as this one from 1871: "Spouse Roasting / The Massachusetts Husband Who Cooked His Wife in Kerosene / A Sample of New England Conjugal Bliss."[11] Storey believed strongly in material causes for all tragedies, with individuals often left helpless, as related in this headline: "The Arsenic Fiend. Full Confession of Lydia Sherman, the Connecticut Arch-Murderess / The Remorseless Murder of Three Husbands and Five Children / A Story of Arsenic, Arsenic, Arsenic / A Constant, Itching Temptation Which She Was Powerless to Resist." His political reporting of the Chicago city council also was grabbing: "Bastard 'City Fathers' / Chicago's Prize Rummers Hold Their Weekly Carnival at the City Hall / And, As Usual, Disgrace the City Over Which They Should Exercise All Care."[12]

Storey became the dictator of Chicago. In the words of his closest *Times* associate, Franc B. Wilkie, "Wilbur Storey was a Bacchus, a Satyr, a Minotaur, all in one. . . . Possessed of no consideration for the feelings of others, he fancied himself infallible." Storey attacked with impunity anyone who crossed his path and did not bow. Sued often for libel, he always managed to avoid heavy penalties. He made up stories which ruined reputations and said he did not care.[13]

10. For more examples of headlines, see Justin Walsh's biography of Storey, *To Print the News and Raise Hell* (Chapel Hill: University of North Carolina Press, 1968).

11. *Chicago Times*, November 21, 1871, 1.

12. Ibid., January 16, 1873, 1.

13. Walsh, *To Print the News and Raise Hell*, 206.

Storey tended to hire editors and writers in his own image. Probably his most famous reporter, "Shang" Andrews, was a drug addict. Storey's city editor once called his staff "a great force. . . . Two of my men are ex-convicts, ten are divorced husbands, and not a single one of them is living with his own wife." *Times* reporters were almost invariably antichurch, producing bitter attacks on "The Preachers of the Period" and "The Peculiarities of Shepherds and Flocks."[14]

Storey's life, though, became evidence for the often-repeated maxim that those who do not believe in Christianity eventually believe not nothing, but anything. The materialist Storey in his fifties became interested in the spiritual, but in his own way: he installed a permanent "spirit-rapping" medium in his home and turned the *Times* into the editorial organ of "Spirit Intercourse." In one article Storey renounced "forever" Christian communion and said he would pay attention to the "mystic and invisible communications" that came to him alone. Through frequent seances he searched for a spiritual realm he could control as he controlled Chicago.[15]

Then doctors found that Storey had contracted syphilis which had advanced to such a stage that his intellect was threatened. Storey moaned to his sister, "Why have I worked so hard, and accumulated money, and planned, and given all my years to building up a great business, when I know that at any moment I may become a helpless mass?" On doctor's advice he took a long tour of Europe in 1878, but seemed to notice nothing. His associate Wilkie wrote that Storey "seemed keenly and unfavorably impressed in a persistent environment of gloom."[16]

Storey lived for six more years, sinking deeper and deeper into what became a permanent depression, raging on in his

14. Ibid., 212.
15. Ibid., 236.
16. Ibid., 261.

newspaper's columns. His third wife hounded him, demanding changes in their prenuptial agreement that precluded her from receiving most of his estate. Nor did anyone else apparently have any fondness for Storey. With the reputation of a rattlesnake, he was seen as being not only critical—*that* his former friends could stand—but also cruel. Storey died hated and alone in 1884 at age sixty-four.

Howe

Greeley's crusading and Storey's sensationalism both included anti-Christian components. A third nineteenth-century editor, E. W. Howe, was the first to see his role as that of community educator in atheism. While writing an influential novel, then editing a Kansas daily and a national weekly from the 1870s into the 1930s, Howe "envisioned himself as a man whose mission was to pull the people of Atchison, and readers everywhere, out of the muck of ignorance."[17]

Calling himself a "lay preacher," Howe told newspaper readers that Christianity was "baseless from top to bottom," with "no foundation in history or probability." Howe said the story of Christ's birth and ascent were taken directly from Buddhism and that the Ten Commandments were stolen from the Egyptians. He also wrote that all intelligent folk knew the biblical stories of creation, original sin, flood, and resurrection were lies, along with all miracles, all prophecies, and all commandments. He told any readers with doubts that they could check those "facts" in *The American Cyclopedia*, a truer book than the Bible.[18]

17. For more information, see Calder Pickett, *Ed Howe: Country Town Philosopher* (Lawrence, KS: University Press of Kansas, 1968), and Howe's autobiography, *Plain People* (New York: Dodd, Mead, 1929). See also Gerald Carson, "The Village Atheist," *Scribner's*, December 1928, and Gene A. Howe, "My Father Was the Most Wretchedly Unhappy Man I Ever Knew," *Saturday Evening Post*, October 25, 1941.

18. Pickett, *Ed Howe*, 177.

Howe's credo, put into effect in his own professional and personal life, was: selfishness, not Christian belief, is the savior of mankind. In his own family an increasingly bitter marriage eventually resulted in a 1901 divorce. Two of Howe's five children died young, and the other three became estranged from their father. But Howe received honorary degrees and much praise, particularly for his "fearless" attacks on Christianity. Yet, when he died in 1937 at age eighty-four, his burial service was conducted in a church, as he had requested.[19]

Following Howe's death his son Gene would write in the *Saturday Evening Post* a remembrance of his father entitled, "My Father Was the Most Wretchedly Unhappy Man I Ever Knew." Gene wrote that his father had been "a master of English, a pioneer in literary style, and he had a great wealth of fire and force and enthusiasm." But the son wrote sadly, "I know of no one endowed as he was who accomplished so little."[20]

Pulitzer

Greeley crusaded for utopian schemes, Storey sensationalized for circulation and power, and Howe proselytized for atheism. Joseph Pulitzer became the most famous editor/publisher in the United States during the last quarter of the nineteenth century by combining the three in both St. Louis (from the 1860s to the 1880s) and New York (from then to his death in 1911). Pulitzer was undoubtedly a genius, with a penetrating intellect, wonderful memory, and superb journalistic instincts. His early years as reporter and editor were happy. But Pulitzer was always looking for love and salvation in all the wrong places. That fruitless search for permanent satisfaction apart from God turned Pulitzer's brilliant promise into one of the great tragedies of

19. E. W. Howe, *Plain People*.
20. Gene Howe, "My Father Was the Most Wretchedly Unhappy Man I Ever Knew."

American journalism history. Pulitzer's desire to be a god unto himself turned him by 1885 into a man who "exudes the venom of a snake and wields the bludgeon of a bully."[21]

That was the verdict of a competitor. Even Pulitzer's friend and top editor, though, said that Pulitzer was the "best man in the world to have in a newspaper office for one hour in the morning. For the remainder of the day he was a damned nuisance." Wanting to be omnipresent, Pulitzer instructed his editors and reporters to spy on each other and send reports directly to him. He purposefully created overlapping authority so that he would have to be called in to break deadlocks. Pulitzer's system, according to one journalist, "produced in time a condition of suspicion, jealousy and hatred, a maelstrom of office politics that drove at least two editors to drink, one into suicide, a fourth into insanity."[22]

Everyone told Pulitzer to stop worrying, but he could not. One reporter wrote, "When anything went wrong, and things seemed to go wrong with him very often, there would come from his office . . . a stream of profanity and filth." Pulitzer's fellow newspaper editor Henry Watterson noted that "absolute authority made Pulitzer a tyrant."[23]

Things became worse when Pulitzer gradually became blind during the 1890s. He called himself "the loneliest man in the world." Even his laudatory biographer, however, noted that "the loneliness, although real, was instead the terrible isolation of the helpless megalomaniac and egocentric, the perfectionist who loved to criticize." Pulitzer separated from his wife and children

21. Readable books about Pulitzer include James Barrett, *Joseph Pulitzer and His World* (New York: Vanguard Press, 1941); Don Seitz, *Joseph Pulitzer: His Life and Letters* (New York: Simon and Schuster, 1924); W. A. Swanberg, *Pulitzer* (New York: Scribner's, 1967).

22. Swanberg, *Pulitzer*, 131, 197.

23. Henry Watterson, *"Marse Henry": An Autobiography*, vol. 1 (New York: Doran, 1919), 209.

for most of his last twenty years because he wanted around him only "compliant attendants." His wife often wanted to join him, writing, "You would be much happier my dear Joseph if you would only believe in the friendly intentions & good feeling of the people about you." But Pulitzer raged at her, then complained that he had to eat dinner with "nobody at my table except paid employees."[24]

Pulitzer could never feel loved. He employed hundreds of assistants over the years, always searching for a friend and confidant. Many admired him at first, but later or usually sooner he would turn on them, then write letters such as the following: "How much I would give if I could only deceive myself with the thought that my anxiety to attach you to me as my long lost and longed for friend is not entirely unappreciated." Pulitzer would swear at an assistant, swing a whip at him, and then plead with the assistant to "tell him why he [Pulitzer] was treated so cruelly."

It seems likely that Pulitzer truly wanted God's love but was too proud to acknowledge anyone above him. When Charles Evan Hughes, later to be the Supreme Court's chief justice, visited Pulitzer in 1903, he reported that "One would have supposed that Mr. Pulitzer was sitting as the judge of all the earth." For a time Pulitzer sent an atheistic employee to church every week to place a new $5 bill on the offering plate and then leave. Another of Pulitzer's assistants explained, "Mr. Pulitzer has then attended church."[25]

Pulitzer spent his last years sailing constantly in a yacht with seventy-five employees trained to cater to his whims. As one biographer put it, "The yacht represented the logical end toward which the eccentric despot, so concerned with democracy, had been working for decades. It gave him complete control. It was an absolute monarchy." But Pulitzer still had no peace of

24. Swanberg, *Pulitzer*, 223, 181, 386.
25. Ibid., 389–93.

mind, and ended his life agitated by what he called his "constant and manifold failures." Having forsaken God, he was left merely to complain that he had been "forsaken and deserted and shamefully treated by fate." Now, on the days Pulitzer Prizes are handed out, Pulitzer is remembered, and perhaps even loved by the winners.[26]

Scripps

The early professional life of E. W. Scripps—the man who developed a central institution of twentieth-century American journalism, the newspaper chain—also was filled with journalistic joy. Born in 1854, he became city editor of the *Detroit Evening News* at age twenty-one and established America's first effective chain during the 1880s and 1890s. Scripps also extended the Greeley-Pulitzer concept of newspapers as voices of the theological and political left. He called his editorials the "teaching department, the statesmanship department and the spiritual department," said he was not out to make a profit, and made enormous profits before dying aboard his yacht in 1926.[27]

Scripps acknowledged that the Christian ethic in which he had been raised gave him the discipline he needed to be successful: "I believe that . . . in 999 out of every 1,000 of my activities, physical and mental, I am prompted to action or thought, or restrained from action or thought, by what might be called Christian tradition." But Scripps made the typical fallacious distinction between "Christ's Christianity of love" and what the Bible actually said about God's justice and mercy. Scripps never wanted to study biblical verses in context, because that would

26. Ibid., 433.
27. The best sources for Scripps are two books of his writings: *Damned Old Crank: A Self-Portrait of E. W. Scripps Drawn from His Unpublished Writings* (New York: Harper and Brothers, 1951) and *I Protest: Select Disquisitions of E. W. Scripps*, ed. Oliver Knight (Madison: University of Wisconsin Press, 1966). Here, *Damned Old Crank*, 101.

put God above his own understanding. Eventually Scripps wrote straightforwardly, "I do not believe in God, or any being equal to or similar to the Christian's God."[28]

Politically, Scripps became a prominent advocate of socialism. Economically, he was a successful capitalist. Yet Scripps was one more person who, looking back late in life, rued his actions. Scripps in 1914 saw "no hope" in socialism. He could see that "socialism is based really upon a spirit of conservatism, of nonproductiveness. The effect of socialism would be that society would not only be satisfied with the knowledge it at present possesses, but that there would be no increase by discovery of new fields of human activity."[29]

Scripps complained further that "the socialist would take possession of the world—material and social—as it exists today, and divide it up into shares, and thereafter have society continue to exist upon the product hitherto accumulated, taking no further step forward into the undiscovered and virgin fields of opportunity." Yet Scripps continued propagandizing for socialism, "despite my will and my reason," because he was "human and normal, and hence weak."[30]

Later he wondered if he had been right in "devoting my energies to denouncing wealth and inspiring the masses to jealousy and revolution." But Scripps also stayed consistent, writing in 1921 an essay, "Wanted—a Tryant," in which he argued that "as Lenin has striven and is still striving to seize and hold power of dictator in Russia, so may we have to depend on some coming strong man." (Edmund Burke's comment on the French revolutionaries comes to mind here: "In the groves of their academies, at the end of every vista, you see nothing but the gallows."[31]) Scripps left to posterity the news service that became United

28. Scripps, *I Protest*, 178.
29. Scripps, *Damned Old Crank*, 137.
30. Ibid.
31. Edmund Burke, *Reflections on the Revolution in France* (1790).

Press International and a maxim for never-ending revolution: "Whatever is, is wrong."[32]

Hearst

William Randolph Hearst was the most powerful journalist of the early twentieth century. Born in 1863 and given the *San Francisco Examiner* by his father in 1887, Hearst moved to New York in 1895 and built a newspaper chain far greater than that of Scripps. By 1935 Hearst controlled 14 percent of daily newspaper circulation nationwide and 24 percent of Sunday circulation. What struck early observers of Hearst and his newspapers, though, was passion as well as money. Early on, Hearst so loved his newspapers that he would examine pages by standing over them and dancing out of sheer pleasure as he turned the pages with his toes.

Hearst, when young, also enjoyed leading his reporters to breaking news stories. The reporters would race to the scene on bicycles or cavalry horses, while Hearst could be seen "leaping wild-eyed and long-legged into a carriage, to be whisked like a field marshall to the scene of battle." Hearst and his editors put out the most exciting newspaper of the late nineteenth and early twentieth centuries, but they rarely moved beyond Wheel of Fortune journalism. Hearst's slogan became, "There Is No Substitute for Circulation," and his practice a mixture of demagogic politics and sensationalism: "Make a great and continuous noise to attract readers; denounce crooked wealth and promise better conditions for the poor to keep readers. INCREASE CIRCULATION."[33]

32. Scripps, *I Protest*, 434.

33. Much of my sense of Hearst comes from reading his lively *San Francisco Examiner* and *New York Journal* and *American*. Some of Hearst's editorials are contained in a public relations book edited by Edmund Coblentz, one of his executives: *William Randolph Hearst: A Portrait in His Own Words* (New York: Simon and Schuster, 1952). Biographies include Oliver Carlson and Ernest Sutherland Bates, *Hearst: Lord of San Simeon* (New

Hearst made an idol out of circulation, but he also tried making one out of himself. He instructed his reporters and editors to praise him at every possibility. He posed as a benefactor of the poor, sending pale children on jaunts to the beach. A reporter sent to cover one expedition, though, later wrote that she received only one container of ice cream to be dealt out on a Coney Island trip: "When at last I placed a dab on each saucer, a little fellow in ragged knickerbockers got up and declared that the *Journal* was a fake and I thought there was going to be a riot. I took away the ice-cream from a deaf and dumb kid who couldn't holler and gave it to the malcontent. Then I had to write my story beginning: 'Thousands of children, pale-faced but happy, danced merrily down Coney Island's beaches yesterday and were soon sporting in the sun-lit waves shouting, "God bless Mr. Hearst." ' "[34]

Hearst made sure his good deeds were surrounded by trumpets for him personally and publicity for his newspaper. His instructions sometimes led to bizarre coverage. When he ordered his writers to mention "comic supplements" in their stories whenever possible, one reporter noted concerning a disaster scene, "I was the first to reach the injured and dying. 'God bless Mr. Hearst,' a little child cried as I stooped to lave her brow. Then she smiled and died. I spread one of our comic supplements over the pale, still face."

The goal of such efforts was not only to sell newspapers but to get Hearst elected president. When he could not get the Democratic nomination in 1904, he called Judge Alton Parker, the party's nominee, a "living, breathing cockroach from under the sink," and labeled the party's chairman "a plague spot in the

York: Viking Press, 1936); Ferdinand Lundberg, *Imperial Hearst: A Social Biography* (New York: Equinox, 1936); John Tebbel, *The Life and Good Times of William Randolph Hearst* (New York: Dutton, 1952); W. A. Swanberg, *Citizen Hearst* (New York: Scribner's, 1961).

34. For this and other Hearst anecdotes, see Allen Churchill, *Park Row: A Vivid Recreation of Turn of the Century Newspaper Days* (New York: Rinehart, 1958).

community spreading vileness."[35] Hearst began using his *New York Journal* as a club against anyone who did not bow down to him. At one time the newspaper had two thousand names on its "S-list" (persons to be mentioned only with scorn).

At first Hearst used his growing newspaper chain as a whip to promote his own political and ideological interests, which included bringing about a big government-big business partnership. Hearst wrote, in a signed editorial, "Combination and organization are necessary steps in industrial progress. We are advancing toward a complete organization in which the government will stand at the head and be the trust of trusts. It is ridiculous to attempt to stop this development." But, frustrated when he actually saw his vision pushed along during the New Deal, Hearst turned on the man he had endorsed, Franklin Roosevelt, and gave up his dreams of government.[36]

Hearst spent his last decades estranged from wife and family. He lived with actress Marion Davies, who ate dinner with a special servant standing behind her throughout the meal to hold powder, rouge, and lipstick, and another servant to bring Miss Davies' dog "Gandhi" sliced ham or turkey on a silver platter. Hearst's house guests abided by a strict rule: "Never mention death in Mr. Hearst's presence." Orson Welles's movie *Citizen Kane* is only loosely founded on Hearst's life, but it nevertheless gives a good sense of the isolation of Hearst's later years as he removed himself from both man and God.[37]

Steffens

A seventh journalistic innovator, Lincoln Steffens, was the modern inventor of "muckraking." He exposed the corruption

---

35. Descriptions quoted often by biographers, including by Carlson and Bates, *Hearst*, 111.
36. Lundberg, *Imperial Hearst*, 141.
37. Ibid., 310.

of a dozen municipal governments early in this century and saw the problem was not so much particular individuals but a general disposition to sin. Steffens read the Bible and almost seemed ready to bow his head. He went to church for several years, only to decide he was superior to those around him. He was superior intellectually, but not spiritually.[38]

Steffens also was aware of the supercilious stares from friends that a Christian conversion would bring. He turned back toward materialism. The political form that materialism took could no longer be liberalism, since he had realized its limitations. He became, instead, a Marxist (of the kind who could be described as "talking revolution and blood—and sucking the guts out of a chocolate eclair impaled on an upright fork"). Steffens became an apologist for the Soviet Union, praising Stalin and others for carrying through "ruthlessly" a plan to change human nature.

The hard-line Communists thought Steffens soft, a playful child of the despised bourgeoisie "wandering among the social battlefields." Steffens proved himself by turning on a fellow Marxist and former friend, Max Eastman, who had been courageous enough to report accurately on the Soviet Union during the 1920s and early 1930s. Steffens won Party praise by joining in what Sidney Hook called "a campaign of brutal repressions, slander and character assassination."[39]

Steffens had come a long way. Previously an apostle of man's reason as the glory of existence, he was saying in 1932 that "there

38. Sources for Steffens include *The Autobiography of Lincoln Steffens* (New York: Harcourt, Brace, 1931) and *The Letters of Lincoln Steffens* (New York: Harcourt, Brace, 1938). Biographies include Justin Kaplan, *Lincoln Steffens* (New York: Simon & Schuster, 1974), and Russell Horton, *Lincoln Steffens* (New York: Twayne, 1974).

39. Steffens portrayed himself in his autobiography as a man of constant honesty and integrity, one with true love for all mankind. Toward the end of his life Steffens wore a small gold cross from his watch chain and called himself "the only Christian on earth" (Horton, *Lincoln Steffens*, 85). The autobiography was a best-seller. For seven months of 1931 so was a Soviet book, *New Russia's Primer*, an explanation for children of the Five-Year Plan.

comes a time to close our open minds, shut up our talking, and go to it." Steffens praised Stalin's purges when they began in 1934, writing that Stalin had "put sixty or more men to death" because he had wisely realized "that the job was not yet done, that security was not yet secured." Steffens apparently realized his lies and contemplated suicide, but he stayed on the path he had chosen, writing in 1936 that "poetry, romance—all roads in our day lead to Moscow."[40]

Steffens thought again of God and sin as he sickened, but he continued to maintain that "treason to Communism" would be a "sin," for "Russia is the land of conscious, willful hope." Eastman called Steffens "a pillar of the Stalinist church in America," and Steffens apparently died that way in August 1936. But he must have had some realization of the stakes, for on the last page of his autobiography he also noted, "I have been contending, with all my kind, always against God."[41]

Duranty

Last of the great journalistic innovators during the 1840–1940 period was foreign correspondent Walter Duranty. Covering the Soviet Union for the *New York Times* during the 1920s and 1930s, Duranty was the father of all those who covered the rise to power of Mao in the 1940s, Castro in the 1950s, and the Sandinistas in the 1970s. Similarly, those who apologized for the Communist regime during Ethiopia's state-caused famine of the 1980s, or who blamed the rise of radical Islam on American imperialism in the 1990s and beyond, merely were following in Duranty's footsteps.[42]

40. Kaplan, *Lincoln Steffens*, lays out best the grisly details of Steffens' political end.
41. Steffens, *Autobiography*, 872.
42. Duranty information is drawn from his writing and from James Crowl's *Angels in Stalin's Paradise: Western Reporters in Soviet Russia, 1917–37 - Case Study of Louis Fischer and Walter Duranty* (Washington: University Press of America, 1982). A documentary about the famine shown on PBS during 1986—due to PBS politicization it ended up on a special evening edition of William F. Buckley's *Firing Line*—supports Crowl's view.

Duranty received a Pulitzer Prize in 1932 for his work's "scholarship, profundity, impartiality and exceptional clarity, and an example of the best type of foreign correspondence." Historical hindsight is not so kind, nor were the few among Duranty's journalist colleagues not tied to the left. Duranty's clarity was actually false analogy, as when he acknowledged that the Russian people were antirevolutionary only because they "are in the position of children at school, who personally might sooner be out at play and do not yet realize that they are being taught for their ultimate good."[43]

Duranty equated Stalin's opponents with the Ku Klux Klan and wrote that "the peasants by and large at last have begun to realize the advantages offered by the new system, just as a plebe at West Point comes later to admire what at first he found so rigorous." Plebes, of course, are not killed, but neither were resisters to Stalin, according to Duranty. Rather, they could redeem themselves by working in Gulag lumber camps, those "communes" where "the labor demand exceeds the supply" and prisoners have the satisfaction of working "for the good of the community."

Duranty ascended in apologia once the Depression began and more Americans began praising Soviet "full employment." In 1930, discussing Stalin's Five-Year Plan, Duranty wrote that there may be problems, but "what does count is that Russia is being speeded up and fermented—and disciplined—into jumping and making an effort." He portrayed Stalin once again as a harsh but kindly teacher, trying to "stir the people up, force new

43. Duranty certainly liked to play, in his way. In 1922, Crowl notes, Duranty brought to Moscow a Buick. He obtained "a fearless driver named Grisha and a screeching horn that was undistinguishable from that used by the G.P.U., the Soviet secret police. For many, the sight of Duranty's Buick plunging through the streets with Grisha's hand against the horn was a terrifying experience. Duranty delighted in making such forays at dusk when the police made their raids, and, on one occasion, his friends refused to unbolt their door for fifteen minutes while they disposed of some possibly incriminating foreign journals." Crowl, *Angels in Stalin's Paradise*, 34–35.

ideas into their heads and make them talk and think and learn despite themselves." Duranty equated the Five-Year Plan with the biblical exodus from Egyptian slavery: "Moses and Aaron can become Lenin and Trotsky, Joshua becomes Stalin."[44]

In 1932 and 1933, though, the Soviet countryside neared collapse in famine. About four million persons probably died in the manner later described by Victor Kravchenko: "Everywhere we found men and women lying prone, their faces and bellies bloated, their eyes utterly expressionless." In Fedor Belov's words, "The people were like beasts, ready to devour one another. And no matter what they did, they went on dying, dying, dying." Alexander Solzhenitsyn later wrote that "long lines of [peasants] dying of famine trudged toward the railroad stations in the hope of getting to the cities . . . but were refused tickets and were unable to leave—and lay dying beneath the station fences in a submissive heap of homespun coats and bark shoes."[45]

Horace Greeley had praised American collectives in the 1840s, but had not covered up small flaws. After a century of progress in journalism, Walter Duranty would praise Soviet collectivization in the 1930s and cover up murder. Stalin needed Duranty's help, because Stalin was shipping grain to the West in order to get cash to buy machinery for the steel industry, and coverage of the famine might have led to protests that could have stopped the big deals. Duranty did help. He wrote, "There is no actual starvation or deaths from starvation," and accused truthful reporters of concocting a "big scare story." Such was the prestige of Duranty, and the ideological mood of the times, that the honest reporters often had trouble with their editors.[46]

44. Just as Satan quotes Scripture for his own purposes, so many pro-Soviet journalists liked to use biblical references. Steffens called Lenin "Moses in Red."

45. Crowl, *Angels in Stalin's Paradise*, 139.

46. Steffens and Duranty may have been at the extreme, but many other journalists during the 1930s were not far behind. In *Bovard of the Post-Dispatch* (Baton Rouge: Louisiana State University Press, 1954), James Markham tells how Oliver Bovard,

Duranty knew what he was doing. Malcolm Muggeridge, then also a Moscow reporter, remembered Duranty acknowledging in conversation the famine but saying "you can't make omelettes without cracking eggs." Some say the Soviets bribed or compromised Duranty, but it was just as likely that he had made an idol of the Soviet Revolution generally and Stalin specifically. Duranty's favorite expression was, "I put my money on Stalin."[47]

At the end of Duranty's tour of duty in Moscow, he wrote that it had really been a tour of love: "Looking backward over the fourteen years I have spent in Russia, I cannot escape the conclusion that this period has been a heroic chapter in the life of Humanity."[48] Duranty's Pulitzer Prize led to other honors, a well-fed retirement in Southern California during which he continued to worship capital *H* "Humanity" rather than capital *G* "God," and a well-attended funeral in the mid-1940s.

Four decades later, books such as James Crowl's *Angels in Stalin's Paradise* and a documentary shown on the PBS show

editor of the influential, Pulitzer family-owned *St. Louis Post-Dispatch*, believed that the Constitution should be amended to abolish guarantees of property rights and due process, so that socialism could speedily be enacted. "To educate readers," Markham writes, Bovard "gave space to Stalin's addresses and the full text of the Soviet constitution," and sent a reporter to the Soviet Union with instructions to stress the theme in his writing that "economically the United States was going to the left, while Russia was tending to the right." Bovard believed, as did others on the left, that Franklin Roosevelt was "a mere schoolboy tinkering instead of getting down to cases, the 'Kerensky of the American revolution.' "

The political climate of the 1930s and the ideology of many journalists make Duranty appear less an anomaly and more the iceberg's tip. According to Malcolm Muggeridge, "If the *New York Times* went on all those years giving great prominence to Duranty's messages, building him and them up when they were so evidently nonsensically untrue, to the point that he came to be accepted as the great Russian expert in America, and played a major part in shaping President Roosevelt's policies vis-a-vis the USSR—this was not, we may be sure, because the *Times* was deceived. Rather it *wanted* to be so deceived, and Duranty provided the requisite deception material." Muggeridge, *Chronicles of a Wasted Time: The Green Stick* (New York: William Morrow, 1973), 255.

47. Muggeridge, *Chronicles of a Wasted Time*, 255.

48. Duranty, *I Write As I Please* (New York: Simon and Schuster, 1935), 340.

Firing Line made Duranty famous once again: this time as an accomplice to mass murder.

Conclusion

Proverbs 26:27 notes that "whoever digs a pit will fall into it." That often happens, but not always. Justice sometimes requires more than one lifespan to complete, and poetic justice in this life is sometimes found in poems but not outside.

Nothing can be proved by eight brief biographical sketches or eighty more, but they suggest certain lines of sight. Individuals often held up as among the most prescient of journalists suffered a limitation of vision. They did not become better journalists for stressing only the material, nor did they hit upon real solutions. They went on one mistaken, idolatrous crusade after another. They lived and died by ideological myths.

4 | Man's Subjectivity vs. God's Plumb Line

"**O**bjectivity**"** was a major goal of twentieth-century American journalism. *New York Times* editor Sydney Gruson demanded "purity of the news columns. Pure objectivity might not exist, but you have to strive for it anyway." Associated Press General Manager Wes Gallagher argued that "all men and women must have a Holy Grail of some kind, something to strive for, something always just beyond our fingertips even with the best of efforts. To the journalists that Holy Grail should be objectivity."[1]

Textbooks and codes of ethics still insist upon "objectivity." Yet, the concept has been under attack since the 1960s, first by fringe groups of "new journalists," now by those thrusting microphones in power-laden corridors. Robert Bazell of NBC, interviewed in 1986, said flatly, "Objectivity is a fallacy. . . . There are different opinions, but you don't have to give them equal weight." Irving R. Levine of NBC noted, "The reporter has got to determine, ultimately, what is valid and what is not." Linda Ellerbee wrote, "There is no such thing as objectivity. Any reporter who tells you he's objective is lying to you."[2]

We will see in this chapter that Christians should align with neither side. First, though, we need a basic definition of

---

1. Quoted in J. Herbert Altschull, *Agents of Power: The Role of the News Media in Human Affairs* (New York: Longman, 1984), 130.

2. Dinesh D'Souza, "Mr. Donaldson Goes to Washington," *Policy Review* (Summer 1986): 24–31.

"objective." For our purposes, we will define "objective" as that which exists independently of our perception of it, or our personal reflections or feelings. Likewise, an objective report is an attempt to report on objective reality and not a personal opinion or view of that reality.

That sounds straightforward enough, but what is reality? A fundamental tenet of Christian theology is the idea that God is real and he created the universe *ex nihilo*, "from nothing." Therefore, according to the Christian worldview, God defines reality, and our understanding of reality should conform to his definition of it. We call this form of journalism "biblical objectivity." As we suggested in chapter 2, and will discuss more fully in this chapter, "biblical objectivity"—accepting God's view of the world as reality—is what defines true Christian journalism.

Atheists, on the other hand, argue that God, as a product of imagination, has no real place in an objective news report. Christians argue that God's existence and sovereignty are objective truth, regardless of an atheist's personal belief in God's nonexistence. Is an objective reporter supposed to treat God as matter of fact (in which case he is joining the theistic side) or matter of opinion (in which case he has assumed the truth of atheism)?

There is a similar debate over what is "fact" and what is not. The *Oxford English Dictionary* defines *fact* as "a thing done or performed . . . something that has actually occurred or is actually the case . . . truth attested by direct observation or authentic testimony; reality." Typical usage in 1794 was, "The evangelists wrote from fact, not from imagination." That definition goes against the common journalistic tendency today to say that anything dealing with religion is a matter of opinion, not fact. That definition may open our minds to understand the four different phases of objectivity within American journalism history.

Phase One Objectivity: Spiritual/Material Interface

Many early American journalists assumed that God is objective reality, with an existence independent of our minds. The first American newspaper, *Publick Occurrences Both Foreign and Domestic*, had statements noting God's "Merciful Providence" as fact, not opinion. Editor Benjamin Harris reported on September 25, 1690, that Plymouth residents "have newly appointed a day of Thanksgiving to God for his Mercy in supplying their extreme and pinching Necessities under their late want of Corn, & for his giving them now a prospect of a very Comfortable Harvest."[3]

Although no one in early American journalism used the phrase *objective reporting*, some editors obviously understood that factuality demanded taking into account the spiritual. The *Boston Recorder* reported that "on a Sabbath, when church members were partaking of the Lord's Supper," members of an "infidel club" went to a nearby creek: "One of them, with the approbation of the rest, administered the Sacrament to dogs."

The *Recorder* did not argue that vicious and unrepentant blasphemers normally die quick and horrible deaths. Obviously, some escape physical punishment in this life. But in this case, "on the same evening, he who had done the impious deed was attacked with a violent inflammatory disease; his inflamed eye balls were protruding from their sockets; his tongue was swollen in his mouth;and he died before morning, in great mental and bloody agony." The *Recorder* saw the horrible death as God's judgment.[4]

3. Harris published only one issue of his newspaper. He had not obtained a license from governmental authorities, and two of his stories did not fit British public relations goals. The first continuing American newspaper was the *Boston News Letter*, published in 1704. Bartholomew Green, editor of the *News Letter* from 1722 to 1733, was explicit about his desire to cover the spiritual so that those "who have the state of religion in the world very much at heart" will better know "how to order their prayers and praises to the great God" (January 21, 1723).

4. *Boston Recorder*, January 25, 1823, 13.

The *Recorder* also reported recoveries from illness as acts of God. One story began with a note that when a ship sank "by the will of Providence" and a merchant lost all he had, his wife "was rendered altogether insane, and that to such a degree, that it was necessary to confine her in order to prevent her from doing herself and others harm."[5]

The wife's insanity continued until her father, who lived one hundred miles away, received a letter describing what had happened, and immediately "gathered together at his house many of the brethren of the Church for the purpose of pleading with God on her behalf. It was a solemn season of united and earnest supplication to the Lord." A few days afterward the father received a letter saying his daughter had suddenly "sat up in bed . . . in an instant restored to her usual health."

The story concluded, "Here we cannot but notice, in grateful acknowledgement, the goodness and mercy, compassion and faithfulness of that God who has said, 'Call upon me in the day of trouble, I will deliver thee, and thou shalt glorify me' for that evening and that hour of restoration, were the same evening and the same hour when many were gathered together, and prayer was made unto God for her."[6]

Just as *Recorder* editors knew that few blasphemers died immediately after notorious offenses with inflamed eyeballs protruding from sockets, so they knew that many individuals recover after prayer, but many others die. Christians sometimes want so much for God to "do justice" right away that we exaggerate reports of his intervention. God does not need public relations help. But when truly miraculous cures do occur, a *Recorder* editorial writer asked, "Can you rationally draw any other inference" than that of God's sovereignty?

5. Ibid., March 15, 1823, 41.
6. Ibid., 40.

Many early American journalists would be amazed to hear that those who ignore the spiritual now consider themselves objective. Then, those who ignored the spiritual were considered subjective atheists, allowing their own feelings to overcome what really was there. The book of Colossians had noted that Christ "is before all things, and in him all things hold together" (1:17). How then could a reporter, in describing reality, not refer to God, the Creator of reality?

Throughout phase one of American objectivity, mentions of God or Providence served more than ritualistic purposes. Journalists evidently saw that the world could not be understood apart from a biblical context. Furthermore, early Christian journalists knew the biblical view that humans are fallen and need regeneration. Humans unaided by God's grace cannot interpret correctly the facts of the universe.

Phase Two Objectivity: Straightforward Materialism

As Christian journalism declined midway through the nineteenth century and materialism became dominant, "fact" came to mean only that which was scientifically measurable. Journalists began to emphasize "facts; facts; nothing but facts. So many peas at so much a peck; so much molasses at so much a quart." Materialists who wanted to pursue their own desires without thought of morality particularly relished their new "freedom" in journalism, literature, and other spheres. Theodore Dreiser enjoyed the journalistic experience he had before gaining novelistic fame: "One can always talk to a newspaper man, I think, with the full confidence that one is talking to a man who is at least free of moralistic mush."[7]

Economic as well as presuppositional reasons backed the materialist trend. Beginning in the 1830s, the "penny press"

7. Michael Schudson, *Discovering the News: A Social History of American Newspapers* (New York: Basic Books, 1978), 78, 86.

79

began pushing for larger and more diversified circulation, which would bring with it the opportunity to raise advertising rates. On some newspapers, avoiding religious offense became critical. Midcentury brought with it development of the Associated Press and an increased push for a lowest-common-denominator view of news content: Describe who, what, when, and where, but often leave out the why and the how.

As the pressure for journalistic speed increased, reporters found that they could turn out more copy by ignoring deeper questions. Some editors resisted this movement toward superficiality, but others proudly proclaimed that their job was to put out a newspaper, not run a theological debating society. They did not understand that an editor inevitably has to do both.

The new definition of objectivity, as coverage of material alone, also required several assumptions about man and the world. Reporters had to be seen as capable of seeing things as they are. An innocent American Adam, before the fall, would name what had to be named. The world would have to be seen as a generally unmysterious place, and the visible equated with the real. Reporters could believe that what they saw naturally was a rational order, and that their own minds were the standard of authority. This represented a considerable departure from biblical notions of fallen man and complicated world.

Soon after gaining ascendancy, though, the concept of reporter as camera began to fall apart theoretically and practically. Early in the twentieth century some journalists rebelled against the idea, not because of questions brought forward by Christians, but because of the impact of Marxism and Freudianism. Marx argued that much of what was called objectivity actually was class subjectivity, with one class-bound vision of the world up against another's, thesis versus antithesis. Freud contended that much of what affected individuals was unknown, even to the individuals themselves, so it could not be assumed that judgments were unimpaired.

Economic society and individual psychology were both in flux, journalists came to believe. Christian objective reporting had depended on the understanding that the material/spiritual interface could be understood by man, with God's grace. Materialist objective reporting had grown up with the notion that a stable, easily understandable material world was there for the taking: what you see is what you get. In the twentieth century, it was being said that all was confusion. How could one reporter figure it out and get it down?

Phase Three Objectivity: Balancing of Subjectivities

Walter Lippmann, probably the most influential newspaper columnist of the twentieth century, was a Marxist in his early years and an admirer of Freudian thought. He used those ideas to become in the 1920s a philosopher of journalism as well. Lippmann was sarcastic about reporters' claims to objectivity, arguing, "For the most part we do not see first, then define; we define first and then see. . . . We pick out what our culture has already defined for us." Lippmann viewed the typical reporter as akin to the traveler who liked trains but did not think it proper to tip station agents and ushers: "His Odyssey will be replete with . . . train escapades and voracious demands for money."[8]

8. Walter Lippmann, *Public Opinion* (New York: Harcourt, Brace, 1922), 21. Lippmann's ideas of subjectivity were picked up by professors and journalists but proclaimed infrequently. One reason might be that widespread acceptance of ideas of reportorial subjectivity would have undermined one of the key reporters' campaigns of the 1930s: the campaign against the publishers. Publishers, often conservative and Republican during the 1930s, tried to rein in their Washington correspondents, often liberal and Democratic. The reporters tried to maintain that they were objective and scientific in their coverage, and thus should not be overwhelmed by the publishers' political considerations. Had they admitted that they tilted as much as the publishers did, but in a different political direction, their defense would have become untenable.

Others during the 1920s had similar scorn for pure fact, whether material or spiritual. Ivy Lee, one of the founders of public relations, said it is "humanly impossible" to state a fact: "All I can do is to give you my interpretation of the facts." Many others came to believe the journalist could not be a camera, since no one viewpoint could possibly be accurate. Henry Luce, founder of *Time* magazine, said, "Show me a man who thinks he's objective and I'll show you a man who's deceiving himself."[9]

"Objectivity" in journalism, therefore, went through its second reconstituting. First, it had been redefined to mean an ignoring of the spiritual. Increasingly, it meant ignoring even the observed material world, for fear of bias. Instead, the reporter would forgo his own reporting in order to assemble as many reports from others as he could.

"Objectivity" came to mean a balancing of multiple subjectivities. The outcome might be neither truthful nor accurate, but who knew what accuracy, let alone truth, really was? The important thing is to reflect different points of view. The desire to reflect multiple subjectivities, in the eyes of its proponents, was not an invitation to nihilism, but a pluralistic recipe for compromise and harmony. Since a variety of views were strongly held, this belief suggested that probably none of them was right, but all of them might have some truth.

The triumph of theological liberalism in major Protestant denominations occurred at the same time as the development of phase three objectivity in newspapers. This was no coincidence, since the balancing-of-subjectivities mode often suggested that there is no right or wrong, just opinion. The idea of absolute truth existing outside of man could not be taken seriously within phase three objectivity, because that would suggest the existence of real objectivity.[10]

9. Ivy Lee, *Publicity: Some of the Things It Is and Is Not* (New York: Industries publishing, 1925), 21; Schudson, *Discovering the News*, 149.

10. "Objectively" quoting the most articulate and convincing proponents of both sides in as evenhanded a way as possible places reporters and readers in the position

To summarize, phase three objectivity became not a reporting of both material and spiritual, nor a reporting of material only, but a reporting of what a variety of observers thought about material. Proponents of phase three objectivity might argue that this phase ushered in an era of balanced, evenhanded reporting. In fact, phase three objectivity became an apologetic for theological, moral, and ethical relativism. Journalists from the 1920s through the 1960s generally did not attempt to hold up the mirror to society. Instead, they urged others to hold up their own mirrors, so that reporters could then describe the funny but often incoherent, nonsensical shapes this house of mirrors produced.

The code of ethics of the Society of Professional Journalists, Sigma Delta Chi, concretized such subjectivity-balancing objectivity: Journalists proclaimed that "Truth is our ultimate goal," but "objectivity in reporting the news is another goal, which serves as the mark of an experienced professional." Such constructions were typical as Bible-based spiritual confidence disappeared. Objectivity might become "another goal," but it could not be part of the goal of truth, since truth, while ultimate, was ever receding.[11]

---

of Eve, who in the garden of Eden did the first balancing act. Wanting to be "objective" in the sense of hearing both sides, she had first heard God's view. Then Satan gave Eve a different set of facts and asked her to be the judge as to which she should accept. As philosopher Cornelius Van Til noted, "The acceptance of this position of judge constituted the fall of man. . . . Before Eve could listen to the tempter she had to take for granted that the devil was perhaps a person who knew as much about reality as God knew about it. Eve was compelled to assume the equal ultimacy of the minds of God, of the devil, and of herself. And this surely excluded the exclusive ultimacy of God." See Van Til, *The Defense of the Faith* (Philadelphia: Presbyterian and Reformed Publishing, 1955), 48–52.

11. Objectivity as traditionally understood—holding up a mirror to the area of coverage—began to receive fewer verbal plaudits during the 1960s. By then, the war of reporters' independence was won. By 1978, Stephen Hess, *The Washington Reporters* (Washington: Brookings, 1981), could state bluntly that publishers' throwing around of their weight had simply disappeared as an issue of reporters' concern. In part, this was because many publishers had moved leftward also; in part, because publishers had been trained to keep hands off the news pages.

As the number of cities with competitive newspapers declined from the 1920s onward, lowest-common-denominator pluralism and superficiality on the news pages was increasingly seen as essential both to profitability and to community service. It would be neither fair nor smart to upset the apple cart in order to search for better apples. Biblical beliefs generally were excluded from the lowest-common-denominator "consensus," but pietistic Christians tended not to complain.

Journalistic Criticism of Subjectivity Balancing

Many journalists came to find phase three objectivity frequently boring, occasionally demeaning, and generally purposeless. Boredom tended to set in because the reporter, if he was not to tip his hand, was forced to tell much less than he knew. Specific detail might be damning to one side or the other. The reporter, typically, would have to quote a variety of positions while keeping the more interesting—but biased—story buried in his notebook.

Some reporters became acerbic about objectivity. Former *New York Times* reporter David Halberstam complained that "objectivity was prized and if objectivity in no way conformed to reality, then all the worse for reality." Douglas Cater put it succinctly: The straight reporter is a "strait-jacket reporter."

A few reporters escaped from the straitjacket by becoming known for "interpretive reporting" or "news analysis." Columnists such as James Reston could claim they had "a wider vision of our duty," and were learning "to put the event of the day in its proper relationship to the history of yesterday and the dream of tomorrow." But only a favored few—such as Reston, whose career extended from the 1930s to the 1990s and included two Pulitzer Prizes—could indulge themselves in that way. Most journalists were demeaned, at least in their own eyes and often objectively, as they became delivery boys, used by politicians and others to carry their messages.[12]

Subjectivity balancing became particularly obnoxious to many liberal reporters during the early 1950s, as Senator Joseph McCarthy gave speeches about 57, then 205, then some other number of Communists in the State Department. The "balancing of subjectivities" approach forced reporters to quote McCarthy, then quote some other "authority" in a sputtering refusal, with the result that fallacious accusations received wide publicity.

Subjectivity balancing also tended to create or reinforce, as investigative journalist Edward Jay Epstein wrote, the "impression that at the root of political controversy is an intelligent argument between evenly matched opponents—an impression fostered by the articulateness of the opponents." When opponents were not equally articulate, the balancing mode favored, particularly on television, the articulate over the inarticulate.[13]

This proved distasteful because journalists knew that most people do not communicate well in public, and that those who do so generally have considerable practice. Since the articulate often are interview professionals, hired to come across well regardless of the validity of their position, balancing stories often do not get at the truth at all. They only create a seller's market for glibness.

Some journalists did find uses for a subjectivity-balancing approach. As late as World War II, reporters felt no need to balance comments by Franklin Roosevelt with those of Hitler.

12. Quoted in William Rivers, *The Opinionmakers* (Boston: Beacon Press, 1965), 59. The post-World War II Commission on Freedom of the Press had argued, "It is no longer enough to report the fact truthfully. It is now necessary to report the truth about the fact." Reston continued that theme, writing that "You cannot merely report the literal truth. You have to explain it."

13. See Edward Jay Epstein, *News from Nowhere: Television and the News* (New York: Random House, 1973).

American journalistic objectivity, like American political debate, extended only as far as the water's edge. But in 1966, reporter Harrison Salisbury of the *New York Times* traveled to Hanoi to get the North Vietnamese side of the story. For the remainder of the war, newspapers that wanted to be neutral could refute charges of lack of patriotism with claims of subjectivity-balancing objectivity.

Most journalists forced into stenography were frustrated, though. Subjectivity balancing satisfied parts of an ingenuous public, but it was unsatisfying to reporters who wanted to express themselves. *Public Interest* noted in 1978, "A significant segment of the media has become impatient with its limited information dissemination role. It is not easy and frequently not exciting for an intelligent person simply to report events. The tendency, therefore, has been for imaginative and socially dedicated journalists to go beyond normal reporting in order to seek fuller expression of their talents or social values."[14]

The movement toward fuller expression of social values led in the 1960s to development of an explicitly subjective "new journalism." Magazine writers such as Tom Wolfe, Gay Talese, and (on the extreme) Hunter Thompson wrote themselves and their ideas into their stories, often with startling effect. New journalism stories often seemed more vivid and honest, with a writer's beliefs showing through.

Television stations and established newspapers, however, tended to oppose "new journalism" methodology. Stations by law, and newspapers by practice, had become by the 1960s very careful about giving obvious offense. For mainstream reporters, the "new journalism" officially could become a subject for gossip but not overt imitation.

14. Max Kampleman in *Public Interest* (Fall 1978): 18; quoted in Rael Jean Isaac and Erich Isaac, *The Coercive Utopians: Social Deception by America's Power Players* (Chicago: Regnery, 1984), 274.

Phase Four Objectivity: Disguised Subjectivity

With subjectivity roaring through America over the past two decades, and each person supposedly an oracle unto himself, many journalists found ways to express their "social values." If they could not do it openly, they would make the world safe for duplicity by doctoring the subjectivity-balancing scales.

Readers and viewers could continue to believe that subjectivity balancing gave them the opportunity to make up their own minds, but journalists frequently selected evidence and structured the debate to produce their desired conclusions. To some extent they had always done this in subjectivity balancing, since no reporter could be completely neutral. However, during phase three reporters were taught to have so much doubt about their own conclusions that they would not want to push their vision too far.[15]

Since the 1960s, though, journalists have often thought themselves more knowledgeable than the people they cover. Former *Washington Post* editor Ben Bradlee argued in the 1960s that "nowadays, when a government expert gives a press briefing on news about economics, missiles, or Africa, there are four or five reporters in the room who know more about the subject than he does." (Maybe the journalists do and maybe they don't, but if they think they do they will write accordingly.)[16] "News analysis" articles became common, and were not always marked as such.

The 1980s saw an extension of "strategic ritual" (pseudo-objectivity that provides defense against criticism).[17] A key aspect of strategic ritual is choice of sources and selection of quotations. Of half a dozen legitimate spokesmen on a particular issue, reporters can readily pick out one who expresses the reporter's

15. Some journalists claim that they are just telling the story lucidly, giving more room to smart people and less to the befuddled. Give true equality to Bible thumpers? How is that possible if we are to improve mankind?

16. Rivers, *The Opinionmakers*, 13.

17. Gaye Tuchman, *Making News: A Study in the Construction of Reality* (New York: The Free Press, 1978).

own position. Norma Quarles was a long-time reporter for NBC and a member of the 1990 inaugural class of the National Association of Black Journalists' Hall of Fame. She was honest enough to admit that she plays journalistic ventriloquism when she wants to make a point: "If I get the sense that things are boiling over, I can't really say it. I have to get somebody else to say it."[18]

Similarly, of the many statements an opponent may make during an interview, reporters can play up one that will make that opponent look foolish. The upshot is that, once again, a reporter often makes a story conform to the "pictures in his head," just as in the era of straightforward materialism. In the late twentieth century, though, the process was far more effective, for readers and viewers had become used to thinking they actually were receiving the debate. When such attitudes imbedded, millions of suckers were born during every minute of airtime.[19]

Some poker-faced reporters continue to insist they merely present "information." Since they do not have to show their hands unless a libel suit results, many readers and viewers never see that they are bluffing. The abortion debate alone provides endless examples of journalistic strategic ritual. As ABC executive producer Av Westin has noted, network abortion stories during the early 1970s followed a formula: First, dramatic photos of bruised, "unwanted" babies, or shots of "a silhouetted woman telling how she nearly died after an illegal abortion." Then, "with the case for legalized abortion powerfully presented, an opponent of abortion would be given a chance to make the pro-life side of the case, usually without dramatic pictures, inserted merely as a 'talking head.' "[20]

The game of strategic ritual is often unsatisfying to reporters, but for a time they had few alternatives. They could not

18. D'Souza, loc. cit.

19. Even when readers and viewers do receive some real debate, it is likely to be liberal materialist versus conservative materialist.

20. Av Westin, *Newswatch: How TV Decides the News* (New York: Simon and Schuster, 1982), 233.

return to phase one, because reporters and editors perceive spiritual matters as grounded in opinion, not fact. They could not return to phase two, because twentieth-century relativists saw correctly that no man is a camera. Phase three forced balance where there was none. (Rita Braver, covering health issues for CBS News, skillfully made the argument from absurdity: "When I cover drugs, it would be absurd for me to look for a person who says PCP is good for kids.")[21] Phase four was the last resort.

Yet, he who digs a pit falls into it. Strategic ritual is based on deception, the idea that reporters are smart enough to indoctrinate subtly and the assumption that readers or viewers are too stupid to get angry. But some readers and viewers got angry, the next several chapters show. Strategic ritual alienated journalists from the communities they were supposed to serve and exhibited the arrogance that people hate.[22] That's why some strategic ritual remains, but a new phase has started.

Phase Five: Undisguised Subjectivity

Recently some major news magazines and television networks have moved toward undisguised subjectivity, for at least four reasons.

21. D'Souza, loc. cit.

22. Strategic ritual receives particular scorn from those who have been libeled in stories that pretend to be objective. Rodney Smolla, in *Suing the Press: Libel, the Media and Power* (New York: Oxford University Press, 1986), 191–92, examined the reaction of one defamed individual, William Tavoulareas: "People like William Tavoulareas do not seem to take offense when reporters draw personal conclusions, as long as they make it clear that they are drawing them. Nor do they take offense when the 'straight' news story neutrally lays out raw facts, leaving all conclusions to the reader. What appeared to irk Tavoulareas and the Washington D.C. jury was the subtle infiltration of judgmental conclusions by the *Post* in what on its face purported to be neutral reportage. What Tavoulareas lashed out against was advocacy wrapped up in the disguise of neutrality—the news story presented as pure fact that was really a selection of facts to support a predetermined opinion." Smolla himself criticizes the *Post* for not having "the courage of its own conviction—the courage to make its editorializing explicit. . . . The *Post* slipped into a wimpish middle ground, hinting that Tavoulareas had cheated the public interest, but putting the story in an objective voice."

First, the movement from three or four channels to hundreds, and a similar proliferation of print news through the Internet, led some networks and publications to stop seeking the whole pie and start settling for a slice. Building a brand—whether that brand is corn flakes, newspapers, or a television network—requires both differentiation and consistency. Great brands make unique promises and deliver what they promise. By the 1990s, staking out a liberal (MSNBC) or a conservative (Fox News) point of view became an efficient way for these networks to promise viewers what they would get on these networks.

Second, we all have a tendency to gravitate toward people who reinforce our own beliefs and ideas. So readers and audiences, voting with their television remote controls, began to encourage undisguised subjectivity. From the 1940s until the early 1980s, the Big Three networks (CBS, NBC, and ABC) had a combined market share of 90 percent or more. But audiences in 2012 no longer reward with their viewership the disguised subjectivity of the three major networks. That's why by 2005, the three major networks had only a 32 percent market share.

Third, technology and the consequent fragmentation of outlets also changed the advertising model of television journalism. We'll have more to say about that in chapter 9. For purposes of our discussion here, we'll simply observe that as fragmentation caused the audiences for individual networks and programs to get smaller, these smaller audiences also became more homogeneous. Their buying behaviors became more consistent and predictable. They became smaller but more attractive advertising markets.

Fourth, media bias became so obvious and pervasive that some journalists and their employers determined that the "liberal" label was less damaging to their credibility than proclaiming neutrality when that label was so obviously false. In October 2010, for example, as the Obama campaign successfully proclaimed "Forward," MSNBC used the tag-line "Lean Forward."

All of this is to say that the undisguised subjectivity of the increasingly liberal media is not an intentional conspiracy, but an unsurprising consequence of technological change and the ongoing secularization of society. The French lawyer and philosopher Joseph de Maistre famously said, "Every country has the government it deserves."[23] The same might be said of our media diet. Media are a powerful force for change in our culture, but media both lead and follow the values of the people. The people and corporations who control twenty-first century media are not cramming anything down our throats. They give us what we are willing to pay for.

New Objectivity New Servanthood

Christians have a solution to the problems of objectivity. It is based on a different understanding of the nature of man, the nature of God, and the nature of man's tasks and man's hopes.

First, the Christian solution is not based on confidence in man. It assumes that fallen man naturally distorts and lies, and that fallen man's wisdom will slide us even deeper into sin and misery. Objectivity in all its non-Christian phases assumes that the major check on pernicious news twisting is journalistic goodwill. Former *Louisville Courier-Journal* editor James Pope called objectivity a compass or gyroscope for fair reporting, a little secret radar beam that stabs you when you start twisting news to your own fancy. But, given a biblical understanding of man's nature, is such a man-made belief likely to function in that way?

Second, the Christian solution is based on confidence in God's objectivity. God alone, the Christian knows, has given

23. "Toute nation a le gouvernement qu'elle mérite," *de Maistre's Lettres et Opuscules Inédits*, vol., 1, letter 53, written on August 15, 1811, and published in 1851. This quotation is often misattributed to Alexis de Tocqueville.

us a biblical measuring rod built of true, godly objectivity. As the prophet Amos saw, "the Lord was standing beside a wall built with plumb line, with a plumb line in his hand." God then told Amos that he was "setting a plumb line in the midst of my people Israel" (Amos 7:7–8). We have that plumb line today, the Bible. Thus, we know what man should do. For the Christian journalist, then, the pursuit of what we have come to call "biblical objectivity" should be a guiding principle.[24]

Third, the Christian solution is based on man's ability, with God's grace, to study God's objectivity and apply it to everyday situations. Christians know that our hope of arriving at accurate views is not to wipe our minds clean, because then we are at the mercy of our fallen vision, but to fill up our minds with God's vision. Walter Cronkite once said that he was a liberal, which he then defined as one "not bound by doctrines or committed to a point of view in advance."[25] But, given our fallen natures, we are all captive to sin unless we are committed to Christ.

Christians are skeptical of self-generated conclusions but sure of God's. When Christians understand the Bible and are able to apply biblical principles, we can have confidence to go beyond subjectivity by responding to problems with God's Word, which is objectivity. Since the Christian presuppositional structure is closer to reality than competing frameworks are, Christians can explain more accurately how the world truly works.

Furthermore, since Christians can measure with God's plumb line, Christians can use all the techniques of phases one, two, and three, and can learn much from talented journalists who were philosophically wrong. Since spiritual causes are not always clear, phase two material description will be all that is sure in some cases. For example, the *Boston Recorder* reminded

24. Marvin Olasky, *Telling The Truth: How To Revitalize Christian Journalism* (Wheaton, IL: Crossway, 1995; Eugene, OR: Wipf & Stock Publishers, 2010).
25. Quoted in Epstein, *News from Nowhere*, 214.

readers of the results of Napoleonic ambition by printing, without editorial comment the following report:

> More than a million bushels of human and inhuman bones were imported last year from the continent of Europe into the port of Hull. The neighborhood of Leipsic, Austerlitz, and Waterloo, and all of the places where during the late bloody war the principal battles were fought, have been swept alike of the bones of the horse and his rider, and shipped to England, where steam engines have been erected, with powerful machinery, for the purpose of granulating them. In this condition they are sent chiefly to Poncaster, one of the largest agricultural markets, and sold to farmers to manure their lands.[26]

The phase three emphasis on quoting various sides is also useful—and we see that God's inspired writers often quoted adversaries. Almost the entire chapters of 2 Kings 18 and Isaiah 36 quote the blandishments of a blaspheming Asssyrian general who demanded surrender and promised exile to "a land of grain and wine, a land of bread and vineyards, a land of olive trees and honey" (2 Kings 18:26; Isa. 36:17). The strategy involved in printing this offer was clear from the context: the Assyrian was merely imitating what God had told the Israelites concerning the land of milk and honey. He offered them in permanence. The Israelites remained silent.

Christian objectivity, then, consists not of a technique but of a plumb line. All kinds of stories can be Christian. Those that end in sadness often teach the wages of sin, those that end well may emphasize the wages of piety, and those that are unclear teach us that much of life is unpredictable and often confusing. Immediate justice often is not forthcoming, except in poetry. Poetic justice tells us what heaven will be like, but an undue

---

26. *Boston Recorder*, January 18, 1823, 11.

emphasis on good guys always winning might make us believe, falsely, that the present, shattered earth is our real home. Christian journalists like to "see what God is doing today," but often do not and cannot supply the didactic "why." Christian objectivity means having both eyes fastened on God.

Can This Be True Objectivity?

This type of objectivity will not be satisfying to the atheist who believes that all religion is subjective. The Bible, though, teaches that our reason is so fallen that apart from God we cannot see anything objectively.

No easy compromise is possible when such fundamental presuppositions are battling each other. God shows Christians that he exists independently of our minds by acting on our minds from outside. Yet, if a person who had not had that experience is unwilling to accept the testimony of others, and thus assumes internally generated psychological change rather than God's grace, he will see Christian fact as imagination, and Christian objectivity as subjectivity.

In the long run, journalistic differences between Christians and non-Christians are inevitable.

PART 2

EXILE

Man without God is a beast, and never more beastly than when he is most intelligent about his beastliness.
—*Whittaker Chambers*

5 | Ethics without Christ?

The hills are alive with the sound of musings. Almost everywhere, it seems, journalists and journalism professors are attending conferences on ethics or writing books on ethics. Some valuable work has illuminated the hazards for reporters in accepting bribes ("freebies"), overt or subtle, or in making up stories.[1] But the discussions of ethics have overlooked some deeper problems.

Part of the impetus for the ethics books and conferences may have come from the shocks to journalism which came in the early 1980s. Novelist John Hersey, writing in a 1980 issue of the *Yale Review*, criticized what he saw as "the great fallacy" of the new journalism, the movement noted in chapter 4 that turned its back on objectivity: "Since perfect objectivity in reporting what the eyes have seen and the ears have heard is impossible, there is no choice but to go all the way over to absolute subjectivity."[2]

1. Some of the better books on journalistic ethics are: Clifford Christians, Kim Rotzoll, and Mark Fackler, *Media Ethics: Cases and Moral Reasoning* (New York: Longman, 1983); Nelson Crawford, *The Ethics of Journalism* (New York: Knopf, 1924); Tom Goldstein, *The News at Any Cost* (New York: Simon and Schuster, 1985); Gene Goodwin, *Groping for Ethics in Journalism* (Ames, IA: Iowa State University Press, 1983); John Hulteng, *The Messenger's Motives: Ethical Problems of the News Media*, 2nd ed. (Englewood Cliffs, NJ: Prentice-Hall, 1985); Edmund Lambeth, *Committed Journalism: An Ethic for the Profession* (Bloomington: Indiana University Press, 1986).
2. John Hersey, "The Legend of the License," *Yale Review* (Autumn 1980): 2.

Hersey argued that such a view "soon makes the reporter the center of interest rather than the real world he is supposed to be picturing, or interpreting."[3] Events of the following year, though, showed there was more to it than even that: As the reporter became the center of interest, the world's actual reality became less important, with imagination (pretending to honesty) assuming the throne.

An episode famous in its own right and as a symbol of the new era of journalistic dishonesty involved the award of a 1981 Pulitzer Prize for the *Washington Post* story "Jimmy's World." The story itself was a series of imaginary events and fabricated quotations about a supposed eight-year-old heroin addict. When *Post* reporter Janet Cooke lied once too often and was found out, the *Post* returned the award. The newspaper defended itself, saying it too was a victim of Cooke's lies, and claiming no editor could be safe from a clever liar.

Some *Post* editors had been suspicious all along. One *Post* reporter drove Cooke through the neighborhood where she claimed Jimmy lived, and saw that she did not know the area. He reported that to the city editor, but no investigation ensued. The story, true or false, was just too juicy to pass up. Cooke's editor, Bob Woodward, previously best-known for helping to break the story of Watergate, said "Jimmy's World" was "so well-written and tied together so well that my alarm bells simply didn't go off."[4]

Ironically, the prize Cooke had to return was awarded to another article that used what the National News Council called

3. Ibid.
4. The sad story of Janet Cooke has been told in many books and articles. One of the fuller accounts is in Normal Isaacs, *Untended Gates: The Mismanaged Media* (New York: Columbia University Press, 1986), 63–81. When the scandal broke, *Post* editors explained that they had not checked the story's facts more carefully or gone looking for Jimmy because a drug dealer had threatened Cooke's life if she identified him. One former editor, Charles Seib, reacted to that explanation by wondering publicly why the editors were "so willing to let Jimmy die." Seib noted, "There was deep concern for Cooke's safety. But not a thought for Jimmy." Goldstein, *The News at Any Cost*, 29.

"overuse of unattributed sources" and "reckless and speculative construction." The same year, a *New York Daily News* reporter admitted he had made up "facts" in a column on violence in Northern Ireland. The reporter, in his defense, said he had done the same thing three hundred times before. In early 1982, the *New York Times* acknowledged that it had published an article about a trip inside Cambodia by a writer who had not gone to Cambodia, and had instead plagiarized passages from a novel written decades before.[5]

Other high-profile cases of journalistic fraud followed in the 1990s and beyond. The *New Republic* determined that Stephen Glass fabricated at least twenty-seven of the forty-one stories he wrote for the magazine between 1995 and 1998. In 2003 the *New York Times* fired rising star Jayson Blair when editors discovered he had fabricated or plagiarized material in at least a half-dozen stories.

Journalists could see part of the problem behind those stories: the movement away from subjectivity balancing to expression of the reporter's own subjective views, generally through subtle "strategic ritual." Editors tended to react by deploring inaccuracies, pledging to cut down on the remnants of "new journalism," and demanding more substantiation from reporters.

Stories such as "Jimmy's World," however, showed not only problems in "objectivity" as it has been most recently defined, but a lack of compassion. *Post* editors did not respond to readers' pleas to try to find "Jimmy" so that he could be helped. A former editor, Charles Seib, pointed out that *Post* editors would have saved themselves much subsequent recrimination if they had shown some compassion for Jimmy, because in searching for him they would have realized that the story was made-up.

5. "News Watchdog Group Scores 'Voice' Pulitzer Prize Winner," *Washington Post*, June 12, 1981, A2; Michael Kramer, "Just the Facts, Please," *New York*, May 25, 1981, 19; James Markham, "Writer Admits He Fabricated an Article in *Times* Magazine," *New York Times*, February 22, 1982, 1Y, 4Y.

Behind most of these and other deceptive stories stand reporters who cared little about real people and real problems, and therefore let imagination reign. When John Hersey noted the present and impending triumph of journalistic subjectivity, he could have gone further and spoken of journalistic solipsism, with many reporters writing as if their private pursuit of stories was the only reality, or at least the only one that counts.

Newspaper treatment of Hilda Pate (she now has a new last name) provides a good example of the failure to place compassion for victims above journalistic cheap thrills. A 1982 court case revealed how Pate was abducted by her estranged husband. He came to her office and, at gunpoint, forced her to go with him to their former apartment in Cocoa Beach, Florida. There he beat her repeatedly and forced her to take off all her clothes.[6]

As police closed in Mr. Pate killed himself. The police entered, found Hilda Pate in a state of shock and emotional distress, and rushed her out of the house to a police car in full view of reporters, photographers, onlookers, and other policemen. She was still naked, but was clutching a dish towel to her body. The local newspaper, *Cocoa Today*, published a photograph of Hilda Pate, her private parts barely covered by the dish towel. The photograph was distributed across the United States through the news services and published in newspapers throughout the country.

Pate sued for invasion of privacy and won a jury verdict, but a Florida appeals court ruled that the photographs were taken in public during a legitimate news event and showed only what a gawking onlooker at the spot could have seen. Photographers and editors were legally in the clear. According to an angry jury, though, journalists had revictimized a sad

---

6. *Cape Publications v. Bridges*, 6 Media Law Reporter 1884; 8 Med. L. Rptr. 2525.

victim, causing her "severe emotional distress and mental pain and anguish."[7]

The Pate case was typical of a pattern emerging during the 1980s: a victim rescued from an assailant, only to face a new victimizer—the press. For example, in 1980 the *Burlington County* (NJ) *Times* printed the name of a rape victim in three separate stories about the rape, despite her request to police that it not be revealed. The victim sued both the newspaper and the hospital which had supplied confidential information to reporters. She charged that identification of a rape victim was not necessary to a rape story but reflected "morbid desire." The *Times* defended its action, saying identification by name strengthened the impact of its stories, and the New Jersey Superior Court agreed.[8]

Similarly, a Florida rape victim testified at the 1982 trial of her assailant after receiving assurance by state authorities that her name and photograph would not be published or displayed. A television station, though, videotaped the trial proceedings and ran the rape victim's testimony on its evening news show. While the videotape ran, the newscaster identified the victim by name to the viewing audience. She sued the station for invasion of privacy, but a Florida appeals court had to note that the state, despite its promise to the rape victim, did not try to restrain the videotaping or use of the woman's name. Since the information was readily available to the public, the television station was legally in the clear.[9]

The station was an ethical derelict in the eyes of the judge. He let the station off "reluctantly," he wrote, "because the information disclosed during the television broadcast appears to us to have been completely unnecessary to the story being presented.

7. Ibid.
8. *Griffith v. Rancocas Valley Hospital*, 8 Med. L. Rptr. 1760.
9. *Doe v. Sarasota-Bradenton Television*, 9 Med. L. Rptr. 2074.

Withholding the name and photograph of the victim in this case would in no way have interfered with or restricted publication of 'news of the day.' " He asked that journalists think about the "individual rights of others."[10]

Judge Campbell also noted the price of journalistic license: "The rape victim," he wrote, "had the unhappy circumstance of becoming a victim of a crime. The publication added little or nothing to the sordid and unhappy story; yet, that brief little-or-nothing addition may well affect appellant's well-being for years to come." The judge was not calling for courts to be closed, nor should Christians generally. Biblically, court proceedings generally were open. Yet, Campbell was asking for compassion. He deplored "the lack of sensitivity to the rights of others" evident among many journalists.[11]

A 1982 Supreme Court decision spotlighted that widespread lack of sensitivity. The Massachusetts legislature, hoping to protect the privacy of minor rape victims, had passed a law excluding the public from sexual assault trials during the testimony of victims under eighteen years of age. The *Boston Globe* wanted its reporters to be present for the victims' testimony during a trial in which the defendant was charged with raping three minor girls. The trial judge said no. The Supreme Judicial Court of Massachusetts refused to issue an injunction and later dismissed the *Globe's* appeal.[12]

The *Globe* kept pushing, and finally found powerful protectors. In 1982 Justice Brennan and six other U.S. Supreme Court justices overturned the Massachusetts ruling. Brennan wrote that the press could be barred only under "narrowly tailored" situations when "necessitated by a compelling government interest." Brennan wrote that the First Amendment did not

10. Ibid.
11. Ibid.
12. *Globe Newspapers v. Superior Court,* 457 U.S. 596, 102 S. Ct. 2613 (1984), 8 Med. Law Rptr. 1689.

"explicitly" justify the Supreme Court's ruling, "but we have long eschewed any 'narrow, literal conception' of the Amendment's terms."[13]

Former chief justice Warren Burger dissented, writing that the legislation was justified in trying "to prevent the risk of severe psychological damage caused by having to relate the details of the crime in front of a crowd which inevitably will include voyeuristic strangers." In most states, that crowd may be expanded to include a live television audience, with reruns on the evening news. That ordeal could be difficult for an adult. To a child, the experience can be devastating and leave permanent scars. Burger concluded that Brennan's opinion showed a "cavalier disregard of the reality of human experience."[14]

The cavalier disregard goes beyond coverage of rape. As we will see in chapter 11, nineteenth-century journalists at times would cover "successful" suicide attempts after they had happened, with the hope of trying to show others that suicide was brutal and nonheroic. Recently, though, some journalists have not acted to prevent suicides, and by their presence have even urged on those aspiring to a brief moment in the headlines.

One notorious instance "starred" a newspaper photographer in Oregon. He could have helped a woman on a bridge who was desperately gripping her husband in an attempt to restrain him from jumping one hundred feet into the Columbia River. The photographer, instead of grabbing on, took five pictures. The man broke loose from his wife and jumped to his death in the river.[15]

A well-publicized episode in 1983 began when a man called television station WHMA in Anniston, Alabama, to say he

13. Ibid., 1692–93.
14. Ibid., 1699.
15. Gene Goodwin, "The Ethics of Compassion," in Ray Hiebert and Carol Reuss, eds., *Impact of Mass Media: Current Issues* (New York: Longman, 1985), 85.

planned to set fire to himself in a nearby town square at midnight. The station's news director dispatched a camera crew. When the news team arrived no one was visible, but when the cameraman climbed out of his car the apparently drunken man approached, poured charcoal-starter fluid over himself, lit a match, and started the fire. The cameraman continued to film as the burning began, but an eighteen-year-old who had a part-time job with the station did try to beat out the flames. The man survived, with serious burns.[16]

Some journalists expressed concern over that episode, and several others. Journalists and the public also paid attention to the tale of a television camera crew following a man trying to pay a ransom to persons who had kidnapped his wife. Despite the man's pleas, the crew kept coming and—according to the FBI—"put that woman's life in danger." The newspaper trade magazine *Editor and Publisher* editorialized that the TV crew had been practicing not "enterprising reporting" but "sheer stupidity. . . . It is this sort of arrogance and brashness that gets media in trouble with the public."[17]

Such episodes are why the 2005 Annual Report on American Journalism from the Project for Excellence in Journalism said the number of people who view news organizations as ethical was 39 percent: "People have long considered the press sensational, rude, pushy and callous. But

16. Some television stations, while not acting in such grotesque ways, have turned suffering to promotional advantage. The Oregon Supreme Court in 1986 reviewed an invasion of privacy case that grew out of a news story. A television cameraman had photographed the scene of an automobile accident in which a man was injured. The evening news showed the man bleeding and in pain while receiving emergency medical treatment. This was legitimate news and the man recognized it as such, but the television station began using the clip for promotional spots in self-advertising; he sued. Oregon judges decided for the television station, thus ruling that the bloodied faces and bodies of accident victims are fair game for television use, not just as immediate news but again, again, and again. *Anderson v. Fisher*, 12 Med. L. Rptr. 1604.

17. *Editor and Publisher*, July 18, 1979, 6.

they have also come to see the press as less professional, less moral, more inaccurate and less caring about the interests of the country."[18]

The trouble amplifies when Hollywood gets hold of the behavior. In the immediate post-Watergate era, the 1976 movie *All the President's Men* turned reporters into heroes and swelled the rolls of journalism schools. Jane Fonda played a television reporter in two 1979 movies: in both *China Syndrome* and *The Electric Horseman* she overcomes her competitive instincts to expose corporate corruption. But Hollywood quickly turned on the profession. The 1981 film *Absence of Malice* showed how careless reporting can injure the innocent.

The selfish, ambitious television reporter has since become a stock movie villain. In the 1988 movie *Die Hard* and its 1990 sequel, a television reporter endangers the lives of others in a quest for ratings and personal glory. In those films and in an over-the-top parody of TV news, *Anchorman: The Legend of Ron Burgundy*, the reporters were not so much villainous as banal and self-absorbed. The 2003 film *Shattered Glass* portrayed Stephen Glass (mentioned earlier) as a chronic liar and virtual sociopath, but most of his fellow journalists were such moral relativists—or so pressured and fearful because of the competitive situation in which they found themselves—that Glass's unethical behavior long went unnoticed.

The movie showed much about journalistic tendencies to falsify that grow with the advent of cable news, the proliferation of news channels, and the growth of the Internet. New technology brings the ability to disseminate news broadly and fast, but the competitive pressure to be first also pressures journalists to dispense with fact-checking and careful editing. In this environment, purely fabricated stories are more likely to slip through cracks that have become fissures.

18. Project for Excellence in Journalism, Annual Report 2005, "Overview," 1.

Broadcast journalists, in particular, face pressure to put on the air sensational but previously taboo material.

For example, local television helicopters now routinely cover police car chases and then air highlights on their evening newscasts. Cable news networks go one step further, often breaking into regular coverage to carry live chases that sometimes end in spectacular wrecks. On September 28, 2012, Fox News covered a chase that ended in a suicide—all broadcast live. Fox later apologized for the incident. Anchor Shepard Smith said it would "never happen again, not on my watch." Perhaps, but in the 24–7–365 world of news in the digital era, it is soon enough someone else's watch, someone who may be less outraged than Shepard Smith was to see such material on the air.

Perhaps the most surreal example of this journalistic lack of compassion happened in 2005. JetBlue Flight 292 with 140 passengers aboard approached Los Angeles International Airport. The crew discovered that the front landing gear would not lock in the proper position. Repeated attempts to remedy the situation failed, so after flying around Southern California for three hours to burn off fuel, the plane landed in what the Associated Press described as a "stream of sparks and burning tires." No one was hurt, but what earns this episode a spot on our list of irresponsible media coverage is that not only was the entire episode broadcast live, but—thanks to satellite television—the passengers on Flight 292 watched the episode themselves.

AP summarized the story, "While satellite TV sets aboard JetBlue Flight 292 were tuned to news broadcasts, some passengers cried. Others tried to telephone relatives and one woman sent a text message to her mother in Florida attempting to comfort her in the event she died. 'It was very weird. It would've been so much calmer without' the televisions, Pia

Varma of Los Angeles said."[19] The Federal Aviation Agency agreed and stepped in where the networks and the Federal Communications Commission would not. The FAA now requires an automatic shutdown of television and Internet service on satellite-enabled flights when the plane drops below ten thousand feet.

Overall, with ethics conferences wading in humanistic homilies, many nonbiblical journalists still salivate like Pavlov's dogs whenever the story bell sounds. This is certainly the public perception of the occupation. According to a survey by the American Society of Newspaper Editors, 78 percent of Americans believe that news reporters "are just concerned with getting a good story, and they don't worry much about hurting people." In the same study, 63 percent said that "the press often takes advantage of victims of circumstance who are ordinary people."[20]

That popular mood has contributed to vigorous criticism and occasional boycotts of local newspapers that print names of rape victims. The Commission on Women of Arlington, Virginia, asked readers to cancel their subscriptions to the *Northern Virginia Sun*, which had a policy of identification by name. The Durham, North Carolina, Rape Crisis Center picketed the *Durham Morning Herald* after it named a rape victim in a front-page story.

Some newspaper editors hit back, though. Michael Rouse of Durham argued that opponents to the printing of names were "seeking to coerce the free press." He wrote that the protesters

19. "JetBlue passengers watch live coverage of plane's equipment problems," *USA Today*, September 22, 2005.

20. Public opinion polls record mixed definitions of "invasion of privacy." In one poll, 70 percent of those questioned said that publication of a photograph of a well-known politician entering a pornographic book shop was invasion of privacy; 26 percent said privacy had not been invaded. Should names of men arrested for soliciting prostitutes be published? Forty-nine percent said that would constitute an invasion of privacy, 47 percent had no objection. Was publication of names of persons under sixteen years old accused of committing crimes an invasion of privacy? Fifty-one percent said yes, 44 percent no. *The People and the Press: A Times Mirror Investigation of Public Attitudes Toward the News Media* (Los Angeles: Times Mirror Co., 1986).

"believed divine guidance was on their side," and added that "newspaper editors lacking the benefit of divine guidance usually call upon their own objective judgment when deciding such matters."[21] Rouse apparently was sarcastic, but the difference between man's best "objective judgment" and divine guidance is clear. Many newspapers do not print names of rape victims, but others do. Major journalistic codes of ethics do not cover the question. Legally, newspapers covering details of rape are generally in the clear. One U.S. Circuit Court of Appeals decreed in very broad language that a reporter's privilege "extends to information concerning interesting phases of human activity." Man's judgment tends to approve of publishing whatever seems interesting.[22]

Real divine guidance, found in the Bible, is very different. Yes, many things are interesting: "The words of a whisperer are like delicious morsels; they go down into the inner parts of the body" (Prov. 18:8). Nevertheless, in Proverbs we are often told to be careful about what we report, for "When words are many, transgression is not lacking, but whoever restrains his lips is prudent" (Prov. 10:19). Subsequent chapters of Proverbs note similarly that "a man of understanding remains silent," and that "whoever guards his mouth preserves his life, but he who opens wide his lips comes to ruin" (Prov. 11:12; 13:3).

The Bible often contrasts those who emphasize the educational with those who blurt out the merely interesting. Proverbs teaches that "whoever restrains his words has knowledge," (Prov. 17:27), but "whoever winks the eye causes trouble, and a babbling fool will come to ruin" (Prov. 10:10). Thoughtless reporting may

21. Michael Rouse, "Rape," *ASNE Bulletin*, February 1982; reprinted in George Rodman, *Mass Media Issues* (New York: Science Research Associates, 1984), 300–303. See also Zena Beth McGlashan, "By Reporting the Name, Aren't We Victimizing the Rape Victim Twice?," *ASNE Bulletin*, April 1982, reprinted in Rodman, *Mass Media Issues*, 304–7.

22. *Campbell v. Seabury Press*, 614 E 2d 395 (5th Cir. 1980), S Med. L. Rptr. 1803, 1829.

have physical consequences: "A fool's lips walk into a fight, and his mouth invites a beating" (Prov. 18:6). It also may have consequences for a community: "A dishonest man spreads strife, and a whisperer separates close friends" (Prov. 16:28). The reporter himself may suffer the spiritual consequences: "A fool's mouth is his ruin, and his lips are a snare to his soul" (Prov. 18:7).

Development of a biblical standard for coverage of rape trials involves three questions of increasing specificity. First, should information about the trials be available to the public? Second, should specific detail from testimony be published? Third, should victims be identified?

On the first question, most trials should be open to the public. Trials in the Bible were generally conducted by "elders" at the "gate," a prominent and public passageway (Deut. 21:19; 22:15; 25:7–9; Ruth 4:1, 11).

On the second question, the Bible's refusal to shy away from harsh reality teaches us that depiction of evil can be useful, if context is provided. The *Winfield* (Kansas) *Daily Courier* was criticized for reporting testimony that after intercourse with one victim (unnamed) the rapist "entered her rectum." Publisher David Seaton, though, argued that citizens needed "to know how severe rape cases are. . . . It seemed to me that there was a sound case to be made for having people face the harsh realities."[23]

The third question, on naming the victim, highlights the question of compassion. Victims generally are powerless during a rape to control what is happening to them. Identification in a news story may be a second assault on privacy, a second situation in which the victim feels powerless to protect herself from consequences such as humiliation, embarrassment, and possible danger. Biblically, we are to have compassion toward widows, orphans, and others who are abandoned or left destitute

23. Rouse, "Rape," 302.

109

in a variety of ways. We certainly owe biblical compassion to rape victims.

The word compassion, however, "makes a lot of journalists squirm," according to former reporter Gene Goodwin: "It describes a condition that runs counter to the strong tradition in journalism of detachment." Harvard University's James C. Thomson wrote that among leading journalists taking sabbaticals under his supervision, "What is usually lacking is empathy or compassion for their subjects, those reported about, or even token nods toward those qualities." Robert Maynard, then-editor of the *Oakland Tribune*, noted that "when people see a TV person shoving a mike in front of a grieving relative," journalists "appear to be boorish and ghoulish." Appearances in this case may not be deceiving.[24]

Again, many newspapers do not print names of rape victims, and—unless the person raped is prominent—it is hard to see any situation in which identifying the victim is vital. Possible apologia for printing names (for example, making the story more "real" for readers) are underwhelming in comparison to the detriments of such action.

The details of revictimization are sad. When one newspaper printed the name of a rape victim without her consent or knowledge, her son learned about his mother's rape through taunting by his playmates. Not only more shame for the victim, but more physical danger as well, may be by-products of journalistic arrogance. Rape victims are far more liable to be threatened again than are victims of other crimes, if newspapers reveal their names.

24. Quoted in William A. Henry III, "Journalism Under Fire," *Time*, December 12, 1983, 76–93. While invading the privacy of victims is poor practice, there is no need to give special privacy protection to those responsible for their predicaments. In *Holman v. Central Arkansas Broadcasting Co.* (1979), a man had been arrested for drunk driving. For five hours at a police station he was "hitting and banging on his cell door, hollering and cursing." A local radio reporter taped some of the noise and broadcast it. That seems fine.

Why, then, do journalistic codes of ethics not prohibit such noncompassionate treatment? To get at that answer, an apparent digression is in order: comparison of the openness to naming rape victims with the blanket prohibition against identification of confidential sources.

The American Newspaper Guild's Code of Ethics states flatly, "The newspaperman shall refuse to reveal confidences or disclose sources of confidential information in court or before judicial or investigative bodies." The Society of Professional Journalists, Sigma Delta Chi Code of Ethics also presents "the newsman's ethic of protecting confidential sources of information." Journalists have frequently protested attempts by judges to make them reveal the names of sources with knowledge of crimes.

Journalistic organizations have made passage of "shield laws" (statutes protecting journalists) a top priority. They note that reporters vulnerable to subpoena might lose access to important information that helps them in performance of a "watchdog" function. They say a closet whistleblower with knowledge of official misconduct but concern for keeping his job might be unlikely to cooperate with a journalist for fear that his identity will be made public. They fear that other sources might "dry up." They fear harassment of newspapers by subpoena-wielding officials. All of these concerns have some validity.

There is another side, though. Criminal defendants have an explicit Sixth Amendment right to compel the attendance of witnesses who could provide helpful information. Furthermore, courts and police like to prevent future crimes and catch fugitive felons. As Justice Byron White once put it, "We cannot seriously entertain the notion that the First Amendment protects a newsman's agreement to conceal the criminal conduct of his source, or evidence thereof, on the theory that it is better to write about crime than to do something about it."[25]

25. *Branzburg v. Hayes*, 408 U.S. 665 (1972).

The Bible in its newspaperless age, of course, never delved into the particulars of such questions, but it does provide clear principles. First, occupation does not allow a reporter to turn his back on crime: "If anyone sins in that he hears a public adjuration to testify, and though he is a witness, whether he has seen or come to know the matter, yet does not speak, he shall bear his iniquity" (Lev. 5:1).

Second, the Bible offers a strong presumption in favor of open accusation that allows witness and defendant to confront one another, and a requirement that at least two sources of indictment are necessary: one witness is not enough (Deut. 19:15). Good reporters today should refuse to report without attribution accusations against or evaluations of a named person by a unnamed "source." If they choose to use confidential material, it should be only to develop leads on stories and witnesses who will testify openly.[26]

Third, reporters can minimize problems by evaluating carefully all motives for requesting anonymity and fighting hard to have everything on the record. As Leviticus 5:4 notes, a person should not thoughtlessly take an oath "in any matter one might carelessly swear about" (NIV). The books of Matthew and James both contain the essential lesson for reporters and many others: "Let your 'yes' be yes and your 'no' be no" (James 5:12; see also Matt. 5:37).

When the reporter does promise confidentiality he should keep his promise, even at the cost of going to jail, for the honest person "swears to his own hurt and does not change" (Ps. 15:4). The biblical presumption, though, is that such promises might only be given in very rare circumstances, and with full knowledge of the possible consequences. Shield laws that promise immunity from hurt may be easy ways out.

26. Many press subpoenas may damage source relationships primarily by compromising the reporter's independent or compatriot status in the eyes of sources, not by forcing revelation of sensitive information. Reporters should limit areas of vulnerability by offering protection only for a certain amount of time, or until after certain events take place. Blanket assurances of confidentiality should be given very rarely.

The biblical presumption against reportorial immunity does not mean that state officials should be free to harass reporters or use them as spies. Justice generally does not require that journalistic sources be revealed. Yet, when the only way to prove that the defendant is innocent is to have the reporter testify, or when all alternative sources of obtaining information concerning a crime have been exhausted, then a reporter's claim to privilege becomes an assertion that his relations with sources are more important than the life or liberty of others.

Connections

Some journalists, as we have seen, do not hesitate to publicize the names of rape victims. Most reporters, though, refuse to give police information relevant to crimes given them by sources. Why so much agony about protecting those sources and not the victim of rape?

One reason is a simple business decision: protection of source yields future stories; protection of subject brings no dividends. It is the nature of man to use and discard others, in this case probably forgetting about them except as a press clipping or a film clip.

But a second reason proceeds from humanistic emphasis on man-made law and on ethics apart from Christ. The problems of the first emphasis are obvious: law deals with short-term "can" and "cannot," not "should" and "should not," or even the long-term implications of legal but unwise actions. The dangers of the second emphasis are more subtle. We might think that training the mind in "ethical reasoning" will create a higher standard of thought and conduct. The Bible, though, tells us that man's fallen mind will always be able to draw conclusions that appear logical, even responsible—but wrong.

Paul said it succinctly: Our minds, without God's grace, "are darkened in their understanding" (Eph. 4:18). Paul also explained to the Romans, "The mind of sinful man is death . . . the sinful mind is hostile to God. It does not submit to God's law, nor can it do so" (Rom. 8:6–7, NIV). In other words, as a result of the fall, we humans are not capable of sound moral judgment apart from Christ. The notion that we humans are "good" who simply need to and are able to evolve to "better" is both a delusion itself, as well as a symptom of a far greater delusion.[27]

How do we overcome ethical anarchy? Modernists oppose the imposition of moral principles in favor of an analytical process. But the Christian worldview teaches that even our analytical faculties are flawed. Ultimately, neither analytical nor merely "moral" principles will overcome our own self-serving justifications. We may claim that we are without sin and capable of coming to righteous conclusions through our own reasoning power, but John noted that in saying so "we deceive ourselves" (1 John 1:8, 10). The same message is clear in 1 Corinthians 8:2: "If anyone imagines that he knows something, he does not yet know as he ought to know." Without God's mercy, we are dead in our transgressions and sins. We must ask him graciously to make us alive through Christ (Eph. 2:1, 4–5).

We are not even able to think wisely of long-term consequences when we are dead in our sins. We tend toward short-term gratification and protection. For example, those shield laws that restrict a judge's ability to apply pressure to a recalcitrant reporter could have a long-term cost: governments would have to "define those categories of newsmen who qualified for the privilege."[28] Shield laws, by giving the state power to sanction

27. Asserting that exposure to ethics courses will enable us to do better, naturally, misses one of the main points of the Bible. Ethics courses could do wonders if man's will and reason were unaffected by the fall, but that is not what the Bible says. An ethics course for non-Christian reporters could most usefully increase their understanding of public reaction to journalistic arrogance. An ethics course for Christians could be useful in making practical applications of biblical truth.

28. Justice White argued in *Branzburg v. Hayes* that protection for reporters at major newspapers but not for independent journalists would be "questionable

some and not others, could lead to that governmental control over the press that many journalists rightfully wish to avoid.

We can learn to act ethically, and wisely, only by first having our hearts changed, and by then following biblical example. In Matthew 18:23–34, Jesus uses a parable about forgiveness to show the source of all deeply motivating compassion. He explains that "the kingdom of heaven may be compared to a king who wanted to settle accounts with his servants. When he began to settle, one was brought to him who owed him ten thousand talents [several million dollars]. And since he could not pay, his master ordered him to be sold, with his wife and children and all that he had, and payment be made."

The parable continues: "The servant fell on his knees, imploring him, 'Have patience with me, and I will pay you everything.' And out of pity for him, the master of that servant released him and forgave him the debt. But when that same servant went out, he found one of his fellow servants who owed him a hundred denarii [a few dollars], and seizing him, he began to choke him, saying, 'Pay what you owe.' So his fellow servant fell down and pleaded with him, 'Have patience with me, and I will pay you.' "

But the first servant refused. Instead, "he went and put him in prison until he should pay the debt. When his fellow servants saw what had taken place, they were greatly distressed, and they went and reported to their master everything that had taken place. Then his master summoned him and said to him, 'You wicked servant! I forgave you all that debt because you pleaded

---

procedure in light of the traditional doctrine that liberty of the press is the right of the lonely pamphleteer who uses carbon paper or a mimeograph just as much as of the large metropolitan publisher." He mulled over the possibilities for confusion beyond even news publishing: "The informative function asserted by representatives of the organized press in the present cases is also performed by lecturers, political pollsters, novelists, academic researchers, and dramatists. Almost any author may quite accurately assert that he is contributing to the flow of information to the public, that he relies on confidential sources of information, and that these sources will be silenced if he is forced to make disclosures before a grand jury."

with me. And should not you have had mercy on your fellow servant, as I had on you?' And in anger his master delivered him to the jailers, until he should pay all his debt."

Compassion comes through our thankfulness for the Master's mercy and our following of that merciful pattern when we deal with others. Relying on the law (which requires payment of such debt) or our own devious ethical analysis is of no avail. Yet, we are unwilling and unable to act rightfully until God transforms our hearts through his saving grace. Journalistic ethics without Christ means arrogance and hypocrisy.

Time spent in most non-Christian ethics conferences would be better spent in reading the Bible and, through God's grace, learning who we are. Christians can benefit from discussion of practical applications of biblical truth at Christian ethics conferences, but each of us also must apply David's words in Psalm 51:3, 6–7, 13 to our specific situations: "Have mercy on me, O God, according to your steadfast love. . . . For I know my transgressions, and my sin is ever before me. . . . Behold, you delight in truth in the inward being, and you teach me wisdom in the secret heart. Purge me with hyssop, and I shall be clean. . . . Then I will teach transgressors your ways, and sinners will return to you."

By reading the Bible and realizing our own sin, we might develop the self-awareness of a New Englander named Shanghai Pierce who moved to Texas, built a great ranch, and in his retirement hired a sculptor to memorialize him in a giant bronze statue set out in the pasture. The story is that Pierce would ride by on horseback, doff his sombrero politely, and say to the statue, "Morning, Shanghai, you old cow thief."

Few journalists are like Shanghai Pierce. Many know the law better than their own selves. The result of journalistic emphasis on externals has been the digging of the deep pit that we will describe in the next two chapters.

6 Libel: Utilitarian Justice vs. Biblical Truth-Telling

oney talks. Big-money court settlements are talked about. Fascination with cash changing hands has made libel law a hot topic among journalists. "Did you hear about the $4.5 million verdict against the *San Francisco Examiner*?" "What about the $9.2 million verdict that forced the *Telegraph* into bankruptcy court?" According to the Libel Defense Resource Center, before 1980 a jury had awarded more than $1 million to a defendant only once. During the 1980s, the average of more than two dozen jury awards topped $2 million.[1] Since then, awards in libel cases have continued to escalate. During the 1990s, the average jury verdict was $2.6 million, and in the 2000s, the average was $3.4 million.

Also during the 1990s, several high-profile cases captured the public's imagination. In 1997, ABC News and its program *Dateline* lost a case against the retail grocer Food Lion. In 1991, Dallas-based Belo Corporation lost a $58 million case, then a record libel award. But it didn't take long for that record to fall. In 1997, a federal jury in Houston awarded $222.7 million to a small brokerage firm for a 1993 article in the *Wall Street Journal*. A judge reduced the award, and an appeals court ordered a new trial. Eventually, the brokerage firm went out of business and dropped the case, but the original jury award sent chills through the journalistic world.[2]

1. *The Cost of Libel: Economic and Policy Implications, A Conference Report* (New York: Gannett Center for Media Studies, 1986), 2.
2. www.nytimes.com/1997/03/21/business/firm-awarded-222.7-million-in
-a-libel-suit-vs-dow-jones.html.

There is more to the money question than court-ordered settlements. Many press organizations lose when they win. When CBS attacked General William Westmoreland, he sued. CBS spent $6 million in lawyers' fees before Westmoreland gave up, realizing he could not prove that CBS had willfully lied. ABC spent about $7 million on another case. *Time* magazine survived the suit of Israel's Ariel Sharon, but at a cost of $3 million. Plaintiffs also pay: Westmoreland and his supporters spent $4 million in a fruitless search for vindication.[3]

Journalists see big defamation suits as "horror stories," but when the telescope is turned around, there is horror in what some publications have done. Healthy individuals have been said to have leprosy, venereal disease, or mental illness. A baton-twirling Miss Wyoming sued after a baton-twirling character with that title was depicted as sexually promiscuous and immoral. *Hustler* magazine lied in depicting Jerry Falwell as an incestuous drunkard.[4]

Some journalists cite instances of libel claimants who seemed more interested in political advantage or monetary gain than in justice. More impressive, though, are the number of instances of libel claimants being doubly abused—first by publication of defamatory falsehood, and second by the reaction of journalists when the claimants complain. According to a University of Iowa survey, many individuals seeking corrections or apologies are chased out of newspaper offices, with reporters screaming obscenities after them. No surprise, a former *Chicago Tribune* city editor noted: "The rudeness in this business is legendary."[5]

3. *Time*, February 4, 1985, 64; *New York Times*, February 19, 1985, 1; February 20, 1985, 13; James Goodale, "Survey of Recent Media Verdicts, Their Disposition on Appeal, and Media Defense Costs," in *Media Insurance and Risk Management* (New York: Practicing Law Institute, 1985); Rodney Smolla, *Suing the Press: Libel, the Media and Power* (New York: Columbia University Press, 1986), 80–99, 198–237.

4. *Pring v. Penthouse*, 695 F. 2d 438 (10th Cir. 1982), 8 Med. L. Rptr. 2409; *New York Times*, December 10, 1984, 15; Smolla, *Suing the Press*, 160–81.

5. Randall Bezanson, Gilbert Cranberg, and John Soloski, "Libel and the Press: Setting the Record Straight," The 1985 Silha Lecture, University of Minnesota,

Journalists who are neither reckless nor rude also are harmed by their defamatory brethren. Libel insurance rates for many newspapers doubled during 1986. One family-owned group of seven small newspapers in eastern Tennessee had never lost a lawsuit. Only one current case was requiring a lawyer. Yet, the newspaper's premiums for 1986 increased by 99 percent.

Ironically, the rise of the Internet and the decline of big-city dailies have eased the libel crisis somewhat. In the 1980s, a small Christian magazine that had never had a libel suit could not find even minimal libel insurance for less than $10,000. As a consequence, many small newspapers simply chose not to have insurance and take their chances. The rise of blogs and online news sites has forced the insurance industry to develop new products. In 2012, an individual blogger could get libel insurance for as little as $1,500 a year for $1 million in coverage. Of course, $1 million in coverage would not come close to covering the average libel lawsuit. Most media outlets need at least $5 million in coverage. Big-city dailies usually carry $100 million or more.[6] The net effect of all of this is that the price of insurance has gone up at the high end, but come down at the low end. Today, the Christian magazine that could not get good insurance in the 1980s has a number of options, and the cost is likely between $5,000 and $15,000 a year, depending upon deductibles and other factors.

Nevertheless, litigation costs have threatened to put some publications out of business. Other publications have become so fearful of any possibility of libel that their editors look for soft soap rather than hard-hitting coverage. Independent journalism also is threatened by those suggesting government regulation of

---

May 15, 1985, 26–27.

6. *The Cost of Libel*; Michael Massing, "Libel Insurance: Scrambling for Coverage," *Columbia Journalism Review* (January/February 1986): 35–38. More recent data comes from *On-line Journalism Review* maintained by the University of Southern California, www.ojr.org/ojr/law/1077150111.php.

newspaper content, with the goal of bringing about "fairness" but more likely to introduce a form of state censorship.[7]

Three major nonlegal answers to the libel problem, and many minor ones, are trotted out regularly.

First, some continue to propose development of national and local "news councils," groups of citizens that would, in a nonjudicial setting, listen to complaints about media coverage. If the news councils were to find media fault, potential litigants would feel vindicated and news organizations could publish retractions or corrections.

News council proposals have a lot going for them, since some defamed individuals (according to the University of Iowa study) are mainly looking for a way to have their names cleared quickly. But only a few news organizations have supported the news council approach. Many legitimately fear outside involvement in their editorial processes. Many wonder about self-appointed memberships of news councils. From the plaintiff side, the news council alternative is less satisfactory than efficient judicial proceedings would be, because news councils have no authority to enforce judgments or award damages.[8]

Second, some editors continue to advocate self-policing by journalists, with the emphasis on making full and immediate corrections whenever there is doubt about accuracy or fairness. But in the absence of spiritual changes among reporters and editors, the arrogance of newsroom power may make self-policing a delusion. A *Washington Journalism Review* article suggested that reporters "should be more polite, respectful, long-suffering and never even a bit arrogant, no matter how overbearing, boorish or criminal the abusive slob on the other end of the phone may

7. *The Cost of Libel*; Michael Massing, "The Libel Chill: How Cold Is It Out There?," *Columbia Journalism Review* (May/June 1985): 31–43; *New York Times v. Sullivan: The Next Twenty Years* (New York: Practicing Law Institute, 1984), 87, 450, 507, 527–28.

8. Interviews by author at Gannett Ethics Conference, University of Kentucky, 1985.

be." As long as there is a tendency to think of the complainant, who may have been smeared unfairly, as an "abusive slob," not much will change.[9]

Third, changing policies of libel insurance companies has had an effect. Most libel insurers now require news organizations to pay 20 percent of all legal fees and expenses above the deductible, generally $5,000 to $50,000, depending on newspaper size. Insurance companies believe that co-insurance rules will force news organizations to keep a tighter rein on their legal firms' expenses, and will also encourage some quick out-of-court settlements.

The new libel insurance policies may change the behavior of some media litigants. Many news organizations have had no-settlement policies, contending that their refusal to compromise would deter frivolous suits and show a willingness to fight for truth to the last dollar (the insurance company's dollar, that is). Now that news organizations have to share the costs, industry leaders such as the *Los Angeles Times* risk manager say that when the going gets tough, "We'll find a way to settle." The drawback, though, is that financial compromise will not bring reputational restitution. Plaintiffs and their lawyers may walk off with some cash, but they will not have what the University of Iowa survey indicates some most want: a clear judicial statement that they were wronged.[10]

At journalistic conventions and meetings, other partial "solutions" have been discussed. Sooner or later, though, almost everyone comes back to the current state of libel law. That is an unhappy subject—a *Journalism Quarterly* article has decried "the disarray that is libel law today"—but an inescapable one. Courts are the only institutions with authority to present judgments and enforce penalties, and it is to the courts that we must now turn.[11]

9. *The Cost of Libel; Washington Journalism Review* (January 1986): 35.
10. Ibid.; Massing, "Libel Insurance."
11. Interviews at Gannett Ethics Conference and at annual convention of the Association for Education in Journalism and Mass Communication, Norman,

Digging the Pit

A 1964 Supreme Court decision, *New York Times v. Sullivan*, opened the door for disarray. The Court decided that a public official could no longer win a libel case by showing that published defamatory falsehood had injured his reputation. Justice William Brennan, writing for the majority, specified that the plaintiff could win only by proving that the published story "was false, and that it was made with knowledge of its falsity or in reckless disregard of whether it was false or true."[12]

The "and" was key: Brennan was breaking with centuries of English and American common-law tradition. Previously, defamatory falsehood by journalists always was potentially punishable, unless it was a generally accurate account of a public proceeding or record, or unless it was opinion based on facts truly stated (most opinions by their nature are not provably true or false). But Brennan was trying to transform what had been issues of right and wrong into utilitarian questions of the greatest good for the greatest number: how do we balance competing claims in order to protect press freedom?

Brennan's expressed concerns had some validity. He wanted to prevent government from using civil libel penalties to inhibit journalists who did have legitimate criticism of public officials. If reporters needed full factual documentation to criticize officials and if those officials withheld necessary facts or had the power to do so, then truth-telling would be hamstrung. But Brennan went further, arguing that even stories proven false should be legally permissible as long as they concerned public officials. (Some errors might result in the process, but if omelets are to be made, eggs must be cracked.)

A majority of justices agreed. After *Sullivan*, journalists could print defamatory falsehoods about public officials and rest easy,

---

Oklahoma, 1986.

12. *New York Times v. Sullivan*, 376 U.S. 254 (1964).

unless it could be proven that the journalists had deliberately lied. That was extremely difficult to do, unless the journalist had been foolish enough to proclaim before many witnesses, or in his notebooks, an intention to lie. There was also the "reckless disregard" clause to fall back on, but the Supreme Court soon interpreted that to mean "something much more than gross negligence; reckless disregard . . . approaches the level of deliberate fabrication" and "must reflect a conscious awareness of probable falsity." In other words, recklessness had to include malice.[13]

One law professor praised Brennan's decision for its willingness to uphold "the strategic sacrifice of some deserving plaintiffs to the more important, at least to society as a whole, goals of the first amendment."[14] That law professor, like a high priest two thousand years ago, evidently believed that it was right for one man to be defamed for the good of the people. But others have asked: Is this fair?

For instance, why did Leonard Damron have to be sacrificed? Shortly after the *Sullivan* decision, a Florida newspaper falsely reported that Leonard Damron, small-city mayor and candidate for tax assessor, was indicted for perjury in a local court. The indicted man actually was Leonard's brother, James, with whom Leonard had no official or business connections. Leonard Damron lost the election and convincingly showed harm to his business. A jury found libel. The Supreme Court let off the newspaper with no penalty at all, since the defamatory article related to qualifications of a public official and candidate for public office, and deliberate lying could not be proven.[15]

Was it good for Leonard Damron to be defamed for the good of the people? The Supreme Court said yes. But if Damron can be sacrificed, why not others? Looking through some recent

13. *St. Amant v. Thompson*, 390 U.S. 727 (1968).

14. Frederick Schauer, "Public Figures," 25 *William and Mary Law Review* (1984): 905, 910.

15. *Ocala Star-Banner Co. v. Damron*, 401 U.S. 285 (1971); cited in Schauer, "Public Figures," 25.

cases, we see that public officials sacrificed for the good of the people include a waterworks auditor, a county motor pool administrator, a county airport board member, and a county social worker.[16]

Was it good for those minor public officials to be sacrificed for the good of the people? If the answer is yes, what about "public figures," prominent individuals outside of government? The Supreme Court, in several early 1970s cases, declared that "public figures" also would have no recourse when they were victimized by published falsehoods, unless they could prove malicious lying.[17]

Some of the cases seemed particularly unjust, and particularly likely to inflame public resentment of news media. Consider, for example, Alonzo Lawrence and James Simpson, two senior citizens who in 1974 were volunteer president and secretary-treasurer respectively of the Rahway (New Jersey) Taxpayers Association. Rahway municipal authorities wanted to build a new firehouse, but Lawrence and Simpson led a successful campaign to get over five thousand signatures on petitions requesting a referendum on appropriations for the firehouse.[18]

It turned out that some of the signatures were illegitimate for reasons such as a husband signing for his wife or vice versa. Typically during petition drives many signatures are thrown out for such reasons. But this time, an inexperienced reporter on the *Rahway News-Record* thought she had a scoop, and the

16. *Kruteck v. Schimmel*, 27 A.D. 2d 837, 278 N.Y.S. 2d 25 (N.Y. Appl. 1967); *Clawson v. Longview Pub. Co.*, 91 Wash. 2d 408, 589 P. 2d 1223, 4 Med. L. Rptr. 2163 (1979); *McMurry v. Howard Pub., Inc.*, 612 P. 2d 14, 6 Med. L. Rptr. 1814 (Wyo. 1980); *Press Inc. v. Verran*, 569 S.W. 2d 435, 4 Med. L. Rptr. 1229 (Tenn. 1978).

17. *Rosenbloom v. Metromedia, Inc.*, 403 U.S. 29 (1971); *Gertz v. Robert Welch, Inc.*, 418 U.S. 323 (1974). For more on the logic of extension from public official to public figure, see Diana M. Daniels, "Public Figures Revisited," 25 *William and Mary Law Review* (1984): 957, 965.

18. *Lawrence v. Bauer Pub.*, 89 NJ. 451, 446 A. 2d 469 (1982); *Cloyd v. Press*, 629 S.W. 2d 24 (Tenn. A1981); *Wright v. Haas*, 586 P. 2d 1093 (Okla. 1978); *Exner v. AMA*, 12 Wash. A215, 529 P. 2d 863 (1974).

following headline resulted: "Forgery Charges May Loom for Lawrence, Simpson." A New Jersey jury found that headline and the accompanying story falsely defamatory, but the New Jersey Supreme Court decided that both Lawrence and Simpson were public figures who would have to prove actual malice or reckless disregard (in the sense of premeditated misstatement rather than mere incompetence).[19]

New Jersey Supreme Court justice Schreiber filed a dissenting opinion, arguing that, because of the majority's decision, "Two highly motivated senior citizens are left without redress for libelous publications holding them up to contempt and ridicule in the community in which they have lived for many years. This is the result of their sincere attempt to participate in local government." But the U.S. Supreme Court refused to hear their case, as only Justice William Rehnquist was willing to grant review.[20]

Those who placed public officials and public figures in journalistic free-fire zones were not entirely indifferent to their fate. Judges suggested that such individuals could use their positions or community prominence to defend themselves against false charges. It turned out that, though some public officials or public figures had that capacity, many did not. Lawrence and Simpson did not have much beyond a mimeograph machine to use in clearing their names. Even a major public official or public figure could be a big fish in a small barrel when *60 Minutes* comes shooting.

Falling into the Pit

The questions were being raised, but many journalists were sanguine, until one other problem developed.

19. *Lawrence v. Bauer Pub.*
20. Ibid.

When the Supreme Court announced its *Sullivan* decision in 1964, philosopher Alexander Meiklejohn predicted that journalists freed from many libel concerns would be "dancing in the streets." It appeared to columnist Anthony Lewis and others that few public officials (and, later, public figures) would be foolish enough to bring suit. What reasonable individual faced with the difficulty of proving what Justice Brennan had defined as "actual malice"—that subjective intention to lie—would want to waste time and money? Even if someone made the effort, it appeared inevitable that judges would see the scanty evidence and make summary dismissals. Even if judges should allow jury trials, juries composed of reasonable men and women would learn the Court's easy-to-remember code words—"absence of malice"—and refuse to convict.[21]

There remained only one threat to journalists within the Brennan dispensation: what if plaintiffs, juries, lawyers, and even some judges were not reasonable? If plaintiffs went against the odds and actually tried to prove malice, then legal costs could become much greater than under the old system of truth or falsehood. After all, it does not take long to read and analyze a newspaper article; but if it is necessary to read through long files and take depositions on comments made and states of mind, legal bills mount. When lawyers have hourly rates of $500 in New York and San Francisco, or $150 to $400 in smaller markets, the bills mount fast.

The threat became reality, for four reasons.

First, many defamed individuals did not give up. They continued to bring suit, despite the odds against them imposed by the proof-of-malice gauntlet. The University of Iowa study showed how desperate many plaintiffs are: "They know that victory is unlikely, and that the final decision is likely in any

---

21. See James Goodale, "Centuries of Libel Law Erased by Times-Sullivan," 191 *New York Law Journal* 49 (1984).

event to be ambiguous and distant." But they still sue, and not for money, according to the study: "Money is rarely the reason for suing. They sue to correct the record and to get even."[22]

Second, some juries showed their respect for attempts by defamed individuals to win despite the *Sullivan* odds. Realizing that "malice" was not provably present, they still refused to accept the idea that a writer or editor could get away with character murder. Such "runaway juries" found news organizations guilty and stipulated large awards to defendants. The verdicts generally would be thrown out by judges and appeals courts, but only after greatly increased legal costs. For instance, one Texas appeals court overturned a $2 million jury award against the *Dallas Morning News*, finding the jury had acted out of "passion and prejudice against newspapers." As law professor Marc Franklin put it, juries are "manifesting general community resentment by imposing liability."[23]

Third, with runaway juries seeking a way to keep producers of defamatory falsehood from going free, trailblazing (or money-hungry) lawyers emerged. They began finding ways to circumvent restrictions on libel cases. Some brought right-to-privacy actions known as "false light." Others asserted that publications had unjustly enriched themselves by violating the property right that an individual holds to his own name. American ingenuity also came up with breach-of-implied-warranty cases (a newspaper cheating its customers by representing as true information that is false).[24]

Fourth, some judges, fascinated by jury uprisings, further encouraged such legal guerrilla warfare through their reluctance to issue summary judgments in libel cases. When Chief

22. Bezanson, et al., "Libel and the Press," 9.

23. Marc Franklin, "Good Names and Bad Law: A Critique of Libel Law and a Proposal," 18 U.S.F.L. Rev. 1, 10 (1983).

24. For examples, see *Libel Defense Resource Center Bulletin* 11 (Summer-Fall 1984): 1–2.

Justice Warren Burger chastised some judges in 1979 for being too quick to dismiss libel suits, the reluctance to issue summary judgments became general. More libel cases survived infancy. More legal bills accumulated. A 1986 Supreme Court decision, *Anderson v. Liberty Lobby*, tried to plug the hole in the dike by expanding a judge's discretion in making summary judgments, but the result of the new change is still unclear.[25]

With four squads of irregulars—angry plaintiffs, sympathetic juries, resourceful lawyers, and even some curious judges—not giving up in the face of *Sullivan* and its follow-up cases, news organizations and their insurers began suffering great financial losses. Cries of "if only" could be heard: If only plaintiffs would keep cool, if only jurors would abide by the *Sullivan* decision, millions of dollars could be saved. But a biblical verse well describes the irony of initial journalistic praise for the *Sullivan* decision, and later concern: "Whoever digs a pit will fall into it" (Prov. 26:27).

Sullivan, in short, put in place a malice stop sign, rationalistically designed to free the press and prevent suits. That sign, though, has become an invitation to a demolition (or defamation) derby. One side must attempt to prove actual malice. The other side must stop that attempt. Both must examine and evaluate internal memoranda among reporters and editors, reporters' notes, or anything else that might show journalists had material available to indicate that what they published was not what they knew. Eighty percent of the expense of defending libel suits is now made up of attorney's fees, with the other 20 percent going for awards, settlements, and administrative fees. Meanwhile, journalists feel pried into and preyed upon. They stop being writers or editors and start being witnesses.[26]

25. *Anderson v. Liberty Lobby*, 12 Med. L. Rptr. 2297 (1986).
26. *The Cost of Libel*, 3; Ethics Workshop interviews.

A 1979 case, *Herbert v. Lando,* showed how far the process could go. CBS documentary producer Lando was deposed in twenty-eight long sessions lasting, on and off, more than a year. Those sessions generated 3,000 transcript pages and 240 exhibits. In some sessions Lando had to scrutinize hundreds of his handwritten notes. In others, he had to go into detail about his thought process. CBS had to produce notes of interviews conducted with 130 people. Herbert had to produce more than 12,000 pages of documents. Lawyers had to examine them, with the meter ticking.[27]

Other utilitarian drawbacks of the Supreme Court's utilitarian decision have emerged. Journalists complain of intrusion into areas of editorial decision making. They worry about attempts to compel identification of confidential sources. As long as *Sullivan* and its follow-ups were merely seen as sacrificing individuals in the "public interest," few calls for change emerged. But when journalistic time and money began to be lost, out came agitated calls for extending even further the Supreme Court's barriers to libel trials.

Some journalists proposed a granting of absolute privilege to journalists in cases involving public officials and public figures. Some wanted to do away with libel law entirely, giving journalists absolute freedom (as long as they could stay two steps ahead of those who would tar and feather them).[28]

Virtually all of the journalistic proposals viewed libel as a problem to be solved by standing on *Times v. Sullivan* and taking it either a bit further or much further. That is like viewing teenage pregnancy as a problem to be solved merely by improving contraceptive technology. During the 1960s two innovations— *Times v. Sullivan* and birth control pills—appeared to open an

27. *Herbert v. Lando,* 441 U.S. 153 (1979).
28. See Congressional Record, July 24, 1985, E3478; Floyd Abrams, "Why We Should Change the Libel Law," *New York Times Magazine,* September 29, 1985, 34, 87, 90–92.

era of journalistic and sexual freedom. But both have had ironic consequences: more libel actions, more illegitimate children or abortions.

Both sets of unforeseen circumstances developed because the legal and medical innovations of the 1960s directly challenged centuries of belief concerning the existence of objective standards of right and wrong. Before *Times v. Sullivan* and the sexual revolution, American leaders generally lambasted both press falsehood and extramarital sex. Suddenly, though, the Supreme Court was excusing reportorial falsehood concerning public officials (later, public figures also) whenever it was produced because of lust for a good story rather than the deliberate desire to smear.

Times v. Sullivan and birth control pills for pregnancy/free extramarital sex were both clever, rational innovations. They were designed to liberate individuals from the consequences of actions that had been considered wrongful. Such liberation, though, has enslaved many. That's the way it always is for "liberation" apart from biblical principles. Perhaps in the area of libel some utilitarians are ready to examine the biblical alternative.

The Biblical View of Defamation

Both the Old and New Testaments take defamation very seriously. At issue is slander, not libel, for the Bible describes primarily oral societies. If there is any ethical difference between libel and slander, though, it seems evident that published or broadcast material should be treated even more harshly than local speechifying, because such material has a wider range and longer life span.

The first slander reported in the Bible was that of Satan in his serpent form against God. The Greek word *diabolis* actually means "slanderer." When Eve listened to and acted upon that slander, in conjunction with Adam, mankind and the world in general suffered tragic consequences. God punished the slanderer in two ways: the serpent thereafter had to crawl upon its belly, and Satan learned he would one day be crushed by Christ, a woman's son.

Other Old Testament false defamations of public officials or public figures, such as Aaron and Miriam's slander of Moses (Num. 12), also resulted in punishment. But it is not necessary to trace descriptive passages throughout the Old Testament, because the prescriptions could not be clearer. Exodus 23:1 declares, "You shall not spread a false report." Psalm 15:3 notes that the one who may enter God's sanctuary is he "who does no slander with his tongue." Punishment for false defamation is inescapable, as Proverbs 19:5 and 19:9 note: "A false witness will not go unpunished."[29]

Prophets did not hesitate to engage in truthful defamation of corrupt public officials and public figures. For instance, Jeremiah vigorously and publicly criticized the priest Pashhur, the false prophet Hananiah, and many others (e.g., Jer. 20; 28). The seriousness of false defamation, though, was clear in Ezekiel's criticism of those "who slander to shed blood" (Ezek. 22:9), as well as in the Levitical injunction, "Do not go about spreading slander among your people. Do not do anything that endangers your neighbor's life. I am the LORD" (Lev. 19:16, NIV).

The New Testament similarly linked slander with other crimes. Jesus attached "evil thoughts, murder, adultery, sexual immorality, theft, false witness, slander" (Matt. 15:19). Paul linked slanderers and God-haters, calling them "foolish, faithless, heartless, ruthless" (Rom. 1:30–31). In recent years, a certain amount of the "foolish, faithless, heartless, ruthless"

29. The specific injunctions against defamation are all subsets of the Ninth Commandment: "You shall not bear false testimony against your neighbor" (Ex. 20:16). Rousas Rushdoony provides a useful discussion of the many aspects of that commandment in his important book *The Institutes of Biblical Law* (Philadelphia: Presbyterian and Reformed, 1973), 542–631.

has been seen as good for society, keeping public officials and public figures on their toes, but Paul had none of that. He noted that slanderers who remain unconverted not only keep up their slandering, but also provide ideological justifications for the practice, and approve of their colleagues in crime.

The Bible clearly takes false defamation more seriously than today's Supreme Court does. No involuntary victim is to be sacrificed for the supposed good of the people. Nor are there any grounds for a double standard, with public officials or public figures deprived of their rights. The Bible is filled with admonitions against unequal justice, whether it involves the showing of partiality to the insignificant or to the great (e.g., Ex. 23:1–8; Lev. 19:15).

Today, we have unequal libel justice in two ways. First, we suffer from the distinction between public officials or public figures and private figures. Second, the frustration of jurors becomes so great that when they can find a way to punish defamation, they are likely to load into one damage award all the damages juries could not award to others. One plaintiff goes away empty-handed; another, perhaps with no stronger case but with an imaginative lawyer and a jury foreman or strong-minded individual who can convince other jurors to "sock it to them," emerges millions of dollars richer (until the appeals court, at least).

If we adopted biblical justice, we would have a much fairer libel law system. Biblically, journalistic false defamation tends to be midway between false witness and gossip. False witness in a court of law, where the issue literally may be life or death, is very serious. Treated less severely, as far as civil penalty, is gossip or talebearing. Libelous journalists are not actually prosecuting anyone. They typically report on or draw conclusions from evidence supplied by sources. They tend to be "bearers of tales," not "false witnesses."

However, lack of truthfulness makes libel a very serious offense. It is a form of theft: stealing a person's reputation, perhaps injuring him in his business or causing other financial harm, and also causing mental suffering. Thieves, after all, take property, but libel robs victims of reputation and peace, perhaps repeatedly as defamatory falsehoods circulate. Penalties need to be serious enough to promote journalistic care and caution.

Biblical Libel Penalties

Biblical penalties for theft are well defined, with the goal of "making whole," not satisfying an itch for vengeance. Precise restitution, not arbitrary court adjudication, is the goal. Normally, thieves would have to pay back double the amount of property stolen (Ex. 22:4, 7). If they deprived the victim of his livelihood, they would have to pay back four or five times the amount stolen (Ex. 22:1).

By applying the principle of multiple restitution to certain types of libel, we can ask the right questions. When Leonard Damron, the Florida public official sacrificed for the supposed good of the many, was damaged in his livelihood by libel, how much damage (including estimated loss of future earnings) did he sustain? When a Miss Wyoming who took chastity seriously had her sexual morality impugned, how much did that libel cost her?

The difficulty and partial irrelevance of that last question, though, indicates the difficulty of assessing many kinds of libel damages. Discussing reputational loss and psychological harassment in terms of dollars and cents is like mixing apples and oranges, or hatchets and hand grenades.

The Bible, however, leaves no doubt that there can be financial penalties for such hard-to-measure damages. Deuteronomy 22:13–19 discusses the situation of a man who defames his wife by saying (in open discussion, not in a courtroom) that she was not a virgin upon their wedding day. If he is proven wrong in that assertion, he could be fined one hundred shekels of silver (about one kilogram, or two and a half pounds). That was a large amount in those days, for the annual poll tax ranged from one-third of a shekel (Neh. 10:32) to one-half (Ex. 30:15).

Such a serious defamation shows severe problems within a marriage, but the biblical court proceedings that would follow such a charge are well worth considering. No depositions concerning state of mind are required. Obviously, the husband dislikes the wife, but the simple job of a defamed woman's parents is to bring proof that she was a virgin to the town elders at the gate and display the cloth before them, and "the elders of that city shall take the man" and punish him (Deut. 22:15–19).

In this case, extreme though it is, resides a model for justice when defamation has occurred. There is no attempt to determine whether what Justice Brennan would call "actual malice" was present. In most cases, only God can know what a person was thinking. Mortals can see only visible evidence, such as blood on a sheet. We examine what is visible, and rest secure in the knowledge that God will do justice concerning what we cannot see. Applying this principle to current libel law, we could eliminate lengthy depositions concerning journalists' state of mind. Judges and juries simply could examine the published story. If it contained defamatory falsehood, an appropriate fine would be levied.

Such a fine could have two parts: one for direct economic injury, one for reputational injury. The latter would be harder to determine, because it depends not only on the particular charges made but on the way a particular society might regard those charges. (Imputation of a lack of chastity might cause major damage in previous generations, and still would in Christian circles now, but might be of minor importance in other social groups.) But whatever the precise penalty, the goal would be restitution in some multiple. If there were only minor damage from a falsely defamatory story, there would be a minor award.

If the biblical view of libel became common, news organizations would have large incentives to take quick action when defamatory falsehoods were uncovered. Biblically, if a thief confesses and voluntarily offers restitution prior to trial, his penalty is only return of the stolen item or its equivalent, plus 20 percent, not 100, 400, or 500 percent. As Numbers 5:5–7 notes: "When a man or woman commits any of the sins that people commit by breaking faith with the LORD, and that person realizes his guilt, he shall confess his sin that he has committed. And he shall make full restitution for his wrong, adding a fifth to it and giving it to him to whom he did the wrong."

Is this applicable to defamation? A parallel passage, Leviticus 6:2–5, gives specific detail on some of the offenses covered: If anyone sins "by deceiving his neighbor about something entrusted to him or left in his care or stolen, or if he cheats him, or if he finds lost property and lies about it, or if he swears falsely, or if he commits any such sin that people may do . . . He must make restitution in full, add a fifth of the value to it and give it all to the owner" (NIV). Applicable to many other kinds of crime, that passage also describes exactly what libelous reporters do: maliciously or unwittingly, they twist words entrusted to them by interviewees, cheat the subjects of their articles, and state or imply that their defamation is true.

Such action demands harsh judgment. But the Leviticus passage also shows God's mercy if a person "commits any such sin that people may do." God understands our fallenness. It is the nature of man to sin. It is the nature of reporters to sin.

This does not mean that the sins we commit are excusable: they are still sins. This does not mean that false defamation, even of public officials or public figures, is legitimate: it is still wrong. But just as punishment is mandatory in such cases, so punishment also is designed to teach, not annihilate. Using biblical principles of libel law, almost all of the large jury awards of recent years would be greatly reduced.

God is a God of both justice and mercy. Some may believe that God is too merciful at times. Should someone who has acted maliciously get away with such a mild penalty, if he decides the legal odds are against him and settles before trial? Matthew 7:1–2 is useful here: "Judge not, that you be not judged. For with the judgment you pronounce you will be judged, and with the measure you use it will be measured to you."

It is very difficult for us to establish motive or to know exactly when a reporter knew that a statement was untrue. The Brennan dispensation attempts to make judges and juries godlike. Only God, though, knows what is inside men's hearts.

Exact measures of punishment will vary from society to society, but the biblical principles remain valid. Falsehood always brings some punishment. The goal is restitution, including a penalty for the wrongdoer. Since the loss resulting from false defamation is more than economic, reputational consequences must be taken into account. Quick restitution can save the thief much grief, as it can save the injured party much suffering.

Conclusion

At heart, libel is an ethical problem, not a legal one. The best way to deal with the libel problem is to train journalists to respect truth and never publish anything that has not been thoroughly checked and checked again. But, given our own fallenness and the congratulations for sin which are often forthcoming in a society where relativism reigns, the sword of the magistrate becomes crucial.

For that reason, good libel law is vital. It punishes, and it also pushes publications toward an emphasis on greater accuracy and fewer falsehoods. Legal penalties signal to both journalists and onlookers an understanding of what is right to do and what is not. Over time, the sword educates journalists, or wounds repeat offenders.

Adoption of the biblical model of libel justice would lead to speed, equal treatment for all, and restitution but not extravagance. With legal fees reduced by the elimination of depositions and discovery proceedings concerning malice, it is unlikely that libel expenses to news organizations would increase, but libel awards to worthy plaintiffs would be spread around more evenly. Falsehood would be taken seriously, but one transgression would not send a newspaper to bankruptcy court.

Some consequences are predictable. Since falsehood would be always punishable, newspapers would be more careful to check accuracy. Fact-checkers would receive funds that now go to lawyers. Insurance companies would relate libel insurance rates to performance rather than circulation size, for a clear record of a newspaper's penchant for printing falsehood would be available.

Journalists, within the structure of biblical libel law, would be able to spend more time working and less time involved in litigation or the fear of it. They would be freed of deposition misery, since lawyers once again would have to look only at the actual published materials. Since there would be enormous advantages to quick correction of error, and no legal liabilities down the road from admitting error, newspapers would rush to make corrections and apologies as quickly as they can.

The most important change would be that some individuals would not have to be sacrificed for the supposed good of the many. Because quick and prominent retraction would eliminate the possibility of fourfold or fivefold restitution, the innocent could have their names cleared more quickly. Citizens would no longer be giving up their right to a good reputation (if earned) merely by taking part in public debate or by becoming public officials.

We would have the biblical pattern of objective justice tempered by the merciful opportunity to make quick correction.

7 | Press vs. Public

In 1986 and 1987, journalists did not head toward the biblical patterns of law and ethics. Instead, the Supreme Court seemed willing to try tinkering once again. In one case, the Court (with Justice Rehnquist writing a dissent) even refused to grasp a splendid opportunity to review *Times v. Sullivan*.

The case, *Coughlin v. Westinghouse Broadcasting*, was a blatant example of investigative reporting run amuck. A television station, investigating the alleged failure of Philadelphia police to enforce state liquor laws, hid a camera across the street from a bar and videotaped police officers entering and leaving the bar. On October 11, 1981, policeman James Coughlin, carrying an envelope, entered the bar to investigate a vandalism complaint. Finding that all was quiet, Coughlin came out a minute later.[1]

The television station ran film of Coughlin's entrance and exit, with a reporter saying, "The only paperwork we saw [Coughlin] doing was carrying this envelope out of the Club less than a minute after he went in." A freeze frame with a circle around the envelope emphasized the clear implication that Coughlin had accepted a bribe.

Actually, the envelope contained Coughlin's incident report book. He sued and received judicial sympathy, but no redress, because of *Times v. Sullivan*. As one appeals court judge wrote,

---

1. *Coughlin v. Westinghouse Broadcasting*, 12 Med. L. Rptr. 2263 (1986).

"The *New York Times* standard makes it hard enough for a public figure to win a libel suit, even when faced, as here, with what any fair observer must agree is egregious conduct on the part of the media."[2]

In a second case, *Hepps v. Philadelphia Newspapers*, the Supreme Court on a 5–4 vote ruled that a news organization even in dealing with a private figure could make defamatory statements of supposed fact that could not be proven. This time, Justice John Paul Stevens wrote a ferocious dissent, calling the decision a "blue print for character assassination . . . a wholly unwarranted protection for malicious gossip." Stevens added, "In my opinion deliberate, malicious character assassination is not protected by the First Amendment to the United States Constitution."[3]

In another case, *Anderson v. Liberty Lobby*, the Court ruled that judges should have more power to dismiss (without benefit of jury trial) most libel charges against the press. The majority opinion, written by Justice Byron White, declared that libel suits filed by public officials and public figures in federal courts must be dismissed before trial unless the evidence suggests plaintiffs can prove libel with "convincing clarity."[4]

White's language stressed the judge's right to decide whether a "fair-minded" or "reasonable" jury could side with the plaintiff. His opinion clearly was designed to reduce the opportunity for runaway juries to act in ways thought by journalists to be "unfair" or "unreasonable." But it was unlikely that the decision would lead to speedier trials. As U.S. Court of Appeals judge Antonin Scalia (whose opinion was overturned by the Supreme Court) noted, under the new standards "disposing of a summary judgment motion would rarely be the relatively quick process it is supposed to be."[5]

2. Ibid.
3. *Hepps v. Philadelphia Newspapers*, 12 Med. L. Rptr. 1977 (1986).
4. *Anderson v. Liberty Lobby*, 12 Med. L. Rptr. 2297 (1986). See also prior U.S. Court of Appeals decision, 11 Med. L. Rptr. 1005.
5. Ibid.

Scalia (soon afterward appointed to the Supreme Court) pointed out that the plaintiff would now have to "try his entire case in pretrial affidavits and depositions." The defendant would also want to use all of his ammunition in response. The real difference would not be time and expense, but the movement of the trial from open court with jury to judge's chambers. Furthermore, it still seemed likely that smart lawyers would find a way around the latest attempt to stifle the popular anti-press uprising.[6]

Ironically, Justice William Brennan, who had unwrapped the Supreme Court's gift to well-paid libel lawyers with his *Times v. Sullivan* decision, was in dissent this time. He complained that the Court majority's decision could "erode the constitutionally enshrined role of the jury." Brennan argued the decision would be "an invitation—if not an instruction—to trial courts to assess and weigh evidence much as a juror would."[7] A few reporters seemed to take Brennan's argument to heart, but even concerned journalists often said there was no choice if press freedom were to be saved: the citizenry from which juries are selected is no longer appreciative of the press.

Those who were historically minded asked, "Why can't today's juries be like the Zenger jury?" They were referring to the famous 1735 trial of John Peter Zenger for criticism of New York's royal governor. During that fondly remembered episode of journalism history, the judges in their red robes and white wigs were ready to impose stiff penalties, and juries had little authority.

Defense attorney Andrew Hamilton, though, turned directly to the jurors and asked them to find Zenger innocent, since he had published the truth. The jury retired and returned quickly with a verdict of "not guilty," after which there were "huzzas

6. Ibid.
7. Ibid.

in the hall." The angered chief justice threatened to put those cheering in jail. In the face of overwhelming popular support for an independent press, though, he could not safely set aside the verdict. Zenger was freed.[8]

The belief that journalists today are modern-day Zengers who are being let down by the public is one of the prevalent current press myths. This chapter, though, argues that the public—as measured by polls and jury reactions recently, and jury verdicts from several centuries ago—has been fairly consistent for three hundred years in its expectations concerning the press. It is the predominant journalistic ethic that has changed.

Truth and Jury

In both England and its American colonies during most of the seventeenth and eighteenth centuries, newspapers legally were supposed to serve as public relations vehicles for government, with the goal of creating warm feelings toward state authorities. British chief justice Holt argued that "it is very necessary for all government that the people should have a good opinion of it," and it therefore would be wrong "to say that corrupt officials are appointed to administer affairs."[9]

Holt's legal concern was not truth or even factual accuracy, but maintenance of the status quo: "If people should not be called to account for possessing the people with an ill opinion of the government, no government can subsist." Holt and his brethren even developed the doctrine that has come down to us as "the greater the truth, the greater the libel." Since something that is

8. James Alexander, ed., *A Brief Narrative of the Case and Tryal of John Peter Zenger, Printer of the New-York Weekly Journal*, 2nd ed., ed. Stanley Nider Katz (Cambridge: Harvard University Press,1972), 101. See also Livingston Rutherford, *John Peter Zenger* (New York: Dodd Mead, 1904), and David Paul Nord, "The Authority of Truth: Religion and the John Peter Zenger Case," *Journalism Quarterly* (Summer 1985): 227.

9. *Rex v. Tutchin*, in Thomas Bayly Howell, compiler, *A Complete Collection of [British] State Trials to 1783. Continued by T. J. Howell to 1820*, vol. 14 (London: 1816–28), 1095.

true is likely to do more damage to a person's reputation than something considered fantastic, judges saw a writer's claim to truth as no defense, and even increased offense.[10]

The political theology of English kings demanded such illogic. As J. F. Stephens explained in his definitive 1883 work *History of Criminal Law in England*, "If the ruler is regarded as the superior of the subject, as being by the nature of his position presumably wise and good . . . it must necessarily follow that it is wrong to censure him openly. . . . Whether mistaken or not, no censure should be cast upon him likely or designed to diminish his authority." Common people were supposed to sit still before governmental officials, minding their manners.[11]

The crown's Court of the Star Chamber, beginning in 1542, could try without a jury those who published opinions considered seditious. It punished, among others, Dr. Alexander Leighton, a Scotsman who declared early in the 1600s that both king and the Anglican state-church were under "laws from the scripture." The Star Chamber had both of Leighton's ears cut off, his nose slit, and his face branded.

The Star Chamber was busy until the Puritans gained power. In 1637, for example, the Star Chamber cut off the ears of John Bastwick, Henry Burton, and William Prynne, three Puritans who also spoke openly of their resolution to follow the Bible only. Later officials hanged John Twyn for writing that the king is accountable to the people under God.[12]

The bravery of men such as Leighton, Bastwick, Burton, Prynne, and Twyn showed that, even as the law was hardening, a Protestant ethic opposed to such arbitrary state power was developing. It had arisen out of the Reformational belief in laws superior to the state

10. Ibid.

11. J. E. Stephens, *History of Criminal Law in England*, vol. 2 (London: 1883), 299.

12. For descriptions of these and other cases, see Frederick Siebert, *Freedom of the Press in England, 1476–1776: The Rise and Decline of Government Controls* (Urbana: University of Illinois Press, 1952).

or to any other human institution. The medieval Catholic Church had presented itself as a divine-human bond of heaven and earth, the kingdom of God on earth. Reformers such as Calvin and Knox, though, had denied that the kingdom of God could be equated with state or church-state. Instead, the goal of journalists and others would be the application of God's truth, as found in the Bible only, to everyday events, regardless of personal consequences.[13]

Puritans, within the theological context of their era, increased the freedom to proclaim truth once they attained power in England. They abolished the Star Chamber in 1641 and allowed a broader range of discussion than had been possible under Henry VIII and his successors. John Milton, poet and Puritan leader, wrote in 1642 that truth and falsehood should be allowed to grapple in a freer press, for "who ever knew truth put to the worse in a free and open encounter?"[14]

The Puritans, and Milton himself, were not always consistent, and in any case the Puritan revolution ended in defeat in 1660, with the English monarchy restored. But the idea was on the record: truth and falsehood should be allowed to fight each other openly. This was a startling view, especially in an age when many governments yearned for unlimited power.

Given that view, those who aspired to journalism faced hazards throughout Europe. In France under Louis XIV, printers and writers were branded, imprisoned, strangled, burned at the stake, or given life sentences in the galleys. In Venice, Italy, in 1650, Ferrante Pallavicino was executed for "disrespectful remarks." England did have a Parliament, but that did not make British political theory all that different from its neighbors. Even when the king lost power to Parliament, it

13. For an example of this application of the thought of Calvin and Knox, see Samuel Rutherford, *Lex Rex* (1644; repr. Harrisonburg, VA: Sprinkle Publications, 1982).

14. John Milton, *Areopagitica*, reprinted in Henry Morley, ed., *English Prose Writings of John Milton* (London: George Routledge and Sons, 1889), 345.

was in the interest not of checks and balances but a new locus of supreme authority.

In such a system, journalists had to fight for even the smallest bit of elbow room—and fight they did, with popular support. Juries primarily concerned with the ethics of truth rather than the law of libel sometimes ignored judges' instructions. As early as 1689, when William Bradford was tried for seditious libel, he insisted that the jury should decide not only whether he had printed the publication considered offensive, but also whether it was seditious. The jury, against the judge's instructions, debated both questions and ended up deadlocked.[15]

Again, when William Maule went on trial in 1696 in a Massachusetts court for publishing a book said to contain "wicked Lyes and Slanders . . . upon Government," the presiding judge asked the jury to return a verdict of guilty. A runaway jury, though, returned a verdict of not guilty.[16] A decade later, two Presbyterian ministers of New York, Francis Makemie and John Hampton, were arrested for sedition, but the jury returned a verdict of not guilty.[17]

The famous Zenger trial in 1735 also was a battle between state power and the Christian faith in truth-telling. Attorney Andrew Hamilton emphasized, in his noted speech to the jury, "The cause of liberty . . . the liberty both of exposing and opposing arbitrary power by speaking and writing Truth." Hamilton argued that "Truth ought to govern the whole Affair of Libels." The jury sided with Hamilton and Zenger, even though the law said otherwise.[18]

15. Isaiah Thomas, *The History of Printing in America: With a Biography of Printers, and an Account of Newspapers. To which is Prefixed a Concise View of the Discovery and Progress of the Art in Other Parts of the World*, vol. 2 (Worcester: Isaiah Thomas Jr., 1810), 12.

16. Matt Bushnell Jones, *Thomas Maule: The Salem Quaker and Free Speech in Massachusetts Bay* (Salem: The Essex Institute, 1936), 30.

17. *A Narrative of a New and Unusual American Imprisonment of Two Presbyterian Ministers: And Prosecution of Mr. Francis Makemie, 1707, by a Learner of Law, and Lover of Liberty*, reprinted in Peter Force, ed., *Tracts and Other Papers Relating Principally to the Origin . . . of the Colonies in North America*, vol. 4, no. 4 (New York: P. Smith, 1947), 24.

18. Alexander, *A Brief Narrative of the Case and Tryal of John Peter Zenger*, 99.

Some eighteenth-century seditious libel cases ended badly, but journalists who were factually accurate generally did well before juries. Thomas Fleet, publisher of the *Boston Evening Post*, went on trial in 1742 for "libelous Reflection upon his Majesty's Administration" that could "inflame the minds of his Majesty's subjects here and disaffect them to his Government." Fleet produced witnesses who attested to the truth of his news item, and the prosecution was dropped. Also in the 1740s, William Parks of the *Virginia Gazette* gained acquittal by proving that the legislator he criticized as a sheep-stealer had been convicted of that.[19]

Throughout the century in England as well, the number of jury revolts increased. In 1752, Chief Justice Lee told a London jury that bookseller William Owen was guilty, but the jury brought in a verdict of not guilty.[20] In 1770, during what became known as the Junius trials, Lord Chief Justice Mansfield told juries they must find guilt if the defendants had published the piece said to be libelous. The defendants acknowledged that they had, but the jury still ignored the judge and declared the defendants not guilty. The issue for the jury, once again, was truth. When editors were able to show that their statements, though sharply critical, had a factual base, they often went free.[21]

Transcripts of the trials themselves readily show the political suppositions of prosecution and defense. In the Owen trial, Attorney General Dudley Rider berated those who spoke of a right to appeal judicial decisions to juries: "An Appeal! To whom? To a mob? Must justice be appealed? To whom? To injustice?" Solicitor General Murray defined the legal situation: "The question is, whether the jury are satisfied that the defendant Owen published the pamphlet. The rest follows of course. If the fact is proved, the libel proves itself, sedition, disturbance, &c."[22]

19. Thomas, *The History of Printing in America*, 143, 144.
20. *Rex v. Owen*, in Howell, *Collection of [British] State Trials*, vol. 18, 1203.
21. *Rex v. Miller*, in Howell, *Collection of [British] State Trials*, vol. 20, 870.
22. *Rex v. Owen*, in Howell, *Collection of [British] State Trials*, vol. 18.

Defense counsel Ford, however, responded by speaking directly to the jury—a jury made up of three merchants, three grocers, three linen-drapers, one baker, one hosier, and one oilman. He called the prosecution's emphasis on judicial power "a doctrine that may be full of the most fatal consequences to all sorts of men." Ford asked, "If legal courts do wrong, must our mouths be shut, and not complain or petition for redress? God forbid!"[23]

Ford then told the jury, "I understand not the shutting of men's mouths. Let every man clap his hand upon his heart and examine how he would like it, was it his own case. . . . Surely, gentlemen, your own breasts, your own consciences, must tell you, which you consider of it—and pray consider it as your own case, fancy each of yourselves here under a rigorous prosecution, like this poor man,—there is no crime proved."[24]

According to Chief Justice Lee, there was crime. He instructed the jury "to find the defendant guilty; for he thought the fact of publication was fully proved; and if so, they could not avoid bringing in the defendant guilty." The jury, however, returned after two hours with a verdict of "Not guilty." Lee then asked a leading question: "Gentlemen of the Jury, do you think the evidence laid before you, of Owen's publishing the book by selling it, is not sufficient to convince you that the said Owen did sell this book?"[25]

Here the jurors were in a fix. According to one commentator, "The Jury could not say, to the question, that the evidence of publishing was not clear, without perjury; and if the jury had answered Yes, and not found the defendant guilty, one does not know what might have been done to the jury." When the judge demanded an answer, "the foreman appeared a good deal

23. Ibid.
24. Ibid.
25. Ibid.

flustered," but he did not answer. He merely kept repeating, "Not guilty, not guilty." Several other jurymen chimed in, "That is our verdict, my lord, and we abide by it." The attorney general wanted to ask more questions, but the crowd was cheering and the noise did not permit more dialogue. The judge gave up.[26]

Similarly, in the 1770 case of *Rex v. Miller*, Solicitor General Thurlow argued for the prosecution that the case was "so plain, and in so ordinary a course of justice, that it would absolutely be impossible to have mistaken, either the application of the proofs of the charges that are laid or the conclusion to be made from them."[27] Defense counsel Davenport, though, asked jurors to go beyond examination of the fact of printing: "It is for you, and you only, to determine whether this paper deserves all the branding epithets with which it is loaded."[28]

Near the end of the trial, Chief Justice Mansfield said with apparent resignation, "I am used to speeches made to juries, to captivate them, and carry them away from the point of enquiry." Nevertheless, he emphasized the legal point: the jurors were to concentrate on the question of publication.

They spent over seven hours discussing the supposedly open-and-shut case, then carried their verdict to Mansfield at his house in Bloomsbury Square: "His lordship met them at his parlour door, in the passage, and the foreman having pronounced their verdict, Not Guilty, his lordship went away without saying a word." Hundreds of people who had assembled outside, though, "testified their joy, by the loudest huzzas."[29]

The thrilling part of this history is the willingness of some jurors to produce verdicts suggesting that government was not a private preserve for rulers. Jurors often reacted harshly when confronted by arrogant demands for punishment of seditious

26. Ibid.
27. *Rex v. Miller*, in Howell, *Collection of [British] State Trials*, vol. 20.
28. Ibid.
29. Ibid.

libel, such as those coming from Chief Justice Hutchinson of Massachusetts in 1767 and thereafter. An English lawyer with the pen name Candor asked in 1764, "What business have private men to write or speak about public matters? Such kind of liberty leads to all sorts of license and obloquy."[30] But juries generally sided with the press against such a political theory, and the press, consequently, worked to extend jury power and restrict that of judges.

Jurors, when they saw individuals threatened by state power, even took direct action at times. When William Bradford had been on trial in 1689, he may have been saved by a juror who "accidentally" shoved with his cane the bottom of the typeform that Bradford had used to print the tract in question. When it collapsed and all the type spilled onto the floor, the evidence that Bradford had done the printing was gone. Similarly, when Henry Woodfall was tried for seditious libel in 1770, he escaped renewed prosecution when a juror walked off with the prosecutor's only copy of Woodfall's newspaper.[31]

Eventually the law was changed to conform to belief in the power of truth. In England, Fox's Libel Act of 1792 proclaimed truth as a defense and provided that the jury rather than the judge would rule on whether published material was seditious. In the United States in 1791, the passage of the First Amendment meant that newspapers would be free (except in extreme situations such as wartime) to publish what they chose without prior restraint. The New York legislature in 1805 spelled out the meaning of the First Amendment by erecting the doctrine of truth as a defense against libel, and other states followed.

One of the most ringing court decisions concerning the central issue of truth and falsehood came in *Commonwealth v. Clap* (1808), with the Massachusetts supreme court observing that publication

---

30. *A Letter from Candor to the Public Advertiser: Containing a Series of Constitutional Remarks on Some Late Interesting Trials, and Other Points of the Most Essential Consequence to Ccivil Liberty* (London, 1764).

31. Thomas, *Collection of [British] State Trials*, vol. 2, 12.

of truths concerning the fitness and qualifications of a candidate for public office, "with the honest intention of informing the people, are not a libel. For it would be unreasonable to conclude that the publication of truths, which it is the interest of the people to know, should be an offense against their laws."[32]

The court added sternly: "For the same reason, the publication of falsehood and calumny against public officers, or candidates for public offices, is an offense most dangerous to the people, and deserves punishment, because the people may be deceived, and reject the best citizens, to their great injury, and it may be to the loss of their liberties." That court statement succinctly described the Christian ethic of publication freedom within limits: truth was a defense against prosecution, but falsehood was no defense.[33]

That was the common understanding of press freedom throughout the nineteenth century.[34]

Changing Sides

Why, then, in the late twentieth century, did jurors become the frequent enemies of journalistic media, rather than the devoted friends they once tended to be? Many hypotheses have been thrown around: Newspapers are now big, established powers. They are often monopolies within their communities. Television stations package news as entertainment and entertainment as news. The class composition of journalists has changed. The public cares less about freedom to tell the truth than it once did.

Most of those generalizations have much to be said for them. Some recent surveys, though, throw suspicion on that last one,

32. *Commonwealth v. Clap*, 4 Tyng 183.
33. Ibid.
34. See, for instance, *Henderson v. Fox*, 83 Ga. 233, 9 S.E. 839; *Sullings v. Shakespeare*, 46 Mich. 408, 9 N.W. 451; *Press Co. v. Stewart*, 119 Pa. 584, 14 Atl. 51; *Haynes v. Spokane Chronicle Publishing Co.*, 11 Wash. 503, 39 Pac. 969; etc.

the idea that somehow the public is losing faith in truth-telling. One Gallup-conducted survey posed this question to a cross section of the American public: "Some people feel that in a free society news organizations should be able to say anything about a person, whether true or false, without having to face libel suits. Others believe that even in a free society news organizations should be subject to libel suits if they say critical things about people that are false. . . . Which position comes closer to your opinion?"

Only 4 percent of those polled said that news organizations should be free to say anything without penalty, while 89 percent took the position pushed for in the eighteenth century and solidified in the nineteenth century by cases such as *Commonwealth v. Clap*: truth is a defense, but falsehood is no defense. (Seven percent answered, "don't know.")[35]

Other survey questions showed very large majorities of the populace also saying that truth is essential in stories involving public officials or public figures, as well as those concerning private individuals.

As we discussed in the last chapter, runaway juries have often decided against newspapers during the past few years. But it is also true that appeals judges often overturn these verdicts. According to a study by the Libel Defense Resource Center, judges overturned, reduced, or returned to the trial court for a retrial 60 percent of libel verdicts from July 1994 to June 1996. But this judicial backstop has only limited the damage. The net result of the appeals decision is often arbitration and out-of-court settlements—thus breaking the backs of media companies who have "no settle" policies.

In any case, this tendency to prefer judges to juries is exactly the opposite of the prevailing tendency in the seventeenth through the nineteenth centuries. The change may

---

35. *The People and the Press: A Times Mirror Investigation of Public Attitudes Towards the News Media* (Los Angeles: Times Mirror, 1986), 35.

say less about beliefs of the citizenry than beliefs among journalists. Opinion polls and jury verdicts tell us of continuing popular concern with basic questions of truth and falsehood—but what about the concerns of many journalists? Has the public abandoned the press, or has the press abandoned the public?

Revolutionary Journalism Past and Present

Complaints about public unwillingness to follow the press have emerged at crucial turning points of the past. Historian James Billington has noted that for leaders of the French Revolution two centuries ago "journalism was the most important single professional activity." As Billington pointed out, "In revolutionary France journalism rapidly arrogated to itself the church's former role as the propagator of values, models, and symbols for society at large." Those citizens who would not go along were excommunicated from the new church of journalists, and sometimes decapitated.[36]

The centrality of the press to the French Revolution is indicated by a statement of Nicholas Bonneville, editor of *Le Tribun du Peuple*. Bonneville wrote that he looked for deliverance not to any political republic, but to "the republic of letters," a rallying of writers who would lead mankind.[37]

Bonneville saw his new journal as a "circle of light," with writers who would transform the world by constituting themselves as "simultaneously a centre of light and a body of resistance." They were to be "legislators of the universe," preparing a "vast plan of universal regeneration." Bonneville published a pledge of allegiance to the nation which began, "I Believe in the Infallibility of the People." But since the people were to be

36. James H. Billington, *Fire in the Minds of Men: Origins of the Revolutionary Faith* (New York: Basic Books, 1980), 33.
37. Ibid., 35.

instructed by journalists, Bonneville and his colleagues were really saying that they believed in their own infallibility.

The French Revolution destroyed itself, as other revolutions since then also have, but it left a legacy. As Billington noted, "The new breed of intellectual journalist during the French Revolution created both the basic sense of legitimacy and the forms of expression for the modern revolutionary tradition." Marx, Lenin, and others spent much of their lives as journalists, both to produce some income and to recruit followers. They believed that journalism could work fast where government often was slow. As one revolutionary Frenchman put it, the press could build a "new democracy" by providing a tribunal for the people that was "higher than the tribunal of judges, the throne of kings, and, I shall say, even the altar of the living God."[38]

That revolutionary idea never caught fire in the United States. It had its moments early on, with a few editors during the 1790s imitating their French brethren. The best-known Francophile editor, Benjamin Franklin Bache, had been educated in France while living there with his grandfather Benjamin Franklin. Bache edited in the 1790s a newspaper filled with malicious gossip, unsubstantiated by fact, directed against American leaders.

Typically, Bache wrote of George Washington that "if ever a nation was debauched by a man, the American nation has been debauched by Washington. If ever a nation was deceived by a man, the American nation has been deceived by Washington. Let his conduct then be an example to future ages . . . that the masque of patriotism may be worn to conceal the foulest designs against the liberties of the people."[39]

38. Ibid., 33.
39. Bernard Fay, *The Two Franklins: Fathers of American Democracy* (Boston: Little, Brown, 1933), is the best source for Bache material.

Bache also attacked John Adams. When only a few Americans backed Bache, he criticized the populace generally for not only letting him down, but for opposing press freedom as well.

Most famous of the journalists who tried to revolutionize the United States during the 1790s was Thomas Paine. Riding on his immense popularity during the American Revolution, when he wrote the pamphlet *Common Sense* with its stirring introductory words, "These are the times that try men's souls," Paine tried to agitate for a very different kind of revolution twenty years later. Paine's belief in intellectual freedom was indicated by his statement to a French friend, Etienne Dumont: "He said to me if it were in his power to demolish all the libraries in existence, he would do it so as to destroy all the errors of which they were the depository." When Paine received little support, he also accused Americans of not caring for freedom of the press.[40]

A few Americans during the nineteenth century tried to popularize a concept of journalistic godliness. In 1833 Joseph Warren of Cincinnati argued that "public influence is the real government of the world," and that printing should "henceforth be the main arm of this governing power." But more typical was the Christian conception of the relationship of citizen, government, and press published in the *Boston Recorder's* explanation of its editorial policy: When it "be necessary to disapprove of public measures, that respect for Government, which lies at the very foundation of civil society, will be cautiously preserved; and in such cases, a tone of regret and sorrow will best comport with the feelings of the Christian patriot."[41]

The same held for other established institutions: they could be criticized, but regretfully. A policy of that sort would be useful today. Christians should not see the press as an enshrined

40. Early biographies of Paine were hostile to him. Twentieth-century biographies have tended to praise him. The most comprehensive biography is Moncure Conway, *The Life of Thomas Paine* (London: G. P. Putnam's Sons, 1892).

41. *Boston Recorder*, January 3, 1816, 1.

fourth estate, legislating without portfolio. Instead, reporters should report without assuming that those in governmental authority are adversaries. As Paul wrote in Romans 13:2, "whoever resists the authorities resists what God has appointed, and those who resist will incur judgment." When leaders rebel against God's authority, though, Christians may advocate opposition.[42]

Some fifty years ago, though, the idea of "adversary journalism"—reflex-action opposition to governmental leaders—took root among leading American journalists. The idea in its modern form originated with the tendency of the French revolutionary press never to give authorities the benefit of the doubt. As noted in chapter 3, publisher E. W. Scripps summarized well the ideology of revolutionary journalism, past and future: "Whatever is, is wrong." But *Oakland Tribune* editor Robert Maynard acknowledged the hard edge in practice when he spoke of journalists who

42. When kings are corrupt and a huge state public relations apparatus is cranking out false prophecies, those who follow God must speak up. In the book of Jeremiah, state-subsidized prophets are predicting that all will be well: "Sword and famine shall not come upon this land" (Jer. 14:15). They control major communications channels with their "visions of their own minds" (Jer. 23:16). No one wants to listen to Jeremiah, yet his task is to tell the people of Judah, "Do not trust in these deceptive words." He is obligated to tell them not to "steal, murder, commit adultery, swear falsely, make offerings to Baal, and go after other gods" (Jer. 7:4, 9).

Jeremiah does his task so well that state officials tell the king, "Let this man be put to death, for he is weakening the hands of the soldiers who are left in this city, and the hands of all the people, by speaking such words to them." Jeremiah is left to die in a cistern full of mud, but one of his supporters intervenes (Jer. 38:4–13). Some journalists today want to deliver jeremiads, but the test is whether what they are saying follows the Bible or their own oracle. In the book of Ezekiel, false prophets and true prophets also are in conflict. God tells Ezekiel, "Woe to the foolish prophets who follow their own spirit and have seen nothing" (Ezek. 13:3). Those individuals "prophesy out of their own imagination," God says (Ezek. 13:2 NIV). The false prophets "have misled my people, saying, 'Peace,' when there is no peace" (Ezek. 13:10). They build a flimsy wall and cover it with whitewash. Ezekiel's task is to be a watchman (Ezek. 3:17; 33:7), warning the wicked and speaking out to dissuade them from their evil ways in order to save their lives. As a true prophet, Ezekiel cannot be a savior. If he has warned the wicked and they do not repent, he is not accountable for their blood. But if he does not warn them, he is.

are "hungry for blood—it sometimes seems to readers that we will not do the story unless we can do someone in."[43]

Adversary journalists assemble regularly to pat each other on the back and highlight for each other their superiority over the audiences. At the 1984 meeting in Miami of a group appropriately called IRE (Investigative Reporters and Editors), Geraldo Rivera orated, "We are part of the process of the positive social change."[44]

Max Frankel of the *New York Times*, complaining about restrictions on press coverage during the Grenada invasion of 1983, expressed his astonishment at the "assumption by some of the public that the press wanted to get in, not to witness the invasion on behalf of the people, but to sabotage it." Given the precedent of the last years of the Vietnam War, the assumption was valid.[45] The Media Research Center for a quarter-century has recorded left-wing pronouncements by leading journalists, and the list keeps lengthening.

Indeed, as the mainstream media have become more self-righteous, even some journalists have had enough. Former reporter Kurt Luedtke noted, "The press is full of itself these days, and frequently, it is simply full of it."[46]

According to adversary journalists in recent decades, a writer in opposition has the right to break most of the Ten Commandments. Top investigative reporter Robert Scheer has stated straightforwardly that it is "the journalist's job" to break into offices or seduce people to get a story.[47] Others would not be as

43. William A. Henry III, "Journalism under Fire," *Time*, December 12, 1983, 76–93.

44. Quoted in Tom Goldstein, *The News at Any Cost: How Journalists Compromise Their Ethics to Shape the News* (New York: Simon and Schuster, 1985), 46.

45. Henry, "Journalism under Fire."

46. Kurt Luedtke, speech before the American Newspaper Publishers Association, *ASNE Bulletin*, May/June 1982, reprinted in George Rodman, *Mass Media Issues* (New York: Science Research Associates, 1984), 190.

47. Ken Auletta, "Would You Lie, Steal or Cheat to Get a Story?" in *Hard Feelings: Reporting on the Pols, the Press, the People and the City* (New York: Random House, 1980), 244.

blunt, but the *New York Times* and other leading newspapers have had no compunction against publishing stolen documents. As the last chapter noted, media false witness is frequent.

Reporter Julius Dascha described how many elite journalists "look upon themselves almost with reverence, like they are protecting the world against the forces of evil." But for many, those forces are now arising mainly from the American middle class. Over and over again, the theme of liberation from middle America emerges. Nicholas von Hoffman of the *Washington Post* praised during the 1960s "now people," those who were "groovy, sexy, beautiful, swinging, mellow, hip and hep." He attacked those who were "old, ugly, square, plastic and out of it."[48]

Similarly, during the 1970s *Post* editor William Greider acknowledged the bias that "turns up in the columns of the *Post, Times* and other members of the media axis. The core of it is the unspoken assumption that the rest of the country is filled with boobs." During the 1980s Tom Brokaw, in a *Mother Jones* magazine interview, called those middle-class values "pretty simplistic, pretty old-fashioned," without "much application to what's currently wrong or troubling a lot of people."[49]

Many journalists also seem to desire "liberation" from Christian roots. In 1980, Stanley Rothman of Smith College and Robert and Linda Lichter of George Washington University surveyed and interviewed a sample of the "media elite": 240 journalists at the three big television networks, the three leading news magazines, and the three most influential newspapers (the *New York Times*, the *Washington Post*, and the *Wall Street Journal*). They found that 86 percent of the elite seldom or never attended

48. Tom Kelly, *The Imperial Post: The Meyers, the Grahams and the Paper that Rules Washington* (New York: William Morrow, 1983), 158. Later, von Hoffman derided President Carter as "Jimmy Peanut . . . the gleamy-toothed, bushy-tailed anointed chipmunk of the Lord."

49. Kelly, *The Imperial Post*, 179; Dinesh D'Souza, "Mr. Donaldson Goes to Washington," *Policy Review* (Summer 1986): 24–31.

church, and only 25 percent favored prayers in public schools (74 percent of the American public favored such prayer).[50]

Polling on social issues that often have a theological component also showed that the journalistic elite had separated itself from the American mainstream. Ninety percent of the elite approved of abortion on demand. (The American public registers at about 20–30 percent on the question of abortion as a woman's "right.") Seventy-five percent of the elite saw nothing wrong with homosexuality. Over half thought adultery was fine (American public: 15 percent). While a good survey of journalists' deeper religious beliefs still needs to be taken, these statistics are evidence of the divide between press and public.[51]

That this divide shows up in the way journalists cover stories should be no surprise. A 2002 study of 116 newspapers by Jim Kuypers found that when journalists covered issues that tended to divide the nation into conservative and liberal camps—such as abortion and homosexuality—news stories tended to omit reasonable conservative voices in favor of the more controversial spokespersons. However, reporters often chose respected moderate voices to represent liberal positions, and omitted more radical and controversial voices from the Left. The net effect was to make the liberal position sound more reasonable and convincing than the conservative position on a whole range of issues.[52]

The results of that divide are evident. Public opinion polls consistently rate press performance poorly. In 1986, the percentage of Americans who viewed network television news "mostly

50. S. Robert Lichter and Stanley Rothman, "Media and Business Elites," *Public Opinion* (October/November 1981): 42–44; *Washington Journalism Review* (December 1982) also had a short Lichter-Rothman piece. Their critique was critiqued, but not very convincingly, by Herbert Gans in "Are U.S. Journalists Dangerously Liberal?," *Columbia Journalism Review* (November/December 1985): 29–33.

51. Lichter and Rothman, "Media and Business Elites."

52. James A. Kuypers, *Press Bias and Politics: How the Media Frame Controversial Issues* (Westport, CT: Praeger, 2002).

unfavorably" or "very unfavorably" was only about 10 percent. By 1993, that number had nearly tripled, to 29 percent. The same survey found that only 25 percent of respondents believe "the news media helps society to solve its problems." A full 71 percent said "the news media gets in the way of society solving its problems."

By 2011, the judgment was nearly complete. According to a study by the Pew Research Center for the People and the Press,

> While the public has long been critical of many aspects of the press's performance, negative attitudes are at record levels in a number of areas. The percentage saying news organizations are often influenced by powerful people and organizations has reached an all-time high of 80%. Other measures, including the press's perceived lack of fairness (77%), its unwillingness to admit mistakes (72%), inaccurate reporting (66%) and political bias (63%) match highs reached in 2009. The public is about evenly divided over whether news organizations are immoral (42%) or moral (38%), but the proportion saying the press is immoral also equals an all-time high.[53]

Such attitudes have real economic consequences. Juries found news organizations guilty in forty-two of forty-seven libel trials during the early 1980s. As we noted in the last chapter, journalists had to go running to judges for protection against "the people" whose tribunes they were supposed to be. As James K. Batten, president of Knight-Ridder newspapers, told fellow publishers, "A lot of the American public don't much like us or trust us. They think we're too big for our britches."[54] *Washington Post* media critic Howard Kurtz was more blunt: "In no other profession would top executives scratch their heads and

53. www.people-press.org/2011/09/22/press-widely-criticized-but-trusted-more
-than-other-institutions/.
54. Henry, "Journalism under Fire."

wonder why it is that a substantial proportion of the customers think they're scum."[55]

It is sad to contemplate the decay of institutions that started off with such hopes and still possess enormous wealth and talent. But *U.S. News and World Report* noted that "America's press, which often views itself as a knight on a white horse, is finding that the public sees its once shining armor has badly tarnished." Even *Time* could see the reason for the tarnishing: Many journalists are "arrogant and self-righteous, brushing aside most criticism as the uninformed carping of cranks and ideologues."[56]

Christians can oppose that arrogance and self-righteousness through prayer, through establishment of alternative media, and through thoughtful criticism of mainline journalism. Sometimes, we have to admit, some of us have engaged in "uninformed carping." The next chapter suggests several informed and specific ways of analyzing journalistic products.

55. Linda Fibich, "Under Siege," *American Journalism Review* (September 1995): 20.

56. Henry, "Journalism under Fire." According to a Michigan State University survey of press attitudes, such isolation has led to a "public-be-damned attitude" among some journalists and professors, complete with frequent speeches about the public's supposedly lackadaisical attitude toward press freedom. A survey for the American Society of Newspaper Editors found that many reporters thought their readers did not appreciate the role of an independent press. Henry Kaufman of the Libel Defense Resource Center argued, "When a libel case gets to a jury, the First Amendment kind of drops to the wayside." University of Illinois professor Thomas Littlewood said, "Rarest of all in many sections of the country is the juror who has even the vaguest appreciation of what the First Amendment is" (*The Cost of Libel: Economic and Policy Implications, A Conference Report* [New York: Gannett Center for Media Studies, 1986], 12). The public may have more appreciation of the original meaning of the First Amendment than many members of the press.

8 | Perceptive Media Watching

S ome Christians are so disgusted with mainline newspapers and news shows that they refuse to read or watch and merely engage in a general carping condemnation. Others understand the problems of "the media" in abstraction, but are news consumers who tend to accept what they read or see as generally accurate: "The camera doesn't lie, does it?"

Sadly, it does. Modern journalistic technology can produce products with great style even when there is ungodly substance, and many journalists have great knowledge and talent, although not the fear of God that is the beginning of wisdom. Using attention grabbers, skillfully constructed stories, and careful placement of articles, such talented individuals are able to pull wool over untrained eyes. This chapter shows how those who attack such practices can add specific detail to their criticism, and those who tend to accept can become more discerning.

Newspaper Headlines, Television Framing

Boiling down a complicated story into a headline's few words or a television station's video graphic and introduction is no easy task. Not only is accuracy vital, but the quick message must be lively enough to sell the story to headline scanners or channel switchers. Ambiguities are common. Does the headline "Women Oppose Bork" mean that all or most women took that position, or were several individuals testifying? Headline choice is vital in newspapers, since most readers are headline scanners and the only information they will have about a particular event or situation is what is conveyed in the headline.

One 1980s report in Detroit about a nuclear plant closed for safety reasons shows the importance of headlines. Detroit's two newspapers, the liberal *Free Press* and the moderately conservative *News*, had similar stories about safety improvements being made at Detroit Edison's Fermi plant, but the headlines reflected a half-empty versus half-full psychology. The *Detroit Free Press* headline was "Panel: Edison Slow to Repair Flaws at Fermi." The *News* headline was, "Outline for Fermi Improves."[1]

Choices of television graphics are also important. When oil prices were rising, some petroleum stories had a graphic of a man in Arab clothing, thus implicitly blaming factors abroad for the price rise. Others had a montage of U.S. oil company logos, thus implicitly blaming corporations for the price rise. Introductions to filmed stories also are crucial to watch. "Tennessee parents are challenging school officials on textbook selection—here's the story from correspondent Jim Bartleby" is very different from "Tennessee fundamentalists are fighting educational authorities—Jim, what's going on there?"

A perceptive reader thinks first about the headline and then turns to the lead (or, in a television report, the "framing" of a story). Leads can be either summary (designed to present succinctly the most important information about the story) or feature (designed not so much to provide news as to grab the reader's attention and get him to read on). Questions to ask about both kinds include: What impression did the lead create? What was its "hook" (the connection to a newsworthy event)? What other angles were possible? Leads are vital because at least half the readers who start a story are likely to read no further.

1. *Detroit News*, June 5, 1986, 1; *Detroit Free Press*, June 5, 1986, 3.

On a national story, it is also worth asking whether reporters took the time to localize it, or whether they reported it dutifully but held it at arm's length while wrinkling their noses. For example, when the *Detroit News* and the *Detroit Free Press* ran front-page stories on AIDS-contaminated blood in blood banks, the conservative *News* lead provided specific detail on how sixty-four donors to Michigan's three Red Cross centers had tested positive for the AIDS antibody. The liberal *Free Press* lead, however, was a general statement about blood banks tracing blood donations.[2]

One final element to examine before scrutinizing the story itself is the story's setting. News organizations try to regularize news coverage through the institution of beats, often associated with government: State Department, city hall, courthouse. Routine channels of that sort account for most news. On local television, death watches (fires, crimes, accidents) account for most of the rest: yellow police tape and flashing red and blue lights are arresting visual images, regardless of the true newsworthiness of the story itself. A television station's decision to send a camera crew to a location that is neither routinized (the beat) nor sensational shows a conscious decision to expend resources in particular ways and not expend them in others. Whose demonstrations are covered, and whose are not? Who gets free publicity, and who does not? Those are key questions that often have ideological answers.

Stories: What to Look For

The best way to check coverage is to compare stories on the same news item in roughly comparable news outlets. That's much easier to do online today than it was twenty-five years ago. We'll look at an old example and a new one.

2. *Detroit News*, June 6, 1986, 1; *Detroit Free Press*, June 6, 1986, 1.

The old one is from Detroit: One day both the *Free Press* and the *News* had at the top right-hand corner of page 1—the most read spot of the newspaper—articles on a keynote speech by union president Owen Bieber at the United Auto Workers annual convention. The placement of the story was no surprise: the UAW is very important in Motown, and each newspaper sent its own reporter to the convention site near Disneyland, rather than relying on wire services.[3]

The headlines, though, made it seem as if two different speeches were covered. The conservative *News* proclaimed, "UAW Chief Threatens Wage 'War.'" The liberal *Free Press* reported, "New UAW Group to Chart Future." Further reading did not lessen the confusion. The *Free Press*'s lead of thirty-four words was: "In a spirited keynote address to the first session of the UAW's 26th Constitutional Convention here Sunday, President Owen Bieber announced the establishment of a new commission to guide the union in the future." The *News*'s lead of thirty-five words was: "The United Auto Workers will 'go to war' with the Big Three auto makers unless substantial gains are made in wages and job security during next year's contract negotiations, UAW President Owen Bieber said Sunday." Same speech, same length of lead, but two very different impressions. The *Free Press*, in its headline and lead, stressed the positive message (in today's culture) of future-orientation, while the *News* provided the negative message of "wage war."[4]

Nor did succeeding paragraphs provide what the leads lacked. The *Free Press* story, continuing onto an inside page, contained twenty-two paragraphs, but nowhere was wage war even mentioned. The *News* story also went onto an inside page and was also twenty-two paragraphs long. It at least mentioned the

3. *Detroit News*, June 2, 1986, 1; *Detroit Free Press*, June 2, 1986, 1.
4. See *Wall Street Journal*, July 27, 1982, 30.

commission, but not until the eighteenth paragraph, by which time most readers would be long gone to the comics, sports, or lifestyle pages.

The coverage of disasters—from car wrecks to hurricanes to terrorist attacks—has long been a journalism staple, but in recent years the ways journalists cover disaster reveal underlying ideologies and biases. For example, were the September 11, 2001, attackers "Muslims," "radical jihadists," or "religious fundamentalists"? The way a journalist answers that question reveals much about his worldview.

WORLD has long thought the coverage of disasters is an important part of its mission. Disasters provide spectacular facts, heroic actors, and—sometimes—cowardly villians. Disasters also raise difficult questions about faith, doubt, and the sovereignty of God. Many disasters also provide opportunities for service and for asking questions about the role of the church, private charities, and the government in the rescue and recovery process. In short, for the Christian journalist, disasters also provide opportunities to fill in the gaps left by secular journalists who have "spiked the spiritual" from their stories.

Consider, for example, coverage of Hurricane Sandy, which devastated the east coast in 2012. An October 30 Associated Press story focused on the role of government in the recovery process. To highlight the centrality of the government in the recovery effort, "Mayor Michael Bloomberg planned to ring the bell at the New York Stock Exchange to reopen it after a rare two-day closure."[5]

WORLD coverage, on the other hand, celebrated individual initiative, entrepreneurship, and community effort. Emily Belz wrote: "Tuesday morning New York awoke with its trademark resilience, though millions in the city had lost power and property. Restaurants and grocery stores that had power and

5. http://news.yahoo.com/slowed–darkened–nyc–begins–stir–life–113733631.html.

minimal damage reopened and bustled even while the city's major financial sector, including the New York Stock Exchange, remained closed."[6]

The Associated Press story did not mention the church, but *WORLD*'s story highlighted it:

> The city's churches assembled to begin relief efforts. Hope for New York, a nonprofit affiliate of Redeemer Presbyterian Church, is helping coordinate relief efforts between churches and nonprofit groups, posting needs on its website (hfny.org/hurricane). All Angels Church on the Upper West Side requested hygiene kits and blankets. New York City Relief asked for clothing and food. Other churches in Queens sent out foot patrols to check on their neighbors.[7]

The *WORLD* story did not ignore the role of the government, but compared its effectiveness to that of grassroots and community efforts in a subtle and ironic way: "The city government's website for registering to volunteer with cleanup (nycservice.org) went down due to heavy traffic."[8]

Readers and viewers need to ask about descriptive words or settings. Are seemingly trivial aspects included in the story? For what reason? Any pattern? In an age when abortion is labeled "termination of pregnancy" and abortionists are "pro-choice," we should note evasive language. Why are pornography shops, patronized by those in arrested stages of development, referred to as "adult bookstores"? Why are homosexuals "gay"? Why did many major media outlets use the words "dictator" or "strongman" to describe autocrats allied to the United States, but the word "leader" to refer to Communist dictators such as Daniel Ortega or Kim Il Sung?

6. www.worldmag.com/2012/10/after_sandy.
7. Ibid.
8. Ibid.

Specific, descriptive detail is the guts of journalism. Reporters quickly learn how to load stories not by distinguishing explicitly their perceived good guys and bad guys, but through the use of evocative descriptives. For example, when Tennessee parents in 1986 protested the teaching of anti-Christian doctrines to their children in public schools, reporters for *Time*, *Newsweek*, and major newspapers did not say, "We think the parents are nutty." Instead, they reported that the parents were objecting to reading about Goldilocks and the Three Bears, Cinderella, the Wizard of Oz, Jack and Jill, and so on.[9] In actuality, the parents were objecting to stories that preach the acceptability of lying, stealing, cheating, and disobeying parents, that motherhood is an inferior activity, and so on. The parents also objected to children being instructed in the writing of witchcraft incantations or the use of New Age meditational exercises.

Newsweek mentioned none of this, but padded its story with description of how the school board's lawyer "spread his hands in exasperation" because the Christian parents apparently were impossible to please. Then the magazine added a bit of local color in the form of an ersatz public opinion poll: "Customers at The Ivory Thimble needlework shop in nearby Church Hill thought the parents were making 'mountains out of molehills.' " Reporters often use such unnamed sources to indicate their own impressions.[10]

Bias in news coverage of demonstrations is relatively easy to spot. At a rally, were news cameras focusing on a few or on a crowd? Were viewers left with an accurate impression of how many people actually were there? (A large crowd can look small and a small one large simply by changing camera lenses.)

These questions became a national issue on October 16, 1995, when the Nation of Islam was a co-organizer of the so-called

9. See, for example, "A Reprise of Scopes," *Newsweek*, July 28, 1986, 19.
10. Ibid.

Million Man March on the National Mall. The National Park Service, which has jurisdiction over the site, had until then made a practice of estimating crowd size at such rallies. The Park Service said the crowd size was about 400,000. March organizers angrily responded with an estimate of between 1.2 and 2 million. Ultimately ABC-TV funded a study that concluded actual attendance was about 830,000—plus or minus 25 percent. The Park Service never backed down from its number, and subsequent studies have supported the 400,000 number. Nonetheless, the media continue to call the event the Million Man March. Two years later, on October 4, 1997, the Christian men's group Promise Keepers held an event on the national mall. Attendance at that rally likely did exceed one million men. However, because of the Million Man March controversy, the Park Service had stopped making crowd estimates. The net effect was that if all you read were media accounts of the two events, you would be hard pressed to conclude which one was larger or had more significance.

Television has even more ways—both obvious and subtle—of influencing impressions. Do cameras focus on kooky stuff or typical activities? It is easy to trivialize a demonstration through emphasis on the silly, or to marginalize it by suggesting that those involved are deviant or irrational. The normal camera angle for news interviews is straight across, simulating the way one adult of average height meets and talks with another adult of average height. If the camera either looks up at the subject (that makes him seem more powerful) or down (that belittles him), the reason is either incompetence or ideology. Worm's-eye or bird's-eye views are such obvious slanting devices that they rarely are used. Differences in distancing are more frequent. Interviewees are typically shot in medium close-up (after perhaps an opening shot to "establish" the setting). Close-ups, though, are used to bring out emotion (in an accident victim) or to show sweat (during an unfriendly interview). On the other hand, a full-length or long shot of an individual during the middle of an interview generally depersonalizes him and distances viewers. Departures from the normal medium close-up should be examined carefully.

Few nonjournalists realize how frequently "experts" and "statistics" are used to bulwark a reporter's ideological position. An "expert" almost always can be found to support virtually any position. Regardless of the statistics involved, skilled makers of line graphs or pie and bar charts can create almost any impression they want. Verticals in line graphs can be compressed, bar charts can leave out center sections, and picture graphs can leave the impression of much greater change than actually occurred.

Reporters often misuse statistics to make political points. Some ten thousand U.S. draft evaders in Canada during the early 1970s were transformed by the *Boston Globe* into "over 50,000," by *Newsweek* into fifty thousand to seventy-five thousand, by CBS into one hundred thousand, and so on.[11] During the late 1950s and 1960s, several hundred abortion-related deaths of women each year turned into annual totals of five to ten thousand, and several hundred thousand illegal abortions per year became one to two million.[12]

Even apparently straight question-and-answer segments may be open to distortion. Some interviewers have been known to change the questions they asked for the camera following conclusion of a taped interview. For example, Geraldo Rivera in one interview asked a subject, "Did you make a mistake?" During the refilming, though, he asked an implicitly more critical

11. Lester A. Sobel, ed., *Media Controversies* (New York: Facts on File, 1981), 73.

12. See, for example, *Newsweek*, November 14, 1966, 92, and *Time*, September 17, 1965, 82.

question: "Do you *admit* that a mistake was made?" He used the original answer and thus made his respondent seem evasive.[13]

Behind the Story: Gatekeepers

Why does one particular story make the front page or network news, when hundreds of other possible stories end up circularly filed? Many scholars suggest that journalists have their prime influence on society not so much by coverage of particular stories as by the choice of what to cover. Journalists are sometimes called "gatekeepers" or "agenda-setters." Readers and viewers should keep asking: Why was the story considered newsworthy? Was it tied to a particular event? Did it have dramatic elements, such as violence or conflict? Was it something unusual? Was it a new development in a continuing issue? Did the activity reported affect many people? Was there a celebrity involved?

A story should be examined in the context of an entire newspaper or program. Where was it placed? How much space or time did it receive? Was it treated as hard news or feature? Could it have been either? How did it compare in interest to stories given more prominent space or time, or less? Other questions are hard to answer from the outside, but they are well worth asking: Who might have been behind the story? Did someone outside the news organization start the ball rolling or shape the story as it developed? Who benefited from the story? Who was damaged?

The best way to see how much of news is discretionary, again, is to compare coverage in different publications, then ask questions about contrast in information and handling. Did a story appear in just one publication or on one program, or many? For example, one day the *Detroit News* gave big play to a report calling the Detroit mayor inactive concerning "hundreds of thousands

13. Kathleen Jamieson and Karlyn Campbell, *The Interplay of Influence: Mass Media and Their Publics in News, Advertising, Politics* (Belmont, CA: Wadsworth, 1983), 49.

of vacant and abandoned homes," "abandoned cars by the thousands with nowhere to store them," and serious problems with the water, sanitation, and other departments. The liberal *Free Press*, which had given consistent support to Detroit's mayor, at first did not cover the charges at all, and the next day buried on page 18A a tiny article about the controversy.[14]

A Classic: The Chambers-Hiss Affair

Leads, stories, and story selection: all the elements come together in a comparison of how the Chambers-Hiss affair mentioned in chapter 2 was covered in the liberal *Washington Post* and the conservative *Chicago Tribune*. A jury in January 1950 found Hiss guilty of perjury.

Historians have no real doubt that the jury verdict was correct.[15] Yet, five of my journalism history students who read about the trial in the *Washington Post*, without any other knowledge of the case, concluded that Hiss was innocent. Five other journalism students who read only the *Tribune* came to the conclusion that Hiss was guilty.

How could that happen? The *Post* downplayed irrefutable courtroom evidence against Hiss: microfilm and stolen

14. *Detroit News*, June 3, 1986, 1; *Detroit Free Press*, June 4, 18A. The *Free Press* is a morning newspaper, the *News* technically an evening one. The *News*, though, actually hits the streets at about noon, too early to include nonemergency coverage of the day's events. The *News*, like the *Free Press*, essentially deals with events of the previous day or before. None of the four Detroit stories referred to in this chapter appeared to be affected by the difference in timing.

15. Two books to read for information about the great case are Chambers' *Witness* (New York: Random House, 1952) and Allan Weinstein's *Perjury: The Hiss-Chambers Case* (New York: Knopf, 1978). Alfred Kazin wrote in *Esquire* of Weinstein's work, "After this book, it is impossible to imagine anything new in this case except an admission by Alger Hiss that he had been lying for thirty years" (March 28, 1978, 21). Liberal historian Arthur Schlesinger Jr., conservative columnist George Will, *Encounter* editor Melvin Lasky, and author Merle Miller all agreed that, in Will's words, "The myth of Hiss' innocence suffers the death of a thousand cuts, delicate destruction by a scholar's scalpel" (*Newsweek*, March 20, 1978, 96).

documents retyped on his typewriter. Instead, *Post* readers learned of the personal battle between "tall, lean, 44-year-old Hiss," with character references from Supreme Court justices, and "short, fat-faced" Chambers, with his "customary air of complete emotionless detachment." In the pages of the *Post*, Chambers wore a "supercilious expression" while Hiss "calmly strode to the stand" and was always "sure of himself, answering the barrage of questions without hesitation, showing no uneasiness or equivocation." The *Tribune*, though, stressed the evidence and supported Chambers.[16]

On June 2, 1949, for instance, Chambers testified that Alger Hiss had furnished government secrets to the Soviets, and also admitted having himself lied while a Communist during the 1930s. The following day the *Washington Post* headline emphasized Chambers' past derelictions: "Lies Admitted by Chambers." The *Chicago Tribune*, though, spotlighted Hiss's activity: "Hiss Aided Reds: Chambers." Each newspaper also described the emotional state of Chambers as he was testifying. The liberal *Post* reported that "Chambers seemed to be showing discomfiture," while the conservative *Tribune* noted that Chambers "never lost his composure."[17]

On June 6 Chambers again provided two possible story emphases: He testified that another federal official had spied for the Soviets, and he also admitted additional lies. The *Post* again played the lying angle big, even running a banner headline across the top of page 1: "Chambers Admits He Lied to Congress," followed by a pro-Hiss lead: "Under vigorous cross-examination which sought to depict him as a confused neurotic, Whittaker Chambers admitted some further conflict in his account." The *Chicago Tribune*, though, headlined

16. *Chicago Tribune*, December 3, 1948, 1; June 16, 1949, 3; *Washington Post*, June 16, 1949, 1.
17. *Washington Post*, June 3, 1948, 1; *Chicago Tribune*, June 3, 1948, 1.

the day's new development: "Chambers Says Wadleigh Was 2d Spy Source."[18]

One week later the testimony of Whittaker Chambers's wife, Esther, became crucial to Chambers's contention, denied by Hiss, that Chambers and Hiss had been close friends during the 1930s. The *Washington Post* transformed one faltering moment on the witness stand—Esther Chambers could not remember whether she had seen the Hisses twelve years earlier at an anniversary party or a New Year's Eve party—into a front-page headline: "Chambers' Wife Alters Testimony."

The *Chicago Tribune*, though, emphasized the main part of her testimony and even suggested comfortable cruelty among the Hisses: "Hiss, resplendent in a cream colored summer suit, and his wife, in a cotton frock and a pert green hat, beamed as the 49 year old witness grew pale and exhausted, hesitated and faltered . . . under a merciless, four hour cross-examination."[19]

Two days later newspapers reported the testimony of a State Department secretary who had worked for Hiss. Part of her testimony was damaging to Hiss's case: she testified that four memoranda in Hiss's handwriting on top secret subjects were not made in the course of regular State Department business. Part could be construed as supportive: she also noted that State Department employees other than Hiss had access to some of the documents Chambers said he had received from Hiss.

The *Chicago Tribune*'s lead was pro-Chambers, describing how the secretary had "stunned the defense at the Alger Hiss perjury trial today with a series of damaging assertions," most notably the one about Hiss's secret memoranda. The *Washington Post*'s story was pro-Hiss, beginning with the headline "State Secrets Open to Many, Hiss Trial Told," and continuing with a

18. *Chicago Tribune*, December 3, 1948, 1; June 16, 1949, 3; *Washington Post*, June 16, 1949 1.

19. *Washington Post*, June 7, 1949, 1; *Chicago Tribune*, June 7, 1949, 2.

direct presentation of the spin put on the story by the Hiss camp: "Trial attorneys for Alger Hiss today emphasized that dozens of other State Department employees had access to documents which Whittaker Chambers said he received from Hiss in 1938."

Throughout the trial, then, *Tribune* and *Post* readers would have received radically different impressions. It so happened in this case that readers of the conservative newspaper would have been much better informed than readers of the liberal *Post*. It is not always that way, since the key dividing point of our era is materialistic versus theist, not liberal versus conservative.

Furthermore, *Tribune* readers would have been no better informed of the theological implications of the story than were *Post* readers. Chambers, throughout the affair, had tried to teach that communism could not be defeated by American materialism. He argued that it was the near-religious vision of communism that attracted to its ranks persons like Alger Hiss. Chambers had stated that only faith in God could allow Americans to stand up to Marxist faith. The *Tribune*, though, generally ignored Chambers's message.

In retrospect, it is clear that Chambers's agenda and the conservative press agendas deviated as he emphasized Christian beliefs and criticized materialism of all stripes. After listening to Chambers's statements, one observer suggested that the question was "no longer whether Alger Hiss is guilty. The question now is whether God exists."[20] Many conservative journalists, like

20. *Saturday Evening Post*, November 15, 1952, 121. Those non-Christian journalists who are conservatives are valuable allies of biblical Christians in many political and social battles because they often see clearly the material manifestations of disobedience to God, even if they refuse to admit the cause. Some, though, are like Hearst's long-time editor Arthur Brisbane, who "wrote approvingly of religion" because "he regarded it as a sort of merciful illusion which sustained people and comforted them when they might otherwise have had nothing on which to lean" (profile by Stanley Walker in *Post Biographies of Famous Journalists*, ed. John Drewry [Athens: University of Georgia Press, 1942], 24–25).

Other non-Christian journalists who are politically involved may be similar to this description of Henry Luce, cofounder of *Time* magazine, by one of his editors, Ralph

many of their liberal counterparts, seemed uncomfortable with the debate on those terms. They did not understand the deeper implications of the ideas of Chambers and the fall of Hiss.[21]

Conclusion: News Perspective

Christians should not assume that news pages are any less biased than editorial pages. Sometimes the only significant difference is the degree of subtlety. It is always important to keep in mind the importance of what writer David Altheide has called "news perspective." As Altheide points out, most stories are too complex to fit into a dramatic and easily understood standard news format. Journalists look for a lead or theme which will help them to structure the story and determine which facts are important. Once they develop that theme, they report news stories on the same subject according to the same theme. They do not pursue details that do not fit the theme.[22]

The Sherri Finkbine abortion story from 1962, discussed briefly in chapter 2, provides a good example of journalistic grasping for a new theme. The problem of what to call the being in

---

Ingersoll: Luce's "first faith had been in God," but in school "it had been challenged. And he had not met the challenge. He had seen that the boys who felt as he felt, truly, were not the 'in' group. . . . he was not drawn to Christ's defense, but to the company of His critics—the popular and the powerful. It was their challenge that he had felt the need to meet, to become one of them, to outdo them. He had given up his faith in God to meet it. He had learned what he really was—a 'back-row Christian.' And something went out of him" (quoted in Roy Hoopes, *Ralph Ingersoll: A Biography* [New York: Atheneum, 1985], 160–61).

21. In a continuation of this study, the *Los Angeles Times* (then a conservative newspaper) and the *New York Times* (a liberal newspaper, although closer to the center then than now) also were examined. *Los Angeles Times* coverage was similar to that of the *Tribune*. *New York Times* coverage was similar to that of the *Post* at first, but when overwhelming evidence against Hiss appeared, the *Times* bailed out and dropped its pro-Hiss stance. Presuppositions create presumptions as to the importance of particular facts or segments of testimony, but in some cases neither liberal nor conservative newspapers will *completely* disregard irrefutable evidence, as long as basic theological questions can be overlooked.

22. David Altheide, *Creating Reality: How TV News Distorts Events* (Beverly Hills: Sage Publications, 1976), 73.

the womb was difficult. Even though the use of the word "baby"
went against the thrust of most stories, the Finkbine articles
early on were sprinkled with references to "unborn baby" and
"child." The *New York Times* on July 26 reported that Finkbine
"feared her child would be permanently affected."[23] The next
day the *Times* referred to "Mrs. Sherri Finkbine, pregnant for
three months with a baby she fears will be deformed."[24] The *New
York Journal-American* mentioned "her baby" and "the unborn
child."[25] The *Los Angeles Times* reported that Finkbine "wants to
prevent the birth of her child."[26] The *Chicago Tribune* referred to
the "expected child [who] is threatened with deformed birth."[27]
Medical language provided the eventual solution: Dump the
word "baby" and substitute the neutral-sounding term "fetus."[28]

Early on, the word *fetus* (and occasionally the word *embryo*)
found use when reporters focused on the medical aspects of the
situation. After the abortion occurred, the *Journal-American* used
the term "fetus" on August 18.[29] The *New York Times* reported on
August 19 that, in the Finkbine case, "the fetus" was deformed.[30]
Journalists needed this new vocabulary to avoid using language
that contradicted themes. Reporters could create sympathy for
the Finkbines by emphasizing their appearance, children, love
for children, professions, etc., but implicitly pro-life language
could create tension by making readers believe that the abortion
would affect a baby and not a thing. Reporters reconciled the
tension by focusing on the possibility of deformity (suggesting

23. *New York Times*, July 26, 1962, 25.

24. Ibid., July 27, 1962, 12.

25. *New York Journal-American*, August 5, 1962, 1; August 19, 1962, clipping from
Journal-American archives, Humanities Research Center, University of Texas at Austin.

26. *Los Angeles Times*, July 31, 1962, 1.

27. *Chicago Tribune*, July 25, 1962, Part 3, 1.

28. *New York Times*, July 25, 1962, 22; July 27, 1962, 12; August 5, 1962, 12; *Arizona
Republic*, July 27, 1962, 4.

29. *New York Journal-American*, August 18, 1962, clipping from *Journal-American*
archives.

30. *New York Times*, August 19, 1962, 12.

that the baby was less than fully human) and took from the medical profession a neutral term, *fetus*.

Use of a dehumanizing term allowed reporters to stress more consistently Finkbine's "unselfish" willingness to sacrifice her privacy to promote "more humane" abortion legislation. The *Los Angeles Times* quoted her as saying, "I hope that in a small way we have contributed toward achieving a more humane attitude toward this problem."[31] The *Chicago Tribune* quoted Robert Finkbine's observation that his wife went public to "help others who may get trapped in the same horrible thing."[32]

Clearly, a new story format for abortion incidents was emerging. The old "abortion as crime" structure viewed the aborted infant as a murder victim, but in the new format sympathy was with Finkbine. Coverage was always from her perspective. The baby was dehumanized or forgotten.

Providentially, though, new developments in medicine are making it more difficult for journalists to use implicitly pro-abortion language. In 1986, doctors announced they had opened a mother's womb by cesarean section, removed her twenty-three-week-old baby for three minutes to correct a urinary tract infection, and put the baby back in the womb. The word *fetus* did not sound quite right even to some hard-boiled reporters. Baby Mitchell, after all, had been a fetus with his own doctor, his own medical records, even his own medical bills. Surgery on unborn children is now common and takes place as early as eighteen weeks. Ultrasound (3D and 4D) is now common at pregnancy care centers nationwide. Among the results: by the 2010s the number of abortions had fallen, and the percentage of Americans who believe we should protect unborn children has grown. This latter trend is particularly pronounced among young people.

31. *Los Angeles Times*, July 31, 1962, 1.
32. *Chicago Tribune*, July 27, 1962, 4.

Ignoring these changes in attitude of the American people, mainline American journalism is still stuck in the ruts of a modernism now grown old. That stubbornness is likely a cause of the economic judgment many media organizations now face, a judgment we discuss more fully in the next chapter. The refusal of many journalists to change should come as no surprise to Christians who recall the description in Psalm 73:9 of those who have power without godliness: "They scoff and speak with malice; loftily they threaten oppression. They set their mouths against the heavens, and their tongue struts through the earth." The refusal is still a sorrowful sight for journalists and for journalism, because God is not mocked.

We should mourn the present and future of leading denizens of the current journalistic night. We should be joyful, though, that God is now raising up new technology, new institutions, and new journalists to take the places of those fallen away. The next section discusses the growing opportunity for part of the prodigal press to come home.

PART 3

RETURN?

Whenever we see ourselves as weak, we should not concentrate on our own frailty, but should gaze—both eyes—upon God's glory.
—*John Calvin*

9

Network News and Local Newspapers: The Coming Economic Judgment

Some media analysts, after examining economic and technological trends, develop reductionist explanations for change. Ignoring the spiritual in this way, as in others, is clearly a mistake. On the other hand, since God works through physical means as well as spiritual power, to ignore economics and technology returns us to the nature versus grace division that sapped Christian energies during late medieval times.[1] This chapter examines economics and technology, not to suggest that they are dominant, but to see how, over time, God "brings princes to nothing and makes the rulers of the earth as emptiness" (Isa. 40:23). This chapter title is unchanged from 1988, though some of that judgment has now come.

Television Network News

During the 1970s and early 1980s, news budgets of all three major networks shot upward. The CBS news division grew from 700 employees in 1970 to 1,500 in 1983, even though requirements

1. For a basic discussion of the nature-grace issue, see Francis A. Schaeffer, *Escape from Reason* (Downers Grove, IL: InterVarsity Press, 1968), 9–29.

for technical staffing decreased due to the introduction of video equipment and simpler cameras/editing machines that took less time to use. ABC and NBC also found that some of their news shows, which had been loss leaders promoted for prestige purposes, were becoming profit centers.[2] Yet, the words of Isaiah 40:24 describe well the brief glory of the news divisions: "Scarcely are they planted, scarcely sown, scarcely has their stem taken root in the earth, than he blows on them, and they wither, and the tempest carries them off like stubble."

The new winds began to blow in 1983. In that year all three network news divisions cut staffs and budgets. The firings were real hardships, the reduction of allowable expenses a psychological blow for those who had become used to lordly treatment. At CBS, for example, first-class travel and catered meals for journalists virtually disappeared. Many media observers, and the networks themselves, thought the cuts temporary. In 1983, the country was still emerging from a recession and 1984 would be an election year, when both advertising revenue and interest in news typically spikes. However, in subsequent years network news departments continued to stagger, with NBC losing $50 million a year on its news operation.

Such news division losses were not problems during the heyday of the networks, the 1950s through the 1970s. But the three networks were losing viewers quickly. During the 1985–86 television season they had a combined 76 share (76 percent of households with televisions turned on had them turned to network shows) compared with an 87 share five years earlier. These viewers were fleeing the networks for cable programming, though by 1986 less than half of American households even had cable. The networks were clearly in trouble. The financial impact of viewer decline became evident in 1985 when advertis-

2. "Behind the Revolt at CBS: An Erosion of Confidence," *New York Times*, September 12, 1986, 1.

ing revenues for all three networks decreased that year for the first time since 1971 (when a ban on cigarette advertising went into effect).

The growth of cable in the 1970s and 1980s was dramatic. Cable had been around since the 1940s, but it was a very isolated and rural phenomenon. Local communities that could not get broadcast programming would put an antenna on the highest place in town and run cables from the antennas to their homes. Lawsuits and FCC rule changes allowed cable to operate more as an industry by the early 1970s. By the end of 1986 cable was in more than forty-two million American households, or 48 percent of the total. By 2006, the percentage had grown to 58.4 percent, or well over one hundred million households. Approximately 20 percent of households had satellite television. The average household now receives dozens of channels on cable and hundreds on satellite. While the three broadcast networks—NBC, CBS, and ABC—are still the largest, they are no longer dominant.

The advent of CNN in 1980 was the beginning of television news on a twenty-four-hour-per-day basis. CNN, now in more than one hundred million households, was not an instant success when it began in 1980. It took time to alter viewing habits and to educate advertisers who had previously paid attention only to network or local station programming. By mid-1985, though, the success of CNN and its headline news service, CNN-2 (which became Headline News, or HLN), was attracting ample advertiser attention.[3]

Satellite technology emerging in the 1980s posed another long-term problem for the networks. Local stations no longer needed the networks for national and international news. An early experiment in satellite news distribution began in 1984

3. Before major advertising revenue came in, large bills had to be paid for the setting up of nine domestic and twelve international news bureaus as well as for everyday production costs. Negotiations with hundreds of domestic and international stations for news coverage exchange also were necessary.

when Hubbard Broadcasting of St. Paul, Minnesota, organized Conus, a satellite news-gathering service. Conus let local stations transmit and receive footage by direct satellite hookup, without going through the networks. Conus also formed a twenty-four-hour news channel in 1989 that for a while was the only direct competitor to CNN.

Conus never became a major player, and it folded in 2002, but it had some immediate and long-lasting effects. For example, in September 1985, when networks asked for help from their local affiliates in covering a bad hurricane season, some of the local stations said they were too busy with their Conus feeds. In 1986 Conus signed an agreement with the Associated Press to form a television news service linking more than six hundred stations. The Associated Press eventually withdrew from that relationship and formed its own television news distribution system, APTV, in 1996. AP rebranded APTV as Associated Press Television News in 2005.

So by the early 1990s, a new television landscape was emerging. Local stations could develop their own linkages because of the nature of networks. CBS, NBC, and ABC each owned only a few stations in major cities, while hundreds of other stations were "affiliates," owned and operated by others. For the most part the network corporations and their affiliates had a friendly, symbiotic relationship, with years of tradition and profits behind them. Affiliates gave the networks access to local airwaves. In return the networks paid the stations for use of their airtime and gave them a core of popular programming around which to sell advertising. Yet, any station could refuse to use network programming at any time. Elton Rule noted when he was president of the ABC broadcast division, "Station owners do pretty much what they want to do."[4]

4. See William J. Drummond, "Is Time Running out for Network News?," *Columbia Journalism Review* (May-June 1986): 50–52. Also, the January 2–9, 1987, *TV Guide* noted

Given that opportunity for decentralization, change could come through God's instruments of technology, economics, and politics. Decentralization accelerated in the 1990s and beyond. One reason was a dramatic shift in the way television was paid for. Until the 1970s, television was free. Broadcasters made money by selling advertising. Cable demonstrated that viewers would pay for more choices. Cable also allowed the mass audience that used to gather around the three major networks to fragment by taste, lifestyle, even racial and ethnic makeup. Advertising remained a key part of television's funding model, but now advertisers could more carefully target their advertising. By the middle of the 1990s, the major network share of advertising dollars was at an all-time low, and cable companies such as Time Warner, Comcast, and Charter had real clout and would not let the networks push them around.

Another major development was the Telecommunications Act of 1996, the first significant overhaul of the nation's telecommunications system since 1934. A full discussion of that law is beyond the scope of our conversation here, but a few details are relevant. First, limits on radio and television station ownership were virtually eliminated. Second, the law established technology standards that extended across platforms. These new standards allowed for a proliferation of cellular and wireless technologies.

Network news shows did not die, but they did change. Deregulation allowed the networks to buy local stations. CBS, which before deregulation was limited in station ownership to just a few, now owns twenty-three stations, all of them in major markets. These new ownership rules virtually guaranteed the ongoing existence of the networks. They had to produce news shows if only to service themselves.

---

that ABC-Cap Cities wanted to cut by 9 percent the amount (thought to be about $125 million annually) that ABC pays to local stations for carrying network programs.

But the main impact of deregulation was a dramatic flowering in new media. To cite just a few examples: Huffington Post began in 2005 and by 2012 was the nation's number-one-rated news site. It became the first Internet-only news organization to win a Pulitzer Prize. Another recent "convergence media" success is The Blaze. When Glenn Beck decided to leave Fox News in 2010, rather than go to another network, he started www.TheBlaze.com as a massive website that aggregates news from other sites, does original reporting, and produces television programming—including Beck's own program that streams live on the site. The site went live in 2011, and in the first eighteen months had more than one billion page views.

During the early 1990s, some local stations, looking at the new technology available to them then, said they were likely to drop network news shows. KCRA's station manager Peter Langlois pointed out, "The public doesn't care where they get their news from. They care that it's accurate, complete and available when they want it. Ten years from now we could be providing a complete newscast covering the world from Sacramento."[5] The irony is that this statement turned out to be completely true, but it is now both network news *and* local affiliates who are fighting for their lives against new media.

The reduction in network power and the rise in new media, even conservative new media, is not automatically good news for Christians. For one thing, "conservative" is not a synonym for "Christian." It's true that in a left-leaning, increasingly materialistic culture, a Christian worldview is often culturally conservative. But that overlap is an accident of history. In the early 1800s,

5. See Desmond Smith, "You Can Go Home Again," *Washington Journalism Review* (June 1986): 44–47. The power shift to local stations was symbolized late in 1986 by the decision of journalist Steve Bell to leave the ABC network in order to anchor a local news show in Philadelphia. Morton Dean of CBS already had gone to New York, Sylvia Chase of ABC to San Francisco, and Bill Curtis of CBS to Chicago, with Curtis saying, "I don't think the future is there anymore for the networks" (ibid., 44).

for example, British politician William Wilburforce—energized by his Christian worldview—crusaded to end the slave trade. In the chapter 11 we look at how Christian journalists crusaded against dueling in the eighteenth century and abortion in the nineteenth century. In their day, these were "progressive" and not "conservative" causes.

But with these warnings about aligning too closely to conservative politics duly noted, we quickly add that the rise of conservative media should give Christian journalists hope. The decline of the networks and the rise of alternative media mean that Christians can exploit profitable niches. Talented Christians now, perhaps for the first time in the electronic age, have the opportunity to show on television the extent of Christ's lordship on public-policy questions and in every aspect of life.[6]

As we will discuss more fully in chapter 13, the time is ripe for a television program resting on Christian presuppositions. The diversity of cable and satellite programming will include—it already does include—much that follows Satan. But if Christians are active it will include, and already does, much that glorifies God.

Av Westin of ABC perhaps best summarized the present and future of network television news: "The whole definition of what a story is, and the network's role in delivering that story, has been changed by the satellite. In the past, we have always referred to the evening news shows as our 'flagships.' Well, as many navies around the world have already discovered, the flagship may prove to be too expensive to maintain." As the flagships are mothballed, Christians will have enormous opportunities—if we understand ways to win and keep an audience.[7]

6. Technological change is increasing the variety of opportunities for both young journalists and viewers. More journalists will get the chance to cover national news stories, if they want it.

7. Desmond Smith, "Is the Sun Setting on Network Nightly News?," *Washington Journalism Review* (January 1986): 30–33.

The Behemoth Local Newspaper

Since 1940, the United States has suffered through a steep decline in the number of cities having competitive daily newspapers. Some of the largest American cities now have only two daily newspapers, and many are down to one. *New Orleans Times-Picayune*, the city's major paper, no longer publishes even daily. It now publishes only three times a week. Cities with more than a million in population, such as Austin, Texas, typically have one daily newspaper; early in the century, with a population only one-twentieth as large, Austin had six newspapers. There are fully competitive newspapers in only thirty American cities, representing just 2 percent of the total of about fifteen hundred cities with dailies.

Clearly, newspapers have not held their ground as other media have emerged. The number of newspapers sold per household per day decreased from 1.32 in 1930 (when radio began making inroads) to 0.79 in 1980. In the twenty largest U.S. cities, newspaper circulation fell by 21 percent between 1970 and 1980. And yet, the daily local newspaper has been until recently very profitable. Newspaper revenues grew 64 percent between 1979 and 1984, and pretax operating income margins increased from 16 to 18 percent. A typical newspaper without daily print competition in its community can convert a third of its revenue to operating profit.[8]

The statistics in the 1980s suggested profitable opportunities for Christians, and others, to jump in with competing newspapers. There was a big catch, though. Usually, when competition is low and profits are high, new competitors are quick to enter a market. But that was not the case with city daily newspapers, for one main reason: the advertising pattern.

8. Ibid. See also Barbara Matusow, "Learning to Do with Less: Lean Days Ahead for Network News," *Washington Journalism Review* (July 1986): 23–25, and Gary Cummings, "Luring Ad Dollars From Network TV," *Washington Journalism Review* (October 1986): 12, 31.

Newspaper advertising for decades typically produced 80 percent of newspaper revenue. Most advertising is local retail, and what those local retailers want is penetration of over 50 percent of the local market. Total circulation was less important than density of penetration in a particular area, for when a newspaper reached over half the households in an area, it often became a must buy for local advertisers. Advertising managers had a motto: "When you get 51 percent of the circulation, you get 70 percent of the advertising."[9]

As the 51–70 rule of thumb would indicate, newspaper circulation leaders within their communities in the late twentieth century tended to become fatter with ads. Their competitors tended to lose advertising inches and revenues. Generally after a struggle, those competitors went out of business. The result was daily newspaper monopoly in most American cities. Those wishing to break the monopoly had to face a Catch-22. Advertising revenues allowed the existing newspaper to publish a fat edition for, typically, twenty-five cents. New newspapers could not get the advertising until they had established themselves by grabbing a big chunk of the market. Yet, unless they had large enough cash resources to cover tremendous losses for several years, they could not sell "full-service newspapers" (complete with columns, special features, and so on) at a competitive price and gain the necessary circulation, until they had the advertising subsidy.[10]

9. Kathleen Jamieson and Karlyn Campbell, *The Interplay of Influence: Mass Media and Their Publics in News, Advertising, Politics* (Belmont, CA: Wadsworth, 1983), 128.

10. Three-quarters of newspaper revenue typically comes from advertising. The typical newspaper advertising mix is 50 percent localized retail ads, 30 percent classified ads, 10 percent inserts, 5 percent national ads, and 5 percent miscellaneous. From the 1970s through the 1990s, large daily newspapers often enjoyed 20 to 30 percent profit margins. They were, in short, cash cows for their owners. That's why a look at the "Forbes 400" list of the wealthiest people in the world often included more than a few of the iconic newspaper families. Thirty-five people on the 2012 list made their fortunes in the media, and at least a dozen of those in print media. (Four descendants of William Randolph Hearst were on the list. Dan Ziff, the son of

The peculiar economics of entry explain why for many years no new, major city newspapers emerged, with the exception of the *Washington Times* (published with millions of Unification Church dollars). And yet, success created weaknesses for behemoth city dailies. To get maximum penetration they have had to provide a little for everyone, but in so doing they often cut down on detailed local news coverage. By providing a little for everyone they produced customers but not supporters, readers who subscribed as long as there was no alternative. In many cases they were ripe for the plucking, if a real alternative came along.

Daily newspaper distribution was also inefficient. Large city newspapers, with their multiple specialized sections, developed the cafeteria line approach to journalism: pick what you want, don't pick the rest. But the comparison had a catch to it. Cafeteria customers do not get a tray with everything on it and then throw 90 percent of their food into the trash can. But most of the typical metropolitan newspaper (72 pages a day and 265 pages—three pounds—on Sunday) was thrown away without being read. Trees fell and newspaper trucks guzzled gasoline to get news across town during rush hours, and most of the effort was a waste as far as news gathering is concerned. A typical 50,000-circulation daily newspaper spent only about one-eighth of its budget on news-gathering and editing. About three times as much went for paper and printing.[11]

Advertising revenues allowed for payment of production and circulation costs with profits left over. When newspaper adver-

---

publishing magnate William Ziff, was the youngest person ever to make the list: he was twenty-one when he first made the list in 1994.) However, the same list in 1982, the first year Forbes compiled it, had nearly double the number of newspaper fortunes on it. These statistics make it easy to see that the virtual elimination of classified advertising from big-city dailies has, even without any other changes in the industry, permanently altered the economics of American newspapers.

11. The American Newspaper Publishers Association (ANPA) provides information about average newspaper size, and some cost data as well. The Audit Bureau of Circulation also produces semimonthly reports. *Editor and Publisher* produces annual reports on the industry.

tising fell, mainline newspapers quickly got in serious trouble. Advances in information technology in the 1980s and 1990s not only made direct mail more efficient, but created whole new industry segments. Websites such as craigslist, eBay, and Monster.com, for example, now dominate what was once a cash cow for newspapers: classified advertising. Classifieds accounted for as much as 70 percent of the revenue of some local newspapers, and for all newspapers it was the most profitable.

The result was a decline in just about every measure of newspaper health. The loss of revenue resulted in less money for news gathering. One obvious impact was the precipitous decline in the number of journalists working in most big-city newspaper dailies. The high-water mark for daily newspaper employment of journalists came in the mid-1980s, at around fifty-five thousand. Between 1987 and 2000, the number held steady, fluctuating only a percentage point or two from year to year. However, in 2001 the number started to fall—at first slowly, then precipitously. Between 2007 and 2008, the number of working journalists fell 15 percent.

Another indicator of newspaper health, circulation, confirms this decline. In 1950, America had about 1,800 daily newspapers. In 2000, the number had fallen to about 1,500. Circulation numbers also fell. Daily newspaper circulation in America peaked in the early 1984 at around 63 million. By 2004, daily newspaper circulation had fallen to 54.6 million. But by 2011, it had fallen another 10 million, to 44.4 million. Since the population of the United States grew by 75 million between 1984 and 2011, these declines are even more dramatic.

Since the 1990s personal computers, followed in the 2000s by smart phones and tablet devices, have allowed us to get news at all times in most places. This capability has obvious benefits. We no longer have to wait for the next day's paper or the evening newscast to find out about important events. But this new capability has also created enormous strains on the news gathering system and consumer expectations.

Over time, due to production and transport costs, newspapers will have to get more expensive, and the migration to digital will accelerate. Earlier, we mentioned that America now has more televisions than households, but it took us seventy years to reach this level of saturation. In 2010, more than 250 million smart phones were sold worldwide. In 2011, that number doubled. Tablets such as the iPad and Kindle are penetrating the market at an even faster rate. Apple released the first iPad in April 2010. By October 2012, more than 100 million devices had sold. Almost all major news organizations have iPad and smart phone apps, and more people are using smart phone and tablet devices for news content. According to the Audit Bureau of Circulation, "paid digital" circulation in September 2012 accounted for 15.3 percent of total U.S. newspaper circulation, up from 9.8 percent just a year earlier.

Christian Opportunities: Publishing

Charging head-on against behemoth newspapers is hard. Outflanking them or taking over niches they have had to abandon has become somewhat easier than it has been in the past. By the 1980s it was feasible for Christians of modest means to establish weekly or monthly newspapers that could cover major stories in ways that point out inaccuracies and biases of the big media outlets, and take into account the spiritual as well as the material. By the late 1990s, as many as one hundred Christian newspapers—most of them monthly tabloids—existed in major cities all across the country.

Such publications can emerge from small staffs with the aid of computers and page layout programs costing under $1,000. Blogs and websites are cheaper still. Writers such as Tim Challies and Ann Voskamp have developed worldwide audiences for their books through their widely read blogs. Though neither Challies nor Voskamp is a journalist, they are showing how writers with an entrepreneurial spirit can have an impact in a digital environment. (We'll have more to say about these possibilities in chapter 13.)

Christians whom God has blessed financially are now discovering the importance of financing conservative and Christian journalism. Billionaire Philip Anschutz is one such financier. His *Washington Examiner*, founded in 2005, is the flagship of a chain of papers operating either print or web editions in dozens of American cities. Though Anschutz is a Christian, and many of the writers and editors who work at his papers are Christians, they do not bill themselves as Christian papers. The *Washington Examiner*, with a free circulation of one hundred thousand (more on Thursdays and Sundays) has met with some success.

The *Daily Caller*, edited by conservative firebrand Tucker Carlson and bankrolled by evangelical Christian and billionaire investor Foster Friess, also affects the public conversation. It panders as well. Next to thoughtful political and cultural analysis sit photos of "Hot Girls in American Flag Bikinis." Christian journalists have better ways of gaining readers, as chapters 11 and 12 will show.

Journalism from a Christian perspective has rarely been done well, but that doesn't mean it can't be done. Individual businessmen, or small partnerships, could take such initiative in smaller cities. Although it sometimes is said that individual enterprises do not have much of a chance in the face of newspaper chains, the largest chain, Gannett, even with its publication of *USA Today*, still has only about 8 percent of nationwide circulation. That is a lot, but in 1935 William Randolph Hearst alone controlled 14 percent of daily circulation and 24 percent of Sunday circulation. Most chains are small, and owned by small businessmen. Some are very profitable. A Christian with money can do well by doing good.

Conclusions

Research into current trends in media economics and technology leads to optimism for Christians. Anyone who is feeling pessimistic about media opportunities should compare the current problems in journalism to those facing Christians in education. Powerful groups with anti-Christian worldviews dominate major media and major educational institutions. In both fields it is often difficult to develop financially sound alternatives. But the contest to reclaim education is much harder than the parallel battle in media, for the schooling contest is rigged. Those pressing for educational alternatives must produce an expensive product that can pull students away from what appears to be a free lunch: state-funded schools and colleges. Christians have seen that state largesse often can lead to isolation and practical disenfranchisement of theological minorities.

Providentially, the public television system is of only minor importance in this country, and we do not have a system of public newspapers as we have one of public schools. God has given Christians the opportunity to engage in fair competition. The number of media outlets indicates the vastness of opportunity: at least 4,000 television stations, over 15,000 radio stations, 1,400 daily newspapers, 6,200 weekly newspapers, at least 12,000 magazines, and newsletters and websites as many as the sand on the seashore.[12]

12. Magazines and radio provide other opportunities for Christian journalists. Americans are a nation of magazine readers. One study showed 143 million adults, 90 percent of the nation's adult population, reading magazines regularly. Each of those 143 million Americans read an average of almost eight magazine copies a month and spent about one hour on each copy. From 1950 to 1980 circulation of American Bureau of Circulation-audited magazines more than doubled, to over three hundred million, while the U.S. population in that same period grew by 55 percent.

Those numbers are growing in most categories. Daily newspapers are the only category to shrink in recent years. Technology has dramatically increased the number of radio and television stations. HD radio now allows radio stations to broadcast two or three or even more different programs on the same frequency. Between 2002 and 2009, more than three thousand HD stations went on the air.[13] Almost all of these new outlets are free of state control or policy dictation from a state religion. These opportunities, though, are just that: opportunities. Christians will not succeed on cable, on radio, in magazines, and newsletters by offering readers or viewers more of the same. Offering more of the same, slightly cleaned up, accomplishes little.

There is a great but hard-to-compute amount of unaudited circulation as well. In addition, the average copy of a magazine has at least four adult readers. Some good magazines, though, die young, often because of a failure to obtain advertising. A typical magazine receives half its revenue from circulation and half from advertising. A few magazines get all their revenue from advertising, but opinion magazines such as the *New Republic* or *National Review* depend primarily on loyal subscribers and some well-heeled financial angels. *WORLD*, which has become the nation's largest Christian news magazine, gets about 70 percent of its budget from subscribers, and about 25 percent from advertising.

With adequate financial backing, non-Christian opinion magazines such as *Harper's* have displayed enormous journalistic influence over the years. *Christianity Today, First Things* (a Catholic-leaning conservative publication founded by Richard John Neuhaus in 1990), and other magazines have had a positive influence, but we desperately need the Christian equivalent of *Harper's* or the *Public Interest*.

The situation is somewhat better in radio. The largest Christian broadcaster in the nation, Salem Communications, is a publicly traded company with a robust news staff and hourly news and information programming. It owns more than one hundred stations. Fox News has a radio product used by many Christian radio stations. However, nothing in Christian radio yet resembles the robust news programming of the government-supported and liberal-leaning National Public Radio. *WORLD* has dipped its toe into radio programming with a daily news program. These syndicated programs now allow Christian stations to have sizable news and information segments. This parallels developments in some non-Christian stations; news, information, and talk shows are the biggest audience getters in New York, Los Angeles, and Chicago. We'll have more on opportunities for a Christian media revival in chapter 13.

13. Statistics available from the National Association of Broadcasters, the Magazine Publishers Association, the American Newspaper Publishers Association, and *Editor and Publisher*.

At times during the 1980s, a defeatist moan has come out of some parts of Christendom: "An elitist group of secular humanists has seized monopolistic control of the networks and major newspapers. They are brainwashing the majority of decent Americans. We can't fight them." Over three thousand years ago, after Moses had sent twelve men to explore the land of Canaan, the majority came back with a similar whine: "We are not able to go up against the people, for they are stronger than we are. . . . All the people that we saw [there] are of great height. . . . We seemed to ourselves like grasshoppers" (Num. 13:31–33).

Because of that lack of trust, the Israelites spent forty years wandering in the wilderness. If Christians today spend time complaining instead of doing, Americans may spend more decades wandering in a media wasteland. Media pessimism is not only wrong in principle and tragic in practice, but unnecessary, for three reasons. First, the deck is not necessarily stacked against Christians in media, as it is in education. Second, technological change is opening up new possibilities for wider competition. Third, and most important, God is in control. With his blessing, mountains move.[14]

Providentially, Americans have an unusual media system. In other countries, governments often own the television and radio stations. Even when they do not own the printing presses, governments frequently offer newspapers and magazines considerable economic support. The American tradition is different.

14. Many media companies are huge. NBC is now part of General Electric. Capital Cities Communications, which owns ABC, and CBS are both about $5 billion companies. The largest newspaper in the country, the *Wall Street Journal*, has a circulation of more than two million and is now owned by News Corporation, which had 2012 revenue of more than $33 billion. Next comes *USA Today*, owned by Gannett, which had annual revenue of more than $5 billion in 2012. Rounding out the top five are the *New York Times* ($3.3 billion in 2010), the *Los Angeles Times* (owned by Tribune, which posted 2010 revenue of $3.2 billion), and the *San Jose Mercury News* (owned by the privately owned Media News Group, which does not disclose revenues.) But faithfulness to God and diligent use of his gifts tends to bring Christians eventual success. Mountains can be thrown into seas.

Newspapers and magazines operate almost entirely without governmental support. Except for the Public Broadcasting System, American television and radio stations also operate without government funds. Limited Federal Communication Commission regulation is becoming less significant year by year.[15]

As cable television takes charge, as diversity and decentralization among local television stations develop, as opportunities to chip away at behemoth newspapers emerge, as low-cost newsletters grow in importance, the question will be whether Christians can produce programs and publications that Americans choose to watch and read. Those who shrink from the task of doing something special, convinced that there are indestructible giants in the land, are not glorifying God. We need the Joshuas and Calebs. We need journalists trained to see that there are ways to gain and keep an audience.

15. Christians should not press government to get involved for short-term gains, even if those could be procured. A system of private ownership and control of television and radio can be exasperating at times, but such a system is based on biblical principles. Furthermore, a private enterprise system always escapes from stagnation, as new challenges arise. Such challenges must receive a response, or economic decline is certain. In countries with state-controlled media, though, stagnation dominates, unless a coup comes along.

The Devil in the Electrons

10

Chapter 9 touched on what the technology revolution now allows Christians to do, and chapters 11 and 12 discuss some strategies—but it's also important to examine the problems that new technology creates. Maybe the place to begin is with the theologian who was also a journalist, Martin Luther,[1] who supposedly said the Devil once threw an inkwell at him. The story mutated in the seventeenth century. By 1650, the story had Luther throwing his inkwell at the Devil.

Historians now believe Luther's enemies concocted the original story as evidence he was a psychopath. The newer version, which Luther's disciples called the true or corrected version of the story, is the one that has persisted. Luther's defenders used the story to build a legend around the Great Reformer as a man who fought the Devil with pen and ink and once stated, "Satan hates the use of pens."

Over the centuries, the idea of a "devil in the inkwell" became a helpful metaphor to describe the sometimes tortured relationship between writers—all artists, all creators—and their art, the things they make. Viewed through a Christian lens, this relationship, and the reason for its tortured nature, comes into sharp focus. We might describe it this way: God is a creator. We are created in his image, so we too are creators and we humans

1. Marvin Olasky, *Central Ideas in the Development of American Journalism: A Narrative History* (Hillsdale, NJ: Lawrence Erlbaum Associates, 1991), chap. 1.

find our highest purpose when we create. However, we are fallen
beings in a fallen world, so our best efforts inevitably fall short
of our highest aspirations.

The metaphor of the "devil in the inkwell" describes how our
fallen nature limits our ability to create. God creates *ex nihilo*,
"from nothing." But we humans are limited by our tools and
our media. How do we make someone see a sunset when all we
have are words? How do we describe our deepest fears with pictures alone? Sometimes bias—anti-Christian and other kinds of
bias—is driven by the form, by the medium, itself. Each medium
has its own capabilities and limitations. Media theorist Neil
Postman famously said that smoke signals can tell you where
I am, but not what I believe. The primitive medium of smoke
signals has a built-in bias against the use of words and ideas.
Obviously, journalism would be poorly served by smoke signals,
regardless of the worldview of the journalist.[2]

The question we will explore in this chapter is whether other
media are also poor servants of journalism, and Christian journalism in particular. And since electronic media are dominant in our
age, we are all—like it or not—shaped by them. The capabilities and
limitations of electronic media shape all other media and define our
media diet. We must understand their capabilities and limitations in
order to be discerning practitioners and consumers of journalism.

A Short History of Mankind and Our Media

Theorists in the emerging field of "media ecology" say we
have seen only a few true revolutions in media in human history. We might call the first revolution the gift of language itself.
Genesis 2 tells us that God gave Adam two vocations: to work the
land (requiring physical engagement with creation) and to name

2. Neil Postman, *Amusing Ourselves to Death: Public Discourse in the Age of Show Business*
(New York: Penguin Books, 1985), 7.

the animals (requiring intellectual engagement with creation). Both jobs required man to understand deeply the nature of God's creation, and to "take dominion" over creation as a necessary part of our own acts of creation—the first of which was this very naming of the animals.

The next great revolution was the shift from an oral tradition to the written word, beginning about five thousand years ago. This shift allowed us humans to refine and preserve our thinking. These new abilities created the possibility for new human endeavors: specifically, those endeavors where the refinement and preservation of ideas are central. Over the next two thousand years we saw the beginnings of law and philosophy develop. In the Judeo-Christian tradition, this was the time of the great lawgiver Moses. Almost concurrently, Hammurabi's Code developed. Then arose the great ancient philosophers of Greece and China. In the arts, the written word allowed the flourishing of the ancient dramas, which still engaged the oral tradition of verse, but which now could contain much more sophisticated philosophical, theological, and psychological content.

The written word also allowed more sophisticated organizations of people as well. As tribes and cultures developed a written language, they often developed cities as well. Likewise, economies evolved from those dependent on agricultural subsistence to those involving more trade and commerce. Again, a written language made all these developments possible.

The next great revolution came with the invention of the printing press about 560 years ago. That shift allowed us to widely distribute what we have thought and learned. This technological breakthrough had dramatic, disruptive effects on law, religion, the arts—virtually all aspects of human civilization. It is hard to imagine, for example, the Reformation unfolding in the way it did without a strong assist from the technology of the printing press. As historian Paul Johnson noted, "The smell of printer's ink was the incense of the Reformation."[3]

We now live in the midst of the third great shift. We stand at the beginning of the electronic age. And like past technological revolutions, the electronic age has brought on massive disruption and change—and much faster change than in the past.

The Rise of Electronic Media

While electronic media came of age in the twentieth and twenty-first centuries, media theorist Marshall McLuhan suggests the electronic age began with the invention of the telegraph in the 1830s. For the first time, messages could travel great distances at speeds approaching the instantaneous. This innovation was not merely the incremental improvement of an older technology. This new technology, and its successors, played a part in just about every major event that followed its invention, from the opening of the West to the Civil War, from the rise of the late-nineteenth-century monopoly trusts to the populist politics that ultimately broke up the trusts.

The first commercial application of the telegraph came on May 24, 1844. It came on a telegraph line that ran from Baltimore to Washington, made possible by a $10,000 appropriation from Congress. Appropriately and—with the passage of time—ironically, the first message tapped out in Morse code on that new telegraph line was a verse from Numbers: "What hath God wrought?"

The eccentric genius Nicola Tesla made key discoveries related to the invention of the radio in the 1890s, but we remember Guglielmo Marconi as the inventor of radio. He conducted several high-profile demonstrations of radio's capabilities, including the transmission of transatlantic airwaves, but the

---

3. Paul Johnson, *A History of Christianity* (New York: Atheneum Macmillan, 1976), 27.

man who deserves the credit for the first real broadcast of entertainment and music to a general audience was engineer and inventor Reginald Fessenden. On Christmas Eve 1906, Fessenden transmitted a short program from Brant Rock, Massachusetts, that included a Handel recording followed by Fessenden's own violin rendition of "O Holy Night." He finished the broadcast with "Glory to God in the highest and on earth peace to men of good will" (see Luke 2:14). He asked listeners to write to him with their locations and their assessments of sound quality. A few military and maritime receivers existed, and he heard from listeners as far as several hundred miles away.

The proliferation of electronic media into the twentieth century was in many ways the great enabler in the spread of knowledge, information, democracy, and prosperity. Democracy was rare when the century opened. By 1950, only 22 of 80 sovereign nations (28 percent) were democratic, according to Freedom House, but fifty years later it counted 120 democracies out of 200 countries.[4] Electronic media facilitated this unprecedented change. One defining moment: Franklin Delano Roosevelt, just a week after his inauguration in March 1933, began the first of his radio "fireside chats." Roosevelt's ability to enter millions of living rooms did much to sell his "New Deal" to the American people and, later, to steel the resolve of Americans facing a global war.

Fifty years later, on June 12, 1987, former actor Ronald Reagan stood at Brandenburg Gate on a set carefully choreographed for television and said, "Mr. Gorbachev, tear down this wall." It was not long before the wall did come down, and journalism played a major role in that semi-miraculous development. Following two months of peaceful protests in 1989, and faced with larger and larger East German crowds massing at the wall,

4. www.hoover.org/publications/hoover-digest/article/7310.

Communist authorities decided to relax travel restrictions. On November 9, 1989, a local party official who had not participated in the decision-making process announced the vague and incomplete plan for the changes at a press conference.

At that point NBC's Tom Brokaw asked when the changes would go into effect. The party official, confused and uncertain, said, "As far as I know, immediately. Without delay." This news, broadcast immediately and around the world, brought out thousands of people from East and West Germany. In a festival atmosphere often accompanied by hymn singing, they started tearing down the wall. In 1970, the soul and funk musician Gil Scott-Heron popularized a protest song predicting "The Revolution Will Not Be Televised." In fact, it was.

Fast-forward another generation to the outbreak of the Arab Spring in 2010. It began in Tunisia with what came to be called the "Twitter Revolution" because of its dependence on mobile devices and social media as an energizing force. Sadly, in Egypt and elsewhere spring turned to Arab Winter as an Islamist machine pushed aside the initial demonstrators.

Mass electronic media have been a powerful force for good or evil in other arenas. In 1984, television crews returned from Ethiopia with footage that united the world in an unprecedented response to famine there. More recently, in the aftermath of natural disasters such as the Indonesian tsunami of 2004, Hurricane Katrina in 2005, and the Haiti earthquake of 2010, television and social media facilitated an outpouring of emergency relief totaling tens of billions of dollars. Of course, we should also note that the massive outpouring of money that the electronic media motivated was often wasted by organizations unprepared to deal with either the disaster or the cash.

The Ubiquity of Electronic Media

New electronic media came at us quickly in the century after the invention of the telegraph, though it didn't seem that way at first.

204

The telegraph stood alone as an electronic medium, and was by no means universally used, for more than thirty years. Then came the invention of the telephone in the 1870s. Then radio, which began as a "wireless telegraph," in the 1890s. Television made its debut in the 1920s. The Great Depression and then World War II delayed its commercial viability, but TV made up for lost time and experienced explosive growth from the late 1940s through the 1960s.

As these new technologies grew, so did our use and—ultimately—our dependence on them. According to a study by the Media Research Center, the average young person will spend fifty-four thousand hours with some form of electronic media by his eighteenth birthday. This is a remarkable statistic because it amounts to nearly sixty hours a week.

If that statistic at first seems implausible, consider just one medium: television. The average number of televisions per American household in 2005 was 2.6, up from 1.7 in 1980. According to the U.S. Census Bureau, the average number of people per American household in 2010 was 2.59, down from 2.62 in 2000. That means that these lines crossed and the American household now has, on average, more televisions than people. And in most households, at least one of these TVs is on most of the day. A 2008–9 survey by Nielson said American households had the television on an average of eight hours and twenty-one minutes of TV per day, and the average individual watches four hours and forty-nine minutes.[5]

This doesn't mean that the average individual was ardently watching television all that time. Sometimes it's background noise. But these numbers do not include televisions we watch in waiting rooms, restaurants, and even the bathrooms of restaurants. These numbers don't count radio, the Internet, and other forms of media to which we are connected in some form, either actively or passively, during virtually every waking hour.

5. www.worldtvpc.com/blog/tv-viewing-figures-reach-all-time-high/.

The Net Effect of Electronic Media

With electronic media now so dominant in our lives, it's worth attempting to answer the question we posed above: Is the complete immersion in electronic media a good thing or a bad thing? As Christians we ask the question more specifically: Is it helping us to develop a more Christian view of the world, or a more secular, materialistic view of the world?

Ecclesiastes 1:9 instructs us there is "nothing new under the sun," so it is important not to overstate the impact of new technology, or to understate the fundamental immutability of human nature. Christian theology teaches us that no matter how sophisticated we become or think we are, we remain sinners in need of a Savior. Nonetheless, each age has its own challenges and opportunities, and given the infiltration of electronic media into all areas of our lives, it strains credulity to say its impact on us is not at least as great we have seen in some of the revolutionary media shifts of the past. So let's look at four characteristics of all media as a way of understanding the impact new media are having on us. We describe these characteristics this way:

- All media have capabilities and limitations.
- All media have positive and negative effects and, therefore, a "net effect."
- New media tend to manifest their positive effects first and their negative effects later, which helps explain why we adopt new technologies.
- All media affect the way we think and experience the world and therefore have the ability to bear both true and false witness.

Let's take these ideas one at a time, beginning with the idea that all media have capabilities and limitations. At the beginning of the chapter, we touched on this idea when we said that each new technology allowed us to communicate in new ways. For example, the printing press of the sixteenth century led to the novel of the eighteenth century. Novels—extended prose fiction narratives—are perhaps the twenty-first century's most common literary form, but the form simply did not exist for most of human existence. The printing press made it possible.

Neil Postman reminds us that while new communication technologies allow new forms and ultimately new cultures, they also tend to destroy old forms and old cultures, and even old conceptions of truth. In Postman's words: "The bias of a medium sits heavy, felt but unseen, over a culture."[6] The printed word tended to destroy the oral tradition, for example. Postman argued that every medium has

> the power to fly far beyond [its] context into new and unexpected ones. Because of the way it directs us to organize our minds and integrate our experience of the world, it imposes itself on our consciousness and social institutions in myriad forms. It sometimes has the power to become implicated in our concepts of piety, or goodness, or beauty. And it is always implicated in the ways we define and regulate our ideas of truth.[7]

Second, all media have both positive and negative effects, which is why Postman says we should evaluate media by their net effect on a culture. For example, in the 1950s and 1960s, television brought the same information and entertainment into the homes of both rich and poor.

But they have also brought negative consequences. Television can also isolate us. Some wise individual once said, "Television

6. Postman, *Amusing Ourselves to Death*, 18.
7. Ibid.

allows thousands of people to laugh at the same joke and still remain alone."[8]

Another example: cell phones may make us feel more secure on dark streets at night, but the feeling of security may mask a reality of greater danger. According to a 2007 survey conducted by the Automobile Association of America, 43 percent of teenagers text while driving. Drivers distracted by their cell phones account for 2,700 fatalities and more than 300,000 crashes a year. As of 2012, at least nine states have decided that the net effect of this new technology tilts too far into the negative category and have banned or restricted cell phone use in automobiles.[9] Between 2007 and 2010, the number of so-called "smart phones" in the U.S. grew from near zero to forty million. Child safety experts say that after decades of decline in the number of child accidents, the number of accidents to children under the age of five rose 12 percent during that same period. Some experts say the rise is a result of parents distracted by their smart phones: "texting while parenting."[10]

A third characteristic of new media—or all new technology that gets adopted by a culture—is that the positive consequences tend to manifest themselves first, and the negative consequences tend to show up later. We might call this the "Happy Hour Effect." If you walk by a bar at 5:00 P.M., you won't see a sign on the door that says, "Come in and we will take your money and make you stupid. If you stay long enough, you might make really bad decisions that negatively change the course of your life." No, the sign on the door says, "Happy Hour."

Consider, for example, the Indiana woman who came home one evening to discover that a thief had stolen thousands of dollars'

8. This aphorism is commonly attributed both to T. S. Eliot and to Bertrand Russell.

9. www.att.com/Common/about_us/txting_driving/att_teen_survey_executive.pdf.

10. Ben Worthen, "The Perils of Texting While Parenting," *Wall Street Journal*, Sept. 29, 2012, C1.

worth of electronics and other goods. The enterprising woman put technology to use and posted a security camera video on her Facebook profile. Because of the video, police identified the burglar and arrested him. If this is all you know about that story, you might think Facebook served the woman and the police well. However, there's more to the story. It turns out the burglar was a "Facebook friend" of the victim. He learned the woman would be out for the evening because of updates to her Facebook status. He chose the time of his robbery based on that information.[11]

What all of this means is that we tend to adopt new technologies before we have all the data we need to evaluate their net effect. We become addicted to the benefits of new technology and that either clouds our judgment about liabilities, or—even if we begin to see plainly the liabilities—we can do little about them.

A fourth major characteristic of new media is that they change the way we think and behave. Marshall McLuhan explained this phenomenon with a metaphor many now call "McLuhan's Light Bulb." Imagine you walk from the bright sunlight into a room without light. The door slams shut behind you before your eyes can adjust to the dark and you can see what's in the room. In short, you are alone in a room that is pitch-black. What would you think and how would you behave? You would likely, at a minimum, be cautious. You would proceed slowly. You might be afraid or annoyed. Now, imagine that someone flips on the light and you discover yourself in a safe place filled with your best friends (who had till the light came on been inordinately quiet!). What do you think and how do you behave now? You likely feel relief, even joy. You throw caution to the wind because you are among friends. You relax. Life is good.

McLuhan observes that the content of the room didn't change, but the medium by which you experienced that room—

11. www.kxan.com/dpp/news/national/northeast/woman-burglar-was-my -facebook-friend.

darkness versus light—changed and radically altered your thinking and your behavior. He argues, therefore, that the content of
a message often carries less information to the receiver than the
medium used for the message.[12] This idea is a powerful insight into
the differences between, for example, television and print journalism. A cover story in WORLD, for example, often runs over two thousand words. A 2012 story on a soldier who lost his legs to a mine in
Afghanistan was more than four thousand words. The lead story on
a typical network television newscast is often less than five minutes.
A transcription of that story would likely be less than five hundred
words. The television story will—or will attempt to—tell more of the
story with pictures than words, and skilled practitioners can do that
extraordinarily well. But setting aside for a moment the judgment
of which story is better or does more justice to the truth, we can
easily see that the stories are materially, demonstrably different.
And that difference impacts the consumers' understanding of the
events covered. Postman says this difference in how we understand
the world affects politics, culture, even religion:

> It is implausible to imagine that anyone like our 27th president,
> the multi-chinned, 300-pound William Howard Taft, could
> be . . . a presidential candidate in today's world. The shape of a
> man's body is largely irrelevant to the shape of his ideas when
> he is addressing a public in writing or on the radio. . . . But it
> is quite relevant on television. The grossness of a 300-pound
> image, even a talking one, would easily overwhelm any logical
> or spiritual subtleties conveyed by speech.[13]

By understanding these characteristics of media—and
applying that understanding to electronic media in particular—
we begin to understand that all media have such a built-in bias.

12. Marshall McLuhan, *Understanding Media: The Extensions of Man* (New York:
McGraw-Hill, 1964), 8.
13. Postman, *Amusing Ourselves to Death*, 7.

That bias is an inherent quality of the medium, and is completely independent of the content—Christian or anti-Christian—that is poured into it. That's why Postman said that media are neither culturally nor morally neutral. They shape our conceptions of truth.

All of which brings us to this question: Do electronic media, by their very nature, have an anti-Christian bias? Let's partially answer that question by looking more closely at the impact electronic media has had on journalism.

Electronic Media's Impact on Journalism

Earlier in this chapter, we noted Marshall McLuhan's assertion that the age of electronic media began in the 1830s with the invention of the telegraph. If so, that age gained new power in the 1980s. The decade began with the inauguration of the first cable news network, CNN. In the middle of the decade, cable television proliferated. Toward the end, the Internet began to make inroads into commercial and consumer markets.

Also at the end of that decade *Seinfeld*—many people call it the first postmodern television program—began. *Seinfeld* gained a top Nielsen spot as a "show about nothing"—except, as television critic Ken Tucker said, the characters are "rooted in jealousy, rage, insecurity, despair, hopelessness, and a touching lack of faith."[14] The 1980s saw the ascendance of postmodernism, a nebulous philosophy hard to define, but one based in either denial of objective truth or radical skepticism toward it.

In the next few chapters we will examine how these sudden changes have disrupted the economic model of journalism and have created opportunities for a revival of Christian journalism. However, if Christians are to seize these opportunities, we need

14. Ken Tucker, "The Fantastic 4," in *Entertainment Weekly: Special Seinfeld Issue*, May 4, 1998, 13.

to be "wise as serpents" so that what we create does not become as trivial, banal, and therefore ultimately as anti-Christian as what we hope to replace.

So what specific characteristics of electronic media in the twenty-first century create both dangers and opportunities for Christian journalism?

Diversity of Outlets and Sources

In chapter 4 we said that in an era of greater diversity of media outlets, more media outlets were openly biased. We called it "undisguised subjectivity," and it has become increasingly common. The good news is that in this environment Christian voices can find a media megaphone: on talk radio, on the Internet, even on cable news.

The bad news is that in such an environment, the increasing difficulty of being heard above the media roar has created a "race to the bottom": increasingly sensational, tabloid-style news that leaves little time for fact-checking or context, especially spiritual context. Tabloid journalism takes the practice of "spiking the spiritual" to a new level. Pulitzer Prize winner Alex Jones wrote, "When watchdog news and accountability news are deemed too boring and news choices are made on the basis of attracting an audience instead of their importance as news, then the tabloid news standard is . . . applied. Effectively, the nation's . . . news organizations are being transformed into tabloid news organizations, and it is happening at a blisteringly rapid pace."[15]

The Need for Speed

Another positive impact of the rise in electronic media has been breaking down barriers between those who have informa-

15. Alex Jones, *Losing The News: The Future of the News That Feeds Democracy* (New York: Oxford University Press, 2009), 51.

tion and those who do not. The speed with which information can travel now makes it possible for billions of people, all around the world, to have access to much of the same information at more or less the same time.

But this capacity for the speedy delivery of news creates a culture in which the new is automatically valued over the old. The poet and social critic Allen Tate called this phenomenon "the new provincialism." The Internet might allow us to know, for example, what a celebrity had for breakfast this morning half-a-world away. But Tate argued that this information had no value or meaning. He argued that technology had broken down geographical barriers, but had erected barriers between us and our history. The "new provincialism" was a provincialism not of place, but of time. Technology has trapped us in the ever-present now, with a never-sated appetite for the new.[16] Statistician and *New York Times* blogger Nate Silver, commenting on the instantaneous, continuously updating, 140-character updates we can now get from Twitter, said, "Twitter is mostly great, but encourages people's worst habits to overrate the marginal utility of new information."[17]

Former ABC News anchorman Ted Koppel summed up the problem of speed in the news business this way: "Putting someone on the air while an event is unfolding is clearly a technological tour de force, but it's an impediment, not an aid, to good journalism."[18]

Christian journalists have no choice but to operate in an environment that rewards speed, but we must not be seduced by these rewards. We should use our Christian worldview to provide a context and a perspective that others cannot provide.

16. Allen Tate, "The New Provincialism," included in *Essays of Four Decades* (Wilmington, DE: Intercollegiate Studies Institute, 1999).

17. Nate Silver's Twitter Feed, https://twitter.com/fivethirtyeight, October 22, 2012.

18. Cited in Jones, *Losing The News*, 149.

That, not some new tidbit of irrelevant information, becomes the competitive advantage of the Christian journalist.

The Importance of Entertainment/The Rise of Infotainment

As the number, diversity, and speed of news sources have proliferated at a geometric rate, new problems have emerged for media outlets. The first is what some are now calling "discoverability." How do you get your website, or your podcast, or your blog discovered? Second, once people discover you, how do you keep them coming back? That quality is sometimes called "stickiness."

Most electronic media outlets—and, in order to compete, many print outlets as well—have solved the challenges of "discoverability" and "stickiness" by resorting to entertainment methods.

We can easily see the downside of resorting to entertainment methods if we think about the word "amuse." The word "muse" means "to think." By adding the prefix *a-*, we modify the meaning of the word: "to *not* think." If something is merely amusing, it is encouraging us to not think. The problem for humans in general and Christians in particular with this condition of "not thinking" should be obvious. The ability to think in complex, rational, and abstract ways is a condition of our humanness. For the Christian, the Bible raises the bar when it tells us to "love the Lord [our] God with . . . all [our] mind" (Matt. 23:27; Mark 12:30; Luke 10:27) and to be "transformed by the renewal of [our] mind" (Rom. 12:2). In short, it is impossible to be a fully mature Christian without a robust life of the mind. It logically follows, then, that any activity that inhibits the life of the mind is diminishing our ability to be either fully Christian and even fully human.

This argument in favor of thinking and against mere entertainment is why, Postman speculates, God gave us a book, the

Bible, as a primary source of his revelation to us. It requires us to think. "Television . . . requires minimal skills to comprehend . . . and is largely aimed at emotional gratification."[19] A book, on the other hand, requires active engagement of the mind and the imagination. "The God of the Jews," Postman wrote, "was to exist in the Word and through the Word, an unprecedented conception requiring the highest order of abstract thinking."[20]

The challenge for the Christian journalist, then, is to be interesting and lively (reflecting life) without being merely amusing.

Changing the Way We Think

By the late twentieth century, biologists and neurologists started to ask if electronic media might even be changing the way we think. By the early twenty-first century, some of those same scientists began to say the answer to that question is yes. Leonard Sax, for example, studied boys aged seven to fourteen and how their brains operate. He found that studying or working a difficult math problem not only increased a boy's intellectual capacity but also increased activity in parts of the brain associated with pleasure. This phenomenon explains the sense of satisfaction we all get when we successfully complete a difficult task.

However, Sax also discovered that playing video games also caused increased activity in the brain's "pleasure centers" while simultaneously shutting off blood flow to the "executive center" of the brain where judgment and rational thought takes place. The net effect is that the boys achieved the same feeling of satisfaction from playing a video game as from completing a difficult task. In effect, these games offered boys the sense that they had accomplished something without actually having done so.[21]

19. Postman, *Amusing Ourselves to Death*, 86.
20. Ibid., 9.
21. Leonard Sax, *Boys Adrift: The Five Factors Driving the Growing Epidemic of Unmotivated Boys and Underachieving Men* (New York: Basic Book, 2007), 91.

Having a Christian worldview means thinking Christianly. It is impossible to think Christianly if we have lost the ability to think. Therefore, any medium that erodes our ability to think, by discouraging active intellectual participation in favor of passive spectating, is by nature anti-Christian.

Conclusion: God's Preferred Medium

An old Hollywood saying goes like this: It all begins with a script. Given the complexity of moviemaking, it is certainly possible to make a bad movie from a good script. But it is almost impossible to make a good movie from a bad script. Words matter. In fact, words seem to have a pre-eminent role, even in moviemaking.

God does have a preferred medium: the Word. In his sovereignty he gave us a written word. He tells us that through the "foolishness of preaching" (1 Cor. 1:21 KJV), the spoken word, he confounds the wisdom of the world. He has such a high view of the word, that through the apostle John he even called his Son the Word: "In the beginning was the Word, and the Word was with God, and the Word was God" (John 1:1).

Now, just because God has a preferred medium, that does not mean God prohibits all other forms. Christian liberty allows, and Christian charity sometimes even demands, that we use the tools of technology to share God's truth with a world whose ability to engage the Word has atrophied.

So it is presumptuous and unsupportable by Scripture to say that God speaks to us only through the written and spoken word, and he prohibits the use of all other media by Christians. But the case for the written and the spoken word being the richest and most nuanced medium for communication is strong. God, in his sovereignty and grace toward us, gave us a book—not a painting, movie, photo, or any other medium. That doesn't mean other media are forbidden, but it should cause us to ask the question why words?

We think the answer to that question is, first, that words both allow and require the active engagement of the mind. Second, the written word likewise requires active engagement with the world. When God told Adam to name the animals in Genesis 2, Adam had to look deeply into the nature of the animals to give each a proper name, a name that fit. In a sense, Adam was the first journalist: he looked out into the world and reported what he saw.

If Christian journalists remain committed to that commandment, to "name the animals" properly, we will take a great step forward toward the revitalization of Christian journalism. But it will take more than just that one step, no matter how great and necessary. Those additional steps are what the next chapters are about.

II Coverage of Sensation and Disaster: The Gaining and Keeping of Audiences

C riticism of journalistic "sensationalism" has been common in the United States throughout the twentieth century. Much of that criticism is merited. The pressures and proliferation of electronic media we discussed in the last chapter have created enormous temptations to race to the bottom and resort to any means possible to get noticed in a crowded media landscape. But this pressure is not new. Theodore Roosevelt in 1909 complained that "sensational" journalism "does as much to vulgarize and degrade the popular taste, to weaken the popular character, and to dull the edge of the popular conscience, as any influence under which the country can suffer." In attacking sensationalism he could point to top circulation newspapers such as the *New York American*. One of its typical issues featured on page 1 a large picture of men attacking women in Alaska. Page 2 was mainly devoted to an illustrated discussion of the question, "Is Woman Human or Animal?" Page 3 discussed a "Woman with a Past," page 4 a torture chamber, and page 5 "The Black Spectre That Frightens Fashionable Brides at the Altar."[1]

1. *Outlook*, March 6, 1909, 510. See also *Nation*, September 26, 1901, 238–39; *Collier's*, March 4, 1911, 18; *Nation*, June 8, 1927, 633–34; *Saturday Review of Literature*, November

Many critics of sensationalism have castigated the desire of editors to appeal to a wide audience, as if popularity necessarily meant lower quality. Newspapers should be solemn, they said. Roosevelt, though, wisely blamed not the mode of presentation itself, but the editors behind the style: "These men sneer at the very idea of paying heed to the dictates of a sound morality." And so the battle is joined: Is sensationalism inevitably a sneer at sound morality? Do the supermarket tabloids represent the only possible kind of sensationalism? Or might there be a Christian variety?[2]

To answer such questions, we have to get our definitions straight. The *Oxford English Dictionary* defines "sensation" as "a condition of excited feeling produced in a community by some occurrence; a strong impression produced in an audience or body of spectators." Sensationalism, then, is the attempt in works of literature or art to produce such responses. One example given of usage, from 1863, is a comment on "the cheap publications which supply sensation for the millions in penny and halfpenny numbers." Sensational stories tend to emphasize death and destruction.

If sensationalism, properly defined, is an attempt to produce excited feelings and strong impressions, often through tales of

---

30, 1935, 18; *Discover*, September 1983; reprinted in Ray Hiebert and Carol Reuss, eds., *Impact of Mass Media: Current Issues* (New York: Longman, 1985), 181–82.

2. The gross kind of sensationalism Roosevelt despised was, during his lifetime, largely a Northern, big-city phenomenon. Turn-of-the-century Southern newspaper editors also tended to criticize the way some of their Northern brethren were "raking the sewers of society high and low for material to fill their columns." One editor argued that New York newspapers were showing evil not to oppose it but to attract more to it: "The great Newspapers vie in an effort to present, in the most lurid style, every disgusting detail of evil-doing [and] to parade, with monster, glittering illustrations and with vivid narration every abnormal phase of life." A Houston editor hoped that the twentieth century would be saved from journalism that "is conscienceless, sensational, and disreputable, and to which nothing is sacred." (See papers by O. E. Dornblaser, in *Proceedings of the Texas Press Association*, 1893, 30; T. H. Napier, in *TPA Proceedings*, 1898, 35; W. A. Johnson, in ibid., 25; E. W. Harris, in TPA Proceedings, 1899, 19–20; and M. E. Foster, in *TPA Proceedings*, 1901, 52. Available at Barker Texas History Center, University of Texas at Austin.)

trouble and disaster, then the inspired authors of the Bible were some of the prime early users of sensationalism. Moses quoted the first news report, Lamech's announcement in Genesis 4:23 that he "killed a man for wounding me." Later in Genesis come the original tales of sodomy, leading to the destruction of Sodom and Gomorrah, followed immediately by the incest of Lot and his daughters (Gen. 19).

Many more sensational events fill the pages of Genesis and the four following books of Moses. That part of the Bible culminates in the blessings for obedience and curses for disobedience found in Deuteronomy 28. The culmination of the curses is especially vivid, with Israelites told that unfaithfulness will lead to terrible war and starvation in which "you will eat the fruit of the womb, the flesh of your sons and daughters, whom the LORD your God has given you. . . . The most tender and refined woman among you, who would not venture to touch the sole of her foot on the ground because she is delicate and tender, will begrudge to the husband she embraces, to her son and to her daughter, her afterbirth that comes out from between her feet and her children whom she bears, because lacking everything else she will eat them secretly" (Deut. 28:53, 56–57).

The slide downhill was speedy during the period described in the book of Judges. When God wanted to show the effect of the Israelites ignoring him—"there was no king in Israel" (Judg. 17:6)—his inspired author wrote of a man murdering his seventy brothers and half-brothers, and of a woman being gang-raped and killed, with her husband cutting her into twelve pieces and then sending the body parts throughout Israel (Judg. 9:5; 19:25–30).

Specific detail in Judges included Jael's assassination of Sisera described in five graphic ways (Judg. 4:21–22; 5:26). Similarly, when Ehud plunged his sword into the belly of the king of Moab, pungent description follows: "And the hilt also went in after the blade, and the fat closed over the blade, for he did not pull the sword out of his belly; and the dung came out" (Judg. 3:22).

By the time of Ahab and his son Joram, some of the curses for disobedience already were being realized. One woman told the king of her neighborly arrangement: "This woman said to me, 'Give your son, that we may eat him today, and we will eat my son tomorrow.' So we boiled my son and ate him. And on the next day I said to her, 'Give your son, that we may eat him.' But she has hidden her son" (2 Kings 6:28–29). Ezekiel promoted similar disgust at what God's covenant people had become when he wrote of how Judah "lusted after her lovers, whose genitals were like those of donkeys and whose emission was like that of horses. So you longed for the lewdness of your youth, when in Egypt your bosom was caressed and your young breasts fondled" (Ezek. 23:20–21 NIV).

Such characterization would not make it into many of today's newspapers, but Jeremiah explained God's methods simply: "Thus says the LORD of hosts, the God of Israel, says: Behold, I am bringing such disaster on this place that the ears of everyone who hears of it will tingle" (Jer. 19:3). How can ears tingle if descriptions are mellow?

Directness carried over to the New Testament as well. The book of Revelation was war reporting at its most vivid. In the New Testament as in the Old, sensationalism showed the difference between God's holiness and man's depravity.[3]

---

3. These words from Ephesians 5:11-13 are key with regard to the question of how far to go in coverage of evil. "Take no part in the unfruitful works of darkness, but instead expose them," Paul wrote. "For it is shameful even to speak of the things that they do in secret. But when anything is exposed by the light, it becomes visible." To some, the expression "shameful even to speak" has meant, "do not write about or talk about evil." That exegesis is hard to justify, though, in the context of the preceding and succeeding verses, and also in the light of Paul's own practice in other epistles (Rom. 1:24–32; 1 Cor. 6:9–10; Gal. 5:19–21; 1 Tim. 1:9–10). John Eadie, *Commentary on the Epistle to the Ephesians* (Edinburg: T. & T. Clark, 1883; repr. Grand Rapids: Zondervan, 1955), 383,

Christians who wanted to produce their newspapers in the image of Scripture regularly practiced sensationalism also. For instance, the *Connecticut Courant* in 1765 sounded very much like Jeremiah in showing the consequences of sin in a land of "indolence and oppression" where the Bible is not read and "no provision is made but from hand to mouth." A famine developed, and "in many places children expired in the arms of their mothers, who devoured them as soon as they were dead." Men tried to sell their wives and children "for a few dollars, to procure a short respite from the pangs of hunger and the approach of death."[4]

The *Boston Recorder* during the 1820s regularly ran sensational accounts. For example, "Earthquake at Aleppo" included both a first-person account of destruction in Syria and an overall report. Benjamin Barker, on the scene, wrote that he was racing down the stairs of a crumbling house when another shock sent him flying through the air, his fall broken when he landed on a dead body. He saw "men and women clinging to the ruined walls of their houses, holding their children in their trembling arms;

---

notes that scholars who have examined the original Greek have suggested several better translations: "Rebuke these sins, even though you should blush to mention them"; "It is a shame even to speak of their sins, yet that should not keep us from exposing and rebuking them"; "Rebuke these sins openly, for it is a shame to make mention of them in any other way than of reproof." Eadie recommends, "By all means reprove them, and there is the more need of it, for it is a shame even to speak of their secret sins."

4. Adultery and its aftermath were depicted in a *Courant* article the following month (April 29, 1765, 2): "On Sunday last the remains of the once prosperous, gay, beautiful, and almost incredibly engaging Miss TERESIA CONSTANTIA PHILLIPS, were interred in the Churchyard in this town." The *Courant* noted "that a catastrophe so striking and melancholy may prove an advantageous lesson to many of the surviving fair; and convince them, however flattering appearances may be, on their first deviation from the paths of rectitude and honour, that no admiration will be lasting, no happiness serene, which is not founded on the basis of rectitude." That article could be compared with an August 2, 1986, article from the *Austin American-Statesman.* The front-page story contained a sympathetic interview with Priscilla Davis, whose lover and daughter had been shot by a masked intruder. An attorney probing the relationship of her adultery and the murder told her, "Priscilla, if you've done anything just pony up to it." Her response was, "Pony up to what? I mean if I had crawled in the sack with 50,000 people what did that have to do with" the case?

mangled bodies lying under my feet, and piercing cries of half buried people assailing my ears; Christians, Jews, and Turks, were imploring the Almighty's mercy in their respective tongues, who a minute before did not perhaps acknowledge him."[5]

The overall report continued the theme of sudden destruction affecting hearts and minds as well as bodies. It began with a description of the poor but peaceful city of two hundred thousand that Aleppo then was, with "nothing remarkable in the weather, or in the state of the atmosphere." But "in ten or twelve seconds" the city was turned into "heaps of ruins," with "hundreds of decrepit parents half-buried in the ruins, imploring the succor of their sons," and "distracted mothers frantically lifting heavy stones from heaps that covered the bodies of lifeless infants."[6]

The *Recorder* noted that "the crash of falling walls, the shrieks, the groans, the accounts of agony and despair of that long night cannot be described." But the *Recorder* described one purpose behind such a sad event: "Earthquakes must be numbered amongst the 'terriblia Dei,' the 'terrible things of God,' in which His irresistible power to punish His sinful creatures is most awfully displayed: and which fill the human mind with greater terror than any other public calamity."[7]

Next, the *Recorder* described great earthquakes of 1638, 1692, 1755, and 1783 and brought the point home: "Should not these awful demonstrations of divine power cause us to fear Him who can so suddenly sweep away a whole city into destruction? Should not sinners tremble to think how awful it is to have such a God for an enemy? Should they not immediately seek reconciliation to Him through the Blood of the Lamb?"[8]

The *Recorder* stressed the material/spiritual interface of earthquakes, which, it argued, were sent as a general punish-

5. *Boston Recorder*, March 29, 1822, 1.
6. Ibid.
7. Ibid.
8. Ibid.

ment for sin, allowing the survivors the opportunity for new reconciliation with God. At Aleppo, according to the newspaper's account, many persons were seen "falling on their knees and imploring the mercy of God; and shortly after crowding the places of worship, eager to learn what they must do to be saved. Thus was it also in London in the year 1755." The *Recorder* then asked why sinners, standing "on the brink of eternity, and liable by a thousand means as fatal to life as an earthquake, to be hurried into eternity," do not "seek the Lord while He may be found."[9]

Later in the nineteenth century many newspapers did not emphasize God's sovereignty explicitly, but they still used sensationalism to stress morals emphasized in books such as Proverbs. Stories about executions of criminals had biblically referenced headlines such as "The Gallows Too Good / The Unrelenting Fiend Should Go to Welcome Haman."[10] Coverage paralleled the assertion in Proverbs that criminals lose out not only in the next life, but this one also: "Do not envy a man of violence and do not choose any of his ways," for "these men lie in wait for their own blood; they set an ambush for their own lives. Such are the ways of everyone who is greedy for unjust gain; it takes away the life of its possessors" (Prov. 3:31; 1:18–19).

Editors sometimes followed biblical example by stressing the consequences of adultery. Just as Proverbs compares a man who sleeps with another man's wife to the man who hopes to "walk on hot coals and his feet not be scorched" (Prov. 6:28), so articles headlined "Shocking Domestic Tragedy" laid out sensationally the "tragic outgrowth of marriage infidelity in high life." As Proverbs compares a man sleeping with a prostitute to "a bird [who] rushes into a snare; he does not know that it will cost him his life" (Prov. 7:23), so the *Houston Daily Post* described how a man was hanged for a murder he committed in "a house

9. Ibid.
10. *Dallas Morning News*, January 1, 1890, 1.

of ill repute." The newspaper was explicit: "The black cap was drawn over his face and the noose arranged, and at three o'clock the cord holding the weight was cut and Doran was hurled into eternity. The body was left hanging eighteen minutes."[11]

Many nineteenth-century newspapers also provided specific examples of the proverbial rule that one crime leads to another, until the person who has strayed "will rest in the assembly of the dead" (Prov. 21:16). Newspaper stories often described the downward spiral of wrong behavior: A man forged another's name on bank papers and then tried to poison him to avoid prosecution, or a husband quarreled with his wife and then killed her with a carving knife.[12] Editors also applied the verse, "Whoever digs a pit will fall into it" (Prov. 26:27; see also Pss. 7:15; 9:15; Eccl. 10:8). They ran headlines such as "A Shooter Shot Dead"[13] (concerning a bandit who prided himself on a quick draw) or "He Is Fixed for Life,"[14] concerning a person who had hoped to steal enough to become financially independent, but ended up receiving a life sentence.

Convention reports from organizations such as the Texas Press Association showed that many editors were aware of their responsibilities. One editor, E. W. Harris, argued that "the press fills its largest and holiest function as the great schoolmaster of the age . . . for the good of humanity and the glory of God." Another editor wrote that "the press is the fair handmaiden of the Christian religion." Editor S. J. Thomas suggested that

11. "Doran Done For," *Houston Daily Post*, August 21, 1880, 1.

12. Dallas *Morning News*, March 11, 1888, 6; *Dallas Daily Times-Herald*, January 31, 1891, 2. Biblically, murderous thoughts are akin to murder itself. A *Daily Times-Herald* reporter on January 31, 1891, showed the close connection of the two in his story of "The Deadly Fence": "John Black and James Goss, two highly respectable farmers . . . became involved in a quarrel today regarding a fence that stood on the dividing line between their farms. Black drew a revolver and began firing at his friend and neighbor. He shot three times, striking Goss in the abdomen. Goss cannot recover. Black escaped. Both are men of family."

13. *Dallas Morning News*, October 2, 1885, 3.

14. *Dallas Daily Times-Herald*, January 28, 1891, 2.

"the journalist is as surely called by divinity to his trade as is the minister of the gospel."[15]

By the late nineteenth century in most parts of the United States the tendency to use sensation to teach biblical morality had diminished, as newspapers had departed from Christian moorings. Yet, a sense of objective right and wrong still found its way into newspaper coverage of some sensational stories.

For example, newspapers did not accept the idea of no-fault, individual-choice suicide, and instead editorialized that suicides should receive more than pity: "It is necessary that we should also take into account the long concatenation of causes which have culminated in the tragedy—follies intellectual, moral, and physical . . . vices which are undeniable tokens of selfishness; passions to which the bridle has been given until it cannot be resumed; with all the waywardness and misemployed persistence of which the race is capable."[16] Underlying the harshness was a theological sensitivity revealed in this 1877 editorial: "The highest wisdom, therefore, even for a wretch whose life is saturated with sorrow, and for whom apparently there is no future, is to wait. Surely, considering how much we need them, faith and persistence should not be lightly abandoned. The very fact that we are not yet called from the scene of wearisome struggle and disaster, seemingly consummate, should prove to us that Providence has some design in continuing our existence."[17]

Throughout the late nineteenth century, newspapers condemned suicide and called it an act committed by a person who had done wrong, but was unwilling to admit responsibility and ask for forgiveness. Newspapers saw suicide as a frequent aftereffect of murder, adultery, or theft. For example, a man who committed suicide in a county jail was said to be receiving

15. E. W. Harris, in *TPA Proceedings*, 1889, 40; S. J. Thomas, in *TPA Procedings*, 1904, 34.
16. *New York Tribune*, February 17, 1877, 4.
17. Ibid., 6.

from his own hand the punishment he deserved for brutally kicking his aged mother to death three months previously.[18] Newspapers also publicized suicide by murderers and adulterers. The *New York Tribune* explained how a convicted wife murderer hanged himself in jail with a handkerchief.[19] The *Los Angeles Times* ran a front-page story about a murderer hanging himself.[20] The *Chicago Tribune* reported that one man took arsenic after learning of his wife's adultery.[21] The *New York Times* had a man killing himself after his wife found love letters another woman had sent him.[22]

Theft also was a leading cause of suicide, a reader of late nineteenth-century newspapers might conclude. A typical 1877 story dealt with the "Suicide of a Defaulting Cashier."[23] Similarly, the *Dallas Herald* noted the cyanide taking of a bookkeeper arrested for theft.[24]

The physical end of suicidal thieves often was described with particular vividness. One front page story, "A Thief & A Suicide," showed how a bank robber shot himself and was found with "his face shattered and covered with blood."[25] Another man, who also had a record of wife beating, slit his throat in the courtroom after being convicted of grand larceny.[26] A bank defaulter was found "with half of his head blown off."[27]

18. *Washington Post*, November 12, 1894, 1.

19. *New York Tribune*, April 2, 1885, 1; September 22, 1894, 1.

20. *Los Angeles Times*, January 6, 1885, 1.

21. *Chicago Tribune*, November 3, 1888, 1.

22. *New York Times*, September 18, 1890, 5. See also *New York Journal*, January 1, 1896, and October 16, 1895.

23. *New York Tribune*, February 28, 1877, 8.

24. *Dallas Herald*, December 24, 1885, 4. See also *Los Angeles Times*, January 6, 1885, 1.

25. *New York Tribune*, January 15, 1895, 1.

26. *New York Times*, October 6, 1887, 1.

27. Ibid., October 7, 1887, 9. Overall, it appears that suicide coverage indicated and strengthened the accepted values of the period. As Professor John Stevens observed, readers of sensational news are "participating, at least vicariously in the redefinition of their own values." Sociologist Kai Erikson noted that "an enormous amount of modern 'news' is devoted to reports about deviant behavior and its punishment." News

Was the violence necessary? The answer to that might depend on whether we really want to follow Jeremiah's procedure of making ears tingle when we communicate the results of sin, and the *Boston Recorder's* policy of emphasizing tribulation to increase awareness of God's sovereignty. As New York reporter Jacob Riis wrote, a murder story can "speak more eloquently to the minds of thousands than the sermon preached to a hundred in the church on Sunday." And yet, sensationalism frequently has been opposed by both materialists and Christians, although for different reasons.[28]

Materialists have tended to criticize the view of man's lowliness that often seems implicit in tales of murder, rape, or other crime. Over 150 years ago the atheistic journalist and reformer Robert Owen wrote, "Do you ask me wherein I put my trust, if religious responsibilities are annihilated? In human goodness. Do ye enquire what I propose as a substitute for religion? Cultivation of the noble faculties of the human mind."[29] During all the years since, those in the Owen mold have been surprised by stories showing human goodness untrustworthy and faculties often ignoble.

Materialists also have proclaimed that children should not be exposed to reports of man's depravity, or else they might also

---

accounts, Erikson suggested, "constitute our main source of information about the normative contours of society." *Journalism Quarterly* (Spring 1985): 53.

There are greater concerns now about invasion of privacy than there were then. Compassion for the family is more evident now. Clearly, though, attitudes toward suicide itself have changed. Some questions need to be asked: Might the tendency in contemporary journalism to cover suicides sympathetically be a factor in subsequent suicides? Might critically sensational coverage lead potentially suicidal individuals to think twice? Dostoyevski suggested that people who might otherwise commit suicide do not kill themselves because they fear physical pain and spiritual judgment. If he was right, newspapers' unwillingness to report pain and discuss the religious questions involved in suicide might actually increase the incidence of suicide. Christians are to act with compassion, but might compassion for those contemplating suicide require some harshness in coverage of those who have?

28. Jacob Riis, *The Making of an American* (New York: Macmillan, 1901), shows Riis's idealism about the power of journalism.

29. *Free Enquirer*, August 4, 1832, 1.

disbelieve in those "noble faculties of the human mind" that are to save us. The biblical view, though, is that children must quickly come to understand that man needs to depend on God for all things and that man without God is sinful and miserable. In any case, as children learn the Bible they will come across the sensational stories inside, and as they get older they learn the facts of tragedy. It is far better for them to learn in a Christian context than elsewhere that we are sinners in the hands of a righteous (and for that reason angry) God.

Christians tended to object not to all sensationalism, but to the kind which preached that sin was not always wrong. From newspaper accounts in the 1920s, for instance, it would sometimes seem as if criminals like Bonnie and Clyde had committed victimless murders; they were glamorized while their victims, and the families of those victims, were ignored. Headlines such as "He Beat Me—I Love Him" or "Thousands Applaud While Woman Is Tortured for Amusement" became typical on some front pages. Meanwhile, the newspapers that could provide biblical sensationalism were either defunct or sunken into antisensational staidness.[30]

Modern sensationalism, in short, proclaims that there is no king in Israel, so every man can do what he wishes. The troubles of others are spectator sport. As one newspaper critic noted about some typical early twentieth-century articles, "Last night

30. These are from the *New York Evening Graphic*, a newspaper that worshiped man and vigorously practiced nonbiblical sensationalism. The *Graphic* was founded by Bernard Macfadden with profits from his *True Story* and *Physical Culture* magazines. It editorialized for eugenics and offered rewards for "physically perfect" men and women to marry and produce offspring ($100 per baby). It crusaded against the wearing of hats by men. The *Graphic* was journalistically innovative, in its way. Crime reporter Jack Grey had done time for safecracking. He brought real expertise to the job. One *Graphic* gimmick, inspired by Macfadden's *True Story* magazine, was the use of first-person headlines; for instance, the story of a man who had killed his wife had the headline, "I Murdered My Wife Because She Cooked Fishballs for Dinner. I Told Her I Would Never Eat Them Again but She Defied Me to the End." Emile Gauvreau, *My Last Million Readers* (New York: Arno, 1974).

this man was worth millions; this morning he has not a cent. Interesting. Yesterday this man was a pillar of his church; today he has two wives. Amusing. Last night he was a respected bank cashier, this morning he is in Canada. Alarming. This morning she was selling lace in a big dry goods store; tonight she is in the East River. Shocking. He quietly entered the house and put a knife into his wife and three children. Horrible."[31]

Sensationalism, as the Bible and the nineteenth-century examples show, does not have to be like that. The type of sensationalism with which we in the twentieth century are most familiar shows the world groaning in sin, yet provides no explanation of why we have such troubles and what we can do about them. The lack of context is not surprising, since in the twentieth century many writers use their pens in an attempt to ink out God. But a Christian sensationalism could win readers while glorifying God.

Christian Sensationalism without Guilt

The journalistic textbooks proclaim that sensationalism is wrong, and cite solemnity as a sign of seriousness. Given the requirements of the media marketplace, such belief ends up turning many current journalists into shamefaced sensationalists. A multiple murder, just in time for the eleven o'clock news, with good film, is impossible to resist, for ratings purposes if nothing else. Journalists give in grudgingly and feel they have sold out. Or, in some cases—as with a frequent lack of suicide coverage—journalists do not cover a story in depth, if at all, and for not taking that job they feel very righteous. The straitlaced *New York Times* is seen as newspaper heaven.

The journalistic goal, though, should not be self-righteousness, but the production of lively and edifying newspapers and

31. *The Nation*, July 30, 1908.

news programs. Non-Christians are increasingly having trouble doing that, since humanistic sensationalism fosters feelings of journalistic guilt. Christians can provide salt, not by censoring coverage but by expanding it; by making newspapers not in our own image but in the image of God's newspaper, the Bible; by helping readers realize not that editors are godlike, but that only God is Godlike.

To contemplate sensationalism constructively, we should keep in mind biblical journalistic purpose. The Christian reporter's goal should be to provide a complete account, material and spiritual, as best he can within the limits of everyday journalism. If a Christian wants to report only the elevating and not the depressing, he is forgetting that in Christianity there is no repentance without an awareness of sin, no triumph without suffering, and no resurrection without the cross. The proper use of sensationalism could help Christians win back an audience of readers from those who purvey tragedy as amusement rather than education.

Readers and viewers should be unashamed about wanting sensational stories of disaster and death. Such stories appeal to us, in part, because they are telling us something important about our postfall human condition. If, though, sensational stories teach readers and viewers to believe that man is not responsible before God, that obedience is not a requirement, that man's sin results from forces outside his control, and that society is responsible for crime because revolution or evolution has not proceeded fast enough, then the stories are appealing to our depravity, our desire to live without God. Sometimes they may even appeal to our sinful tendencies to gloat or to enjoy the suffering of others.

Biblical sensationalism, however, can provide bad news and good news by showing sin and repentance, and the reasons for thanksgiving day by day. Biblical sensationalism can portray man as sinner, fully responsible before God who requires obedience. It can make ears tingle at the news of punishment for breaking God's law. It can educate readers or viewers and inoculate them against the belief that sin is without consequences.[32] It can be the two-by-four that is often necessary to gain our attention. And it can do all this in a way that people will read.

Christians should report about sin as sorrowful participants rather than gleeful spectators. After all, Paul explained in Romans that all have sinned and fallen short of God's glory. Christians who understand man's tendencies toward evil realize that every murder or suicide is neither an exotic man-bites-dog story nor a result of environmental pressure. Christians know that the murderous thoughts inside all of us are akin to murder; so the tale of murder itself is not bizarre, but a reminder to all of us. (If "news" is defined as deviation from the norm, then good news—taken for granted by those with faith in man—is truly news for Bible-believing Christians.)

Furthermore, Christians should be among the best at producing human interest stories of all kinds, because Christians are commanded to be truly interested in humans. For non-Christian reporters coverage of the macro issues of politics is prestigious, while the crime beat is something for newcomers or those who could not hack it elsewhere. A prevalent non-Christian belief was summarized well by Lincoln Steffens, the muckraker encapsulated in chapter 3. The cause of trouble in the garden of Eden was not Adam, Eve, or even Satan, but the apple.[33]

---

32. Biblically, the general penalties for disobeying God's rules are clear. When God commands a proclamation of bad news, Jeremiah is told that the Israelites will ask him, "Why has the LORD decreed all this great evil disaster against us? What is our iniquity?" God tells him to say, "Every one of you follows his stubborn, evil will, refusing to listen to me [God]" (Jer. 16:10, 12).

33. Lincoln Steffens, *The Autobiography of Lincoln Steffens* (New York: Harcourt, Brace, 1931), 571–74.

Steffens was arguing that the real story of man is economic and the personal just reflects the societal. People are victims of circumstance, not truly responsible for our own actions, not truly important. For Christians, though, the most important battles are not fought out in Washington: they are fought out in the human soul. "Big questions" are reflections of that largest-of-all struggle.

Cautions and Conclusions

Christians who wish to reinvigorate sensationalism must be careful to avoid malicious gossip. Human disasters cannot always be connected to specific, personal sins that may have preceded them. Those who force such connections are in the position of Job's friends, who gave bad advice because they did not know the war in the heavens was claiming one more victim. Particularly when writing against deadline, we must be discerning to avoid false inference from inadequate evidence.

Christian reporters are not inspired. In our zeal to apply biblical explanations for tragedy, we must avoid premature explanation, exaggeration, or malicious whispering. Forcing an explanation that seems to agree with a particular doctrinal or ideological perspective is also a danger. Christian journalists must remember that true justice, not poetic justice, pervades the world. This means we know that the Judge of the whole world does right, but—with Satan still going to and fro in the world—many tragedies are unpredictable from our human vantage point and may not have a journalistically discernible cause.

To some, it might seem strange to mention coverage of sensational events and truth-telling in the same paragraph, since the two have so often seemed opposed in non-Christian publications. God's world, though, is full of wonderful and terrifying things, and Christians are often faced with the question of whether to downplay the latter. We must resist that tempatation

234

if we are to witness fully to our faith in God's sovereignty and justice, come what may. God does not need our public relations.

Disciplined truth-telling cannot be based on our own character development alone, but on the belief in God's sovereignty that only faith can bring. Telling the truth about a sorrowful incident is not easy. Augustine, after describing some of the difficult situations a person must face, noted that he found it very difficult "to resist when someone says to me: 'Look, here is a patient whose life is endangered by a serious illness and whose strength will not hold out any longer if he is told of the death of his dearly beloved only son. He asks you whether the boy is still alive whose life you know is ended.' "

Augustine then posed the hard question: "What will you answer when, if you say anything except 'He is dead' or 'He is alive' or 'I don't know,' the patient will believe that he is dead, because he realizes that you are afraid to say and do not want to lie? It will be the same no matter how hard you try to say nothing. Of the three convincing answers, two are false: 'He is alive' and 'I don't know,' and you cannot utter them without lying. But, if you make the one true answer, namely, that he is dead, and the death of the anguished father follows hard upon it, people will cry that he was slain by you."

Augustine wrote that he was "moved by these arguments," but then he "put before my mind's eye the intellectual beauty of Him from whose mouth nothing false proceeded," and was "so inflamed by love of such great beauty that I despise all human considerations that call me back from there."[34]

In a hard case of that sort, it takes enormous discipline born of faith to think of the "intellectual beauty" of God's truth. Yet, those who see the beauty realize that our most vivid teaching

34. Augustine, "Against Lying," quoted in *Treatises on Various Subjects*, vol. 16, chap. 2, ed. R. J. Deferrari, Fathers of the Church series (New York: Catholic University of America Press, 1:1952), quoted in Sissela Bok, *Lying: Moral Choice in Public and Private Life* (New York: Random House, 1978).

about man's fallenness comes from the large and small disasters we see around us. The *Boston Recorder*, at the end of its coverage of the Aleppo earthquake, asked a hard question: "Must we tempt God to visit us also with an earthquake?" Sensational destruction forced many in Aleppo to consider their Creator, and the *Recorder* suggested that God could use its sensational accounts to make some readers think of spiritual questions while they still could.[35]

We know, therefore, that even disaster accomplishes something. It requires faith to understand that God protects, in life or in death, those who believe in him. In the words of Paul to the Colossians, Christ has "reconcile[d] to himself all things, whether things on earth or things in heaven, by making peace through his blood, shed on the cross" (Col. 1:20). But if news organizations do their job properly, disaster also brings edification for those who look on with wonder and horror. When even Christian news organizations play down news of fallenness and the long-term consequences of the original fall, they are denying a truth that Martin Luther proclaimed: "It is impossible for a human heart, without crosses and tribulations, to think upon God."[36]

Sensationalism, in short, gains audience, but it also can educate that audience. The inspired writers of the Bible wanted to make ears tingle. So did American Christian journalists in the early nineteenth century. Tingling ears often are learning ears. They tend to belong to people who will come back for more stories of life and death, sin and misery, repentance and revival.[37]

35. *Boston Recorder*, March 29, 1822, 1.

36. Martin Luther, *Table Talk*. Luther also noted, "No man ought to lay a cross upon himself . . . but if a cross or tribulation come upon him, then let him suffer it patiently, or know that it is good and profitable for him" (ibid.).

37. Circulation opportunities for newspapers practicing Christian sensationalism are tied to the economic questions discussed in the previous chapter. With newspapers selling less than 50 copies per 100 households now, compared to 124 copies for 100 households in 1950, many people are not reading. Part of the decline may be due to

In the nineteenth century, pride—a refusal to take audience tastes into account—contributed to the fall of many Christian publications. Their refusal to employ sensationalism actually meant that some editors were thinking themselves better than God, who showed in the Bible that he wants many sensational things reported. We should not make that mistake again. With God's grace, biblical sensationalism is the key to successful Christian publishing and programming.

---

television, but some nonsubscribers might be looking for a different kind of newspaper. For more on Christian sensationalism, see Marvin Olasky, *Telling the Truth: How To Revitalize Christian Journalism* (Eugene, OR: Wipf & Stock Publishers, 2010).

12

Crusading on Social and Political Issues: Personalization and Persistence

ccording to the leading journalism history textbook, "The crusading spirit is as old as journalism, but never in American history had there been more opportunity for 'the people's champions' than in the years following 1900."[1] Joseph Pulitzer's *New York World*, the textbook states, "commanded deep respect for its intelligent and fair-minded approaches to issues of public importance, for its progressive and hard-hitting crusades. . . ." The textbook also praises Scripps, Steffens, and other "famous crusading liberals."[2]

It is ironic that the words *crusade* or *crusading* should be used nine times in three pages to praise the efforts of atheists. According to the *Oxford English Dictionary*, the word *crusade* (originally *croisade*) found its way into the English language around 1575, from the French. The word first was used in reference to the military expeditions in Palestine from the eleventh through the thirteenth centuries; then it was used to designate any war fought for supposed Christian ends; only in relatively recent

1. Edwin Emery and Michael Emery, *The Press and America: An Interpretive History of the Mass Media*, 5th ed. (Englewood Cliffs, NJ: Prentice-Hall, 1984), 311.
2. Ibid., 313, 316–18, 322.

times has it been generalized to refer to any movement against something considered evil.[3]

The current usage is ironic for two reasons. The first irony lies in the history of the word *crusade*, and its French connection with *croisement*, being marked by the cross. The second and most important irony is that non-Christian editors who want to crusade against evil are unaware of where true evil resides: not in specific individuals or institutions, but in the nature of man apart from God.

Without understanding original sin, non-Christian crusaders may gain relatively rapid passage of new laws and eviction of old leaders, only to find, with victory declared, that little has changed. With an understanding of man's nature, Christian crusaders find that reform takes longer to bring about, since the goal is not just the exchange of one leader for another, or passage of a government program. The goal is to make people aware that all of us are, to use Jonathan Edwards' phrase, "sinners in the hands of an angry God."[4]

One practical outworking of this belief in changed hearts rather than (as a primary goal) changed laws is that Christian journalistic crusading does not emphasize the work of civil government: use of the state is a last resort. Paul told the Christians in Rome to subject themselves to the governing authorities (Rom. 13:1)—plural. Parents, church leaders, employers, teachers, and so on are all representatives of different types of governing authority. Change must come in many different spheres for true reform to take root. Once accomplished, though, Christian reforms are likely to last longer, with God's grace.

How should Christian journalists today conduct crusades? Two of the outstanding nineteenth-century successes point the way.

---

3. The "Christian" justification for the original Crusades, of course, is somewhat dubious.

4. Jonathan Edwards' most famous sermon is included in Perry Miller and Thomas H. Johnson, eds., *The Puritans* (New York: Harper and Row, 1963).

Example: Dueling

The *Boston Recorder* carried on a crusade against one early nineteenth-century practice, dueling, within the context of its biblical political views.[5] Politically, the *Recorder* had argued that man's sin required diffusion of power and decentralization. Comparing God's holiness to man's depravity, *Recorder* writers concluded that man could hardly be trusted to rule himself politically, and could not be trusted to rule others: therefore, the less civil government, the better. The *Recorder's* goal was to bring the power of multiple governments to bear on manifestations of sin.[6]

In developing an antidueling crusade, the *Recorder* first emphasized use of family, one type of government. The *Recorder* argued frequently that potential duelists should respect the wishes of parents and spouses, rather than satisfying their own vanity, and ran many parental pleas to avoid duels, along with tales of mothers mourning over sons.[7] A typical tale in 1823 began with one man challenging another to a duel. The challenged man accepted, on condition that they should breakfast together at his house before going out to fight. After breakfast,

5. Readable histories of dueling in America include William Oliver Stevens, *Pistols at Ten Paces: The Story of the Code of Honor in America* (Boston: Houghton Mifflin, 1940), and Harnett Thomas Kane, *Gentlemen, Swords and Pistols* (New York: Morrow, 1951).

6. *Recorder* recommendations anticipated what Alexis de Tocqueville was to note in 1835: "Americans of all ages, all conditions, and all dispositions constantly form associations. . . . If it is proposed to inculcate some truth or to foster some feeling by the encouragement of a great example, they form a society . . . what political power could ever [do what Americans voluntarily] perform every day with the assistance of the principle of association?" *Democracy in America*, vol. 2 (Vintage: New York, 1945), 116.

7. *Boston Recorder*, June 22, 1822, 100: "The young man succeeded in concealing his intentions from his relatives until it was too late to interpose a check to the fatal meeting. He had a mother. She doted on him. From this mother he was most anxious to conceal his designs. She heard what her son was going to do, but not till it was too late . . . she saw her boy, only nineteen years of age, brought home, pale, bleeding, and just sinking in the cold embrace of death! It was too much for her. The dreadful shock hurled her reason from its throne, and she went mournfully about, pensively asking, 'where's my son—where's my son?' "

the challenger asked if the host was ready. " 'No sir,' replied he, 'not till we are more upon a par, that amiable woman, & those six innocent children, who just now breakfasted with us, depend solely upon my life for subsistence—and till you can stake something equal in my estimation to the welfare of seven persons, dearer to me than the apple of my eye, I cannot think we are equally matched.' 'We are not indeed!' replied the other, giving him his hand."[8]

Second, the *Recorder* proposed that voluntary associations, schools, churches, and businesses criticize duelists at every opportunity, and that newspapers print names of all those involved in duels. Since some saw duels as heroic, the *Recorder* asked societal leaders to poke fun at duelists at every opportunity. One of its own stories told of a man awaiting his opponent's arrival, until "he observed some bushes near him shaking, and supposing it was his adversary skulking" fired. The man found he had shot a cow.[9]

Third, since all authority came from God, the *Recorder* argued that Christians governed by God's law, not their own, would avoid situations in which they might commit murder. The lesson of Admiral Stephen Decatur's fatal 1820 duel—"there is no honor, which is valuable and durable, save that which comes from God"— was stressed repeatedly.[10]

Other Christian newspapers, and some non-Christian ones, joined the antidueling crusade, first in the North, later in the South.[11] Like the *Recorder*, they did not merely quote biblical verses against murder and preach an abstract sermonette. Instead, they used specific detail to make their points. They did not emphasize

8. Ibid., April 22, 1823, 57.
9. Ibid., March 31, 1826, 52.
10. Ibid., April 22, 1820, 57.
11. Some Southern editors who did not join the antidueling crusade were digging their own pits and eventually falling in. Editors in Richmond, Vicksburg, and other cities died in duels with offended readers.

governmental action. Dueling already was against the law, but antidueling laws, like others, were regularly breakable unless they were written in men's hearts.

As the early nineteenth-century Christian newspapers became less vigorous, others carried on the crusade. Social changes contributed to the demise of dueling, but newspaper coverage seems to have had an effect. By the late nineteenth century dueling pistols were still very much in demand, but as collector's items.

Example: Abortion

It is no accident that the abortion story comes into play in several chapters of this book. Abortion is not only a major manifestation of sin in our age, but a deadly fad whose rise and fall and rise again and prospective fall are interwoven with the history of American journalism.

Part of chapter 1 discussed the role of one newspaper, the *New York Times*. Segments of chapters 2 and 8 noted treatment of one aborting mother, Sherri Finkbine. The goal in this chapter is to learn a lesson from the way journalists treated the abortionists themselves. As Pulitzer and his contemporaries knew, personalization is vital to a successful crusade. To keep readers' or viewers' attention throughout a long campaign, they must be able to see a bad guy rather than an abstraction. Christian crusaders must learn how to personalize in a way that spotlights the activity and its reprehensibility, and does not ignore the nature of original sin.

In the nineteenth-century abortion battle, the chief bad guy for forty years was a woman, Madame Restell. Born Anna Trow in 1812, she worked in New York as a seamstress and occasional midwife, and married a printer. In the late 1830s she opened an abortion business and took the name Madame Restell (the French were considered most up-to-date in such matters).

Madame Restell found that word-of-mouth would take her business only so far. Hoping to get her message on abortion availability to thousands of pregnant women and desperate men, she began to advertise in New York's newspapers.[12] She had to be careful, because abortion was illegal by statute in New York; she did not have to be too careful, because anti-abortion laws rarely were enforced.[13] She ran euphemistic ads in non-Christian newspapers, such as this one in the *New York Sun*:

MADAME RESTELL FEMALE PHYSICIAN, office and residence 148 Greenwich Street, between Courtlandt and Liberty St., where she can be consulted with the strictest confidence on complaints incidental to the female frame. Madame Restell's

12. Such an advertising strategy would not have been possible shortly before. Advertising until the 1830s often was a moral as well as an economic exchange. Christian-based newspapers did not allow ads editors considered "objectionable." The *New York Journal of Commerce*, the *New England Palladium* of Boston, and many other newspapers would not accept advertisement of theaters, lotteries, or business to be transacted on the Sabbath, let alone abortion.

That sense of editorial responsibility changed as Christian newspapers declined in importance. The *Boston Daily Times* was typical of the new media when in 1837 they said: "It is sufficient for our purpose that the advertisements are paid for. . . . One man has as good a right as another to have his wares, his goods, his panaceas, his profession, published to the world in a newspaper, provided he pays for it."

13. The anti-abortion laws were rarely enforced for two reasons. First, there were no pregnancy tests. Until "quickening" (generally the fifth month of pregnancy, when fetal movement becomes evident) there was no invariably accepted proof that a woman was pregnant.

Consequently abortion before quickening was often termed merely "an attempt to remove female blockages," and prosecution was impossible. Nor was after-quickening prosecution likely either, since witnesses would be very hard to come by. (If the abortion was successful and the woman survived she would be unlikely to testify; if she died, pathologists at that time could not know for sure that an abortion had taken place.)

There also was some public unwillingness to attempt the enforcement of abortion statutes because there was widespread questioning of the pre-quickened infant's humanity, despite biblical testimony. A common understanding from the 1830s through even the 1870s is indicated by a statement given to the Michigan State Board of Health: "There is very generally current among the people the notion that before . . . the fourth month of pregnancy, there is no real life in the fetus, or at least that it is not a 'living soul,' and to destroy it is no real crime." James Mohr, *Abortion in America: The Origins and Evolution of National Policy* (New York: Oxford University Press, 1978), 73.

experience and knowledge in the treatment of cases of female irregularity, is such as to require but a few days to effect a perfect cure. Ladies desiring proper medical attendance will be accommodated during such time with private and respectable board.[14]

Madame Restell also publicized her "FEMALE MONTHLY REGULATING PILLS" that would cure "all cases of suppression, irregularity, or stoppage of the menses, however obdurate."[15] This was accurate in that the leading cause of menstrual stoppage among women of childbearing age was pregnancy.

According to contemporary observers, "every schoolgirl" knew what references to "female irregularity" and "perfect cure" meant. While no financial records of her business are known to exist, response to her advertising was so great that she soon opened up a chain of abortion offices in New York, Boston, and Philadelphia.[16]

Other abortionists began advertising their "willingness to treat the private ailments of women" in terms that clearly indicated the availability of abortion services. Advertising of generally ineffective abortifacients, like that of patent medicines, also boomed. Abortionists advertised "Dr. Peter's French Renovating Pills [as] a blessing to mothers . . . and although very mild and prompt in their operations, pregnant women should not use them, as they invariably produce a miscarriage." Dr. Monroe's French Periodical Pills displayed prominently the "precaution" that they were "sure to produce a miscarriage." Dr. Melveau's Portuguese Female Pills alerted consumers that they were "certain to produce miscarriage."[17]

14. *New York Sun*, March 3, 1846, 1.

15. Ibid., December 11, 1839, 1. Also see *New York Herald*, March 6, 1840, 1; August 26, 1841, 3; September 22, 1843, 4; December 13, 1843, 4; January 25, 1844, 4; April 13, 1844, 4; January 11, 1845, 4.

16. *New York Herald*, March 6, 1840, 4; January 15, 1845, 4.

17. Ibid., October 25, 1841, 3; April 15, 1842, 4; December 13, 1843, 4; July 23, 1844, 4; January 29, 1845, 4.

Those with "blockages" not removed by medication often turned next to surgical methods. By the mid-1840s Amos Dean of the Albany Medical College, *Medical Jurisprudence* editor R. E. Griffith, and many others wrote of a dramatic increase in the number of abortions. Changes in the intellectual and social climate had an effect on the abortion rate, but advertising clearly was important. When abortionists occasionally were arrested, pregnant and unmarried young women testified that they had seen abortion advertisements and had begun thinking about what appeared to be an easy way out of trouble.[18]

Some doctors fought back. Dr. Gunning Bedford, in the *New England Journal of Medicine*, called Madame Restell "a monster who speculates with human life with as much cruelness as if she were engaged in a game of chance." He wrote of one patient who told him that "Madame Restell, on previous occasions, had caused her to miscarry five times." The patient also described one Restell abortion in which the aborted baby "kicked several times after it was put into the bowl." Bedford wrote angrily that Restell's "advertisements are to be seen in our daily papers. . . . She tells publicly what she can do; and without the slightest scruple, urges all to call on her who might be anxious to avoid having children."[19]

In the 1840s the *New York Times* did not yet exist, and other Christian newspapers seemed reluctant to become involved. One newspaper, the *National Police Gazette*, did begin an anti-abortion crusade. Its name came from a willingness to specialize in news of crime at a time when other newspapers often refused to get their hands dirty. Later the *Gazette* went through several changes of ownership and began to glamorize crime rather than expose and oppose it. In the 1840s and the 1850s,

18. *National Police Gazette*, November 15, 1845, 100.
19. Ibid. See also Gunning Bedford, "Madame Restell and Some of Her Dupes," *New York Medical and Surgical Reporter*, February 21, 1846, 158–65.

though, the *Gazette* was the only newspaper consistently attacking abortion.[20]

The *Gazette* began its great crusade in 1845 by proclaiming that it would publish articles about abortion "because we believe that full expositions of the infamous practices of abortionists will tend to present these human fiends in a true light before the eyes of those who may become their dupes. We shall follow up this business until New York is rid of those child destroyers."[21] Even though Madame Restell originally saw such attacks as part of a day's work, and even claimed they were good publicity—those who wanted abortions would definitely know where to go—the *Gazette* persisted.

The *Gazette* emphasized community action. It complained in February 1846 that "Restell still roams at large through the influence of ill-gotten wealth and will probably still continue until public indignation drives her and her associates from our midst."[22] Week after week the *Gazette* kept after Madame Restell, predicting that a "day of vengeance" would arrive for her and other "fiends who have made a business of professional murder and who have reaped the bloody harvest in quenching the immortal spark in thousands of the unborn."[23] Week after week the *Gazette* attacked "Restell, the murderess paramount in the dark scheme of professional destruction, openly defying decency and the statute, and proclaiming to the world to stifle human life at so much per deed."[24]

20. Dan Schiller, *Objectivity and the News: The Public and the Rise of Commercial Journalism* (Philadelphia: University of Pennsylvania Press, 1981), has two chapters on the *Gazette*, but does not mention the anti-abortion crusade.

21. *National Police Gazette*, November 15, 1845, 100.

22. Ibid., February 14, 1846, 205.

23. Ibid., February 21, 1846, 218.

24. Ibid. The *Gazette* hit hard at the enormity of Madame Restell's crime: "We are not now demanding justice upon the perpetrators of a single crime, but upon one who might be drowned in the blood of her victims, did each but yield a drop, whose epitaph should be a curse, and whose tomb a pyramid of skulls. . . . We call again for action from the authorities in relation to this woman. She has been for nearly ten

With authorities still not acting, popular hostility fueled by *Gazette* accounts and anti-Restell handbills erupted. At noon on February 23, 1846, a crowd of perhaps seven hundred gathered in front of Madame Restell's house to "protest the inertness of the authorities." Reporters quoted cries from the crowd of "Haul her out," "Where's the thousand children murdered in this house!," "Hanging is too good for the monster." The *New York Morning News*, describing "a universal cry for vengeance and retribution," made comments about "wholesale female strangler . . . vital spark of the unborn . . . rude and savage butchery."[25]

Under great pressure, police finally arrested Madame Restell in 1847 for procuring an abortion. At the trial a young woman, Maria Bodine, testified that during the abortion Madame Restell "hurt me so that I halloed out and gripped hold of her hand; she told me to have patience, and I would call her 'mother' for it."[26]

Found guilty, Madame Restell was given a one-year jail term, but political connections preserved her from great misery. She received permission to put aside the lumpy prison mattress and bring in her own fancy new featherbed instead. Madame Restell also brought into the "prison suite" her own easy chairs, rockers, and carpeting. Visiting hours changed so that her husband was able to visit at will and "remain alone

years involved in law, and her money has saved her, as yet, from the direct penalty of a single dereliction."

25. *New York Herald*, February 24, 1846, 1; *New York Tribune*, February 24, 1846, 2; *New York Morning News*, February 23, 1846, 1. Madame Restell, it seemed, had been warned and had gone to a friend's house. The crowd eventually dispersed. The *Morning News* concluded, "We trust that from the experience of yesterday, Madame Restell is now convinced of the necessity of immediately closing her unlawful business. . . ." So was the New York state legislature, which passed a new law making abortion of a quick child a felony except when the abortion was necessary to preserve the mother's life. At this point the *Gazette* began a strong campaign for enforcement, complaining on April 25, 1846, of police "neglect of duty before the face of Heaven," and emphasizing once again that abortion is "murder . . . strangling the unborn."

26. Alan Keller, *Scandalous Lady: The Life and Times of Madame Restell* (New York: Atheneum, 1981), 38.

with her as long as suited his or her pleasure," according to Warden Jacob Acker.[27]

After release from such a jail, Madame Restell proclaimed the trial and imprisonment to be worth $100,000 to her in advertising. She moved to larger and better offices and in the 1850s spent $20,000 on advertising per year, at a time when eggs were six cents a dozen and decent apartments in New York City cost $5 or $6 a month. Madame Restell also became known as the favorite abortionist of the wealthy and powerful. She boasted that mistresses of senators, governors, and other high officials used her services. One 1850 newspaper editorial explained her lenient treatment by police: "She held in her keeping the dread secrets of many a high-toned family, and fear of exposure led those people quickly to defend her when she got into the toils."[28]

Some newspapers would have given up, but the *Gazette* kept at it. Popular pressure led to a re-arrest of Madame Restell in 1856. This time her political connections were so strong that she gained release at once. Growing still wealthier and continuing to expand her clientele, she moved to a mansion at Fifth Avenue and 52nd Street that, according to the *New York Times*, "never fails to attract the attention of the passerby, on account of its architectural beauty and magnificence." Madame Restell traveled the avenues behind a pair of matched grays and a driver with plum-colored facing on his coat lapels. According to one writer, she also carried a small muff of mink in which she hid her hands, much like the ones "famous pianists or violinists used to protect their hands from harm."

By the mid-1860s she was said to be a millionaire. Other New York abortionists also had, in the words of the *British Medical Journal*, a "large and lucrative business," one in which they were "never in want of engagements." One anti-abortion doctor,

27. Ibid., 68; *New York Tribune*, April 2, 1978, 1.
28. Quoted in Keller, *Scandalous Lady*, 71.

J. H. Toner, had to admit that abortion "has become a regularly established, money making trade." Some opponents of abortion gave up, just as some give up now: the opposition seems too strong. And yet, the *Gazette* kept at it.[29]

In the 1860s the great crusade finally began to make real progress with the coming aboard of the *New York Times*, as described in chapter 1. Following the exposes by the *Times*, even the Greeley-edited *New York Tribune* ran anti-abortion editorials, examining the business aspects of "an infamous but unfortunately common crime—so common that it affords a lucrative support to a regular guild of professional murderers, so safe that its perpetrators advertise their calling in the newspapers, and parade their spoils on the fashionable avenues."[30]

29. Mohr, *Abortion in America*, 86–118. No one knows for sure how many abortions were performed in the United States during the 1850s and 1860s. Statistics were not kept, but both pro- and anti-abortion physicians estimated or guessed that 20 percent of all pregnancies ended in planned abortion. The *New York Times* noted that abortion during the 1860s was "very common." One doctor complained that both unmarried and married women frequently had abortions because of unwillingness to undergo "the care, the expense, or the trouble of children, or some other motive equally trifling and degrading."

Most ministers at that time did little to oppose the pro-abortion bandwagon. Missouri anti-abortion doctors in 1868 noted that "our clergy, with some very few exceptions, have thus far hesitated to enter an open crusade against . . . criminal abortions." An Illinois anti-abortion doctor contended that ministers "have been very derelict in handling this subject too delicately, and speaking of it too seldom."

Some ministers were personally opposed to abortion but thought it impolitic to say so. One minister said that sermons on abortion would "turn the pulpit and church into a place that many people would not like to visit." A reporter noted that congregations were hearing "rose water balderdash, politico-religious harangues and cream-cheese platitudes *ad nauseum*" from ministers who were silent on abortion "lest the namby-pamby sensibilities of fashionable fops should be hurt."

Those who believed abortion to be murder wanted to cut through that indifference. The ministers, for the most part, were not going to lead the way. Neither were the politicians. The American Medical Association was anti-abortion at that time, and doctors such as Gunning Bedford and Hugh Hodge had great persistence. See Hugh Hodge, *Foeticide* (Philadelphia: University of Pennsylvania, 1869). For the most part, though, it was the newspapers during the late 1860s that began to, in the words of an Indiana minister, "sound the cry of MURDER!"

30. *New York Tribune*, August 30, 1871, 4.

The *Tribune* called for an end to newspaper advertising of abortion services: "Abortion at any period is homicide" and should not be "allowed to flourish openly as a recognized industry." Non-Christian newspapers, even the *New York Herald*, bowed to public pressure and at various points during the 1870s began refusing to run ads for known abortionists.[31] Madame Restell's business began to decrease, but as revenue slackened she seemed to spend more and more, putting part of her savings back into the Fifth Avenue house.[32]

Increasingly though, her house itself became known as a symbol of ill-gotten gains. With newspapers attacking her personally, as a way of focusing attention on the issue, a new generation of officials did not automatically protect her. Assistant District Attorney Fellows complained that "Every brick in that splendid mansion might represent a little skull, and the blood that infamous woman has shed might have served to mix the mortar." Community pressure increased, and Madame Restell became isolated. Loud cries against "Madame Killer" would sometimes follow her carriage down Fifth Avenue. With anti-abortion laws not only tightened but, due to public sentiment, enforced, she began to lie low.[33]

Early in 1878, personalization and persistence finally paid off. The *New York Times* reported, "Mme Restell Arrested" for

31. Ibid.

32. Keller, *Scandalous Lady*, 120. A description of the mansion's interior written by James McCabe in 1872 indicates the way Madame Restell lived: "On the first floor are the grand hall of tessellated marble, lined with mirrors; the three immense dining-rooms, furnished in bronze and gold, with yellow satin hangings, an enormous French mirror in mosaic gilding at every panel . . . more parlors and reception-rooms; butler's pantry, lined with solid silver services; dining room with all imported furniture. Other parlors on the floor above; a guest-chamber in blue brocade satin, with gold-and ebony-bedstead elegantly covered . . . [many bedrooms and lounges]. . . . Fourth floor—servant's rooms in mahogany and Brussels carpet, and circular picture gallery; the fifth floor contains a magnificent billiards room, dancing-hall, with pictures, piano, etc. . . . The whole house is filled with statuettes, paintings, rare bronzes, ornamental and valuable clocks, candelabras, silver globes and articles of many origins and rare worth" (ibid.).

33. *New York Times*, January 26, 1871, 3.

"selling drugs and articles to procure abortion." The *Times* noted that "The residence of Mme Restell is one of the best known in New York. . . . Her wealth is entirely the proceeds of her criminal profession. Her patrons are said to belong to the wealthiest families." But Madame Restell's patrons were not able to protect her from newspaper reporters who followed every detail of her arraignment and trial.[34]

Some of the developments were low comedy. Madame Restell could not immediately raise bail from her own funds, since her investments in bonds and real estate were illiquid. Bondsmen said they would put up sufficient funds only if the judge would order reporters not to print the bondsmen's names in the newspaper. The judge refused and the bondsmen refused. Madame Restell's lawyer turned to one bondsman and asked him to help out, saying, "Will you not allow a Christian feeling to govern you?" But there was nothing Christian about Madame Restell, the *Times* suggested, as it quoted the bondsman refusing not from opposition to abortion but from dislike of publicity: "I've got a wife and a family of girls, and I'll be hanged if I'm going to have my name in the papers as a bondsman for an abortionist."[35]

Madame Restell eventually left jail, but she could not leave behind newspaper attacks. She had lived by the press and was now dying by it. She asked her lawyers if there was some way to suppress the newspapers, but was told that nothing could be done, for the press was without standards. One of Madame Restell's colleagues complained angrily, "Money! We've plenty of that. But what good is it with the newspapers against us?" Madame Restell's lawyer asked both judge and editor to have mercy on his client, a "poor old woman," but he was laughed at. Madame Restell could not seem to understand the causes of the judgment she was facing: "I have never

34. Ibid., February 12, 1878, 8.
35. Ibid., February 14, 1878, 8.

injured anybody," she complained. "Why should they bring this trouble upon me?"[36]

Madame Restell at age sixty-five became an avid newspaper reader, but she found no peace. The *New York Times* described how she was "driven to desperation at last by the public opinion she had so long defied." At night she paced her mansion halls like a latter-day Lady Macbeth, looking at her hands and bemoaning her plight. Early on the morning of the day trial was scheduled to begin, Madame Restell was discovered in her bathtub by a maid, with her throat cut from ear to ear, an apparent suicide.[37]

The end was sad: Madame Restell apparently never repented. But she served during her life as the symbol of evil. She had flaunted wealth gained through murder. Just as the *New York Times* seized on the death of a young woman to drive home its abortion lesson, so the *Gazette* and then other newspapers concentrated on Madame Restell. Was the treatment of Madame Restell compassionate? Her only hope was to realize that abortion was wrong and to change, as Dr. Bernard Nathanson and many other late twentieth-century abortionists did.[38]

Learning from their successful treatment of Madame Restell, and going with/contributing to the changed flow of opinion, many newspapers in the 1870s and 1880s emphasized the large monetary rewards many abortionists received. They thus suggested "murder for profit" rather than an offering of

36. Ibid., February 14, 1878, 4; February 24, 1878, 5; March 2, 1878, 1; April 2, 1878, 1.

37. Ibid., April 2, 1878, 1. The *New York Times* announced this denouement at the top of page 1: "End of a Criminal Life. Mme Restell Commits Suicide." The *Times* reported rumors that "Mme. Restell was murdered through the instigation of wealthy people who had patronized her in her criminal business, in order to prevent disclosures which they deemed inevitable at her trial." Reporters found no proof for these allegations and called them "improbable." *Times*, April 3, 1878, 1.

38. Nathanson, responsible—by his own admission—for 60,000 abortions, became convinced of the humanity of unborn children and went on to make *The Silent Scream*, a 1984 movie credited with bringing "many converts to the pro-life cause." Michael J. New, "The Pro-Life Legacy of Dr. Bernard Nathanson," *National Review*, February 22, 2011.

professional services. Newspapers almost invariably described arrested abortionists as rich. At one abortion inquest, a "Madame Ihl" was "dressed handsomely in black silk." Another abortionist was "plainly but richly dressed in a costume of black silk."[39]

Always, the motto was personalization and persistence. In 1890 the *New York Times* wrote that an arrested abortionist, Dr. McGonegal, "has the appearance of a vulture.... His sharp eyes glitter from either side of his beaked nose, and cunning and greed are written all over his face." McGonegal's accomplice, Fannie Shaw, was described as "wholly repulsive in appearance, vice and disease having made her a disgusting object."[40]

The *Times* even sent a reporter to McGonegal's neighborhood in Harlem to learn how he was regarded by people he said he was trying to help. The reporter concluded, "To the good people of Harlem, and especially to the poorer class, this grizzly old physician had long been an object of intense hatred. They were certain of his unholy practices, although he had escaped conviction, and when he drove through the streets in his old-fashioned, ramshackle gig, they hooted and jeered at him in derision."[41]

39. *New York Times*, March 17, 1875, 7; March 19, 1875, 6; March 20, 1875, 12. Newspapers continued to report gruesome developments in the 1880s. The *New York Times* reported from Philadelphia that policemen, on a tip, dug in one downtown cellar and found "the bodies of 21 infants who had been killed before birth." The abortionist was sentenced to seven years hard labor after a trial in which jurors were shown a cigar box containing the bones of the murder victims: "Wherever the box was moved, they rattled like hard withered leaves. There were many bits of skulls among them, some almost complete." In Indianapolis, one story told of an abortion attempt in which a baby was expelled from the womb still alive. By the time a reporter arrived, he was able to witness only "the remains of a newly-born infant of the male gender, the umbilical cord showing the child to have been forcibly torn from its mother while yet alive, while upon its skull is the mark of a cruel blow, as if the helpless one had been swung by its heels against an unyielding surface, and its skull crushed until life was extinct."

40. *New York Times*, July 23, 1890, 8.

41. Ibid., July 24, 1890, 2. McGonegal was sentenced to fourteen years. See also stories on July 25, 1890, 8; July 26, 1890, 2; July 27, 1890, 13; July 28, 1890, 8; July 29, 1890, 8; July 30, 1890, 8; July 31, 1890, 8; September 19, 1890, 8; September 23, 1890, 8; September 24, 1890, 9; September 25, 1890, 3; September 26, 1890, 2; September

By 1900, though, the *New York Times* and other newspapers were not paying much attention to abortion. The practice had been driven underground, but it was far from ended. Magazine articles occasionally discussed abortion and abortionists, and slowly the slant of personalization began to change. *Time* magazine in 1936 called the pro-abortion gynecologist Frederick Taussig "a handsome man" who performs "strict and meticulous clinical work."[42] Eight years later *Time* was more forthright, reporting that "one of the best abortionists in the U.S. went to jail last week." "Best" was not just a slip of the pen; *Time* called the imprisoned abortionist a "good practitioner."[43]

By the end of the 1950s, with sweeping changes in the religious and intellectual climate, and in attitudes of doctors and many journalists, pro-abortion forces could reemerge. Conferences installed the intellectual carpeting. Then the techniques of persistence and personalization were used to sell abortion. A typical *Newsweek* article on abortion in 1960 highlighted quotations by pro-abortionist Alan Guttmacher, described by the magazine as a "strong-faced outspoken crusader." An excerpt from Guttmacher's book, *Babies by Choice or by Chance*, appeared in the January 1960 *Reader's Digest.*[44]

The next step for pro-abortion personalization was television. In April 1962 the CBS show *The Defenders* aired an episode entitled "The Benefactor," with an abortionist as the hero of the title. This "benefactor" had become an abortionist not for profit

27, 1890, 8; October 1, 1890, 8; October 2, 1890, 9; October 3, 1890, 3; October 4, 1890, 1; October 16, 1890, 9.

42. *Time*, March 16, 1936, 52–54.

43. Ibid., March 6, 1944, 60. My thanks to Rick Rutledge, a student at the University of Texas, for uncovering the *Time* stories.

44. For these and more details on the pro-abortion movement of the 1950s and early 1960s, see an article written by Marvin and Susan Olasky, "The Selling of Abortion," in *Eternity*, January 1986, 20–24. See also Marvin Olasky, *The Press and Abortion, 1938–1988* (Hillsdale, NJ: Lawrence Erlbaum Associates, 1988), and Marvin Olasky, *Abortion Rites: A Social History of Abortion in America* (Washington, DC: Regnery Publishing, 1995).

but merely to help young women in trouble.[45] The idea that altruists could honorably kill unborn children was part of American popular culture. Shortly afterward, the Sherri Finkbine incident hit the headlines.

A Willingness to Give Offense

To combat the perverse equation of abortion and altruism, Christian journalists and allies have to be willing to give offense when needed. Some Christians are uncomfortable with attempts to shock readers by providing unpleasant descriptions of the abortion itself, and sometimes even "bloody pictures" of aborted infants. Many have discomfort about the plastering of abortionists' names on billboards. Attack the institution but not individuals, some say.

The history of effective crusading shows the importance of personalization. So does the work of the leading anti-abortion newspaper in the United States during the late twentieth century, the *National Right to Life News.* One issue provided examples of all four types of stories useful in a persistent crusade: bad news, good news, exposure of institutions, and exposure of individuals.[46]

The bad news story, "Murder Trial Set for Man Accused of Fatally Injuring Unborn Child," reported the follow-up to the death of a baby girl born prematurely after the accused man allegedly beat the baby's mother when she would not get an abortion. A California judge ordered the man to stand trial and rejected the defense attorney's motion to limit the charges to no more than second-degree murder.[47] This case seems like one

45. Ibid.
46. *National Right to Life News* is a published by the National Right to Life Committee and edited by Dave Andrusko (National Right to Life Committee, 512 10th St. NW, Washington, DC 20004). After many years operating as a biweekly print publication, it is now web-only: www.nationalrighttolifenews.org.
47. *NRL News*, December 18, 1986, 9.

taken almost directly out of Exodus 21:22–23. In those verses, if a man hits a pregnant woman and she gives birth prematurely but there is no serious injury, a fine is in order; but if there is serious injury, more severe penalties go into effect, even up to life for life.

The good news story was of an operation in which doctors opened a mother's womb by cesarean section, removed her baby for three minutes to correct a urinary tract infection, and put the baby back in the womb. Nine weeks later a healthy baby named Mitchell was born. Doctors did not publicize the operation until a year after it took place. By then, according to Mitchell's mother, the baby could "walk holding on to the couch and he smiles all the time. We've decided he's an angel."[48]

The institutional expose was of a cozy relationship between the most powerful pro-abortion group, Planned Parenthood, and the supposedly objective National Academy of Sciences. The Academy published a pro-abortion report, "Risking the Future." *NRL News* showed how the report came about. Planned Parenthood employees and allies "produced much of the 'research,' wrote the evaluation (of their own research), and critiqued their own findings and conclusions. Nice work, if you can get it."[49]

The individual expose was the most gripping story on the front page. "Malpractice Result of 'Burnout,' from 2,600 Second Trimester Abortions, Garrett Claims" told of a New Jersey abortionist who pleaded "no contest" to malpractice charges involving forty patients, including one fourteen-year-old girl who died. The abortionist, E. Wyman Garrett, blamed his action in the cases on stress caused by performing 20,000 abortions,

48. Ibid., 4. Fetal surgery outside the mother's womb raises one more set of provocative questions for pro-abortionists: Does it make sense that a baby, once outside, could be put back inside and then legally aborted? Can an unborn baby still be referred to by the dehumanizing name "fetus" when he has had his own doctor, his own medical records, even his own medical bills?

49. Ibid., 2, 9.

2,612 of which were dilation and evacuation (D&E) abortions done in the second trimester. (In a D&E, the unborn child is crushed and dismembered before being removed from the mother's womb.)[50]

In at least one case, Garrett allegedly left the head of an aborted baby in the woman's body. Another abortionist, testifying in Garrett's defense, said he "could have predicted" that Garrett would suffer burnout from doing abortions because most doctors who specialize in obstetrics and gynecology (as Garrett did) do so to be part of the "life and birth" process, making abortion—especially D&E abortions—stressful.[51]

Did *NRL News* lack compassion to spotlight one particular individual? Did nineteenth-century newspapers lack compassion when they hounded Madame Restell? First, we have to remember the mountain of tiny skulls on which abortionists stand. Second, we must pray for the abortionists. They also have souls which will never die, souls which are scarred anew when each abortion is performed. Trained to save life, they are taking it. They know, deep down, that what they do is wrong (Rom. 1:32).

The best thing that could have happened to Madame Restell would have been for her to stop doing abortions. She kept on, and ended up committing suicide. The best thing that could happen to today's abortionists, for their own good as well as for the good of children, would be for them to cross over from death to life, physically and spiritually. Newspapers that pressure them could aid in the process.

In any case, compassion is not the only question worth considering. Augustine's emphasis on truth-telling is fundamental to good reporting. While we are concerned about the ultimate fates of Madame Restell and E. Wyman Garrett, we cannot ne-

50. Ibid., 1.
51. Ibid., 11. "It is something that is not natural," *NRL News* reported the other abortionist as testifying. "You have to convince yourself intellectually that what you are doing is necessary because some patients need it."

glect truth and God's justice. The inspired author of 2 Kings did not write with gentleness of the death of Jezebel, Ahab's queen: "They threw her down. And some of her blood spattered the wall and on the horses, and they trampled on her." As Elijah had predicted, dogs quickly ate Jezebel's flesh: "When they went to bury her, they found no more of her than the skull and the feet and the palms of her hands" (2 Kings 9:33, 35).

From Specific to General: The Nature of Crusading

The four *NRL News* stories cited represent part of one issue. Every issue is full of specific detail and personalization, not sermonettes and abstraction. Some Christian publications that style themselves newspapers are not. They present opinion, sometimes well stated, but not much news. The essence of newspaper crusading, though, is news: showing, not just talking about, the evil amid us and the need for change.

The willingness to be specific, even if feelings are hurt, is based on some theological discernment. It is not enough for us to go around saying, "God loves you." He does, but Christ's sacrifice, the greatest love of all, can only be fully understood in terms of Adam's fall. Grace is a meaningless concept if sin is not taken seriously and condemned by journalists and others.

Crusading requires certain cautions, both in selection of issue—are we exposing something the Bible defines as evil, or just something we do not like?—and in method; carelessness may lead to ethical and legal problems, as indicated in the chapter 6 discussion of libel. Today's law allows some reporters to get away with character assassination, but Christians have a higher standard. A Christian journalistic crusader should never go to print unless his accusations are confirmed by the testimony of two witnesses.

Reporters must also remember that personalization is a dramatic technique; we should never think that if we depose one individual we have disposed of sin. Personalization, just like sensationalism, can be misused, if we do not remember that "all have sinned and fall short of the glory of God" (Rom. 3:23). God's holiness and God's redemptive love go together. Paul's verse of bad news is followed by the good news that we "are justified by his grace as a gift, through the redemption that is in Christ Jesus" (Rom. 3:24). Christian journalists who keep both verses in mind can avoid distortion while crusading.

This chapter gave examples of crusading against abortion, one manifestation of sin. The same principles of specific detail, persistence, and personalization may be applied journalistically in other social and political areas, and on economic issues as well. In every situation, it is vital to stress news rather than sermonettes, and to banish thoughts of easy victory.

13 A Christian Journalism Revival?

Technology provides the opportunity for a Christian comeback. Use of biblical sensationalism and crusading personalization will allow Christians to gain and keep an audience. But none of this will make much difference unless Christian communities view journalism as a vital calling and Christian journalists as ministers worthy of spiritual and economic support. Christian editors and reporters, after all, are like fish in a lake. Some Christian newspapers made mistakes in the nineteenth century, as indicated in chapter 1, but the lake itself was drying up fast.

The water level of Christian lakes appears to be rising. The environment for successful Christian publications earlier in American history was a Christian population willing to fight on social and political issues. Jolted by the atheism of many French revolutionaries and their American supporters, Christians resolved to publish rather than perish. Jolted in recent decades by similar revolutionary doctrines in modern wineskins, Christians are relearning what the *New York Times* proclaimed during its abortion campaign of the 1870s: "The evil that is tolerated is aggressive," and the good "must be aggressive too."[1]

In the mid-1980s, the Coalition on Revival (COR) was one of the aggressive groups affirming "that all Bible-believing Christians must take a non-neutral stance in opposing, praying

1. *New York Times*, November 3, 1870, 4.

261

against, and speaking against social moral evils." Among those evils listed were abortion, infanticide, and euthanasia; adultery and homosexuality; unjust treatment of the poor and disadvantaged; state usurpation of parental rights and God-given liberties; and atheism, moral relativism, and evolutionism taught as a monopoly viewpoint in public schools.

Crucially, COR's statement included admissions of sin: "We have neglected our God-ordained duties to be the world's salt, light, teacher, and example. . . . We, and our fathers, have settled for a sub-standard, false version of Christianity in our local churches and denominations. . . . We have allowed our churches to become irrelevant, powerless ghettos."

The statement asked for forgiveness by God, fellow Christians, and, significantly, non-Christians: "Forgive us for our failure to demonstrate to you biblical answers for your difficulties and problems in life. Forgive us for failing to occupy our proper position as servants in the affairs of law government, economics, business, education, media, the arts, medicine, and science as the Creator's salt and light to the world, so that those spheres of life might offer you more help, justice, hope, peace, and joy."

COR's Call to Action proclaimed several truths essential to the revival of Christian journalism: "We affirm that living under the total Lordship of Jesus Christ in every area of life is not optional for those who would call themselves Christians." Furthermore, we cannot be smiling all the time: COR stressed the "need for loving confrontation over matters of falsehood and unrighteousness in the Church and in the world." Regular confrontation, exhortation, and rebuke are vital to the leading of biblically obedient lives and the transforming of culture.[2]

Other Christian organizations also are speaking out forcefully, and sometimes effectively. Focus on the Family, founded in

2. *A Manifesto for the Christian Church: Declaration and Covenant*, July 4, 1986 (Mountain View, CA: Coalition on Revival, 1986).

1977, has grown into a behemoth that owes much of its success to sophisticated use of radio, with a daily program that often features interviews with newsmakers. It has a monthly magazine, *Citizen*, and other daily and weekly radio features that air on Christian radio stations around the country.

In the 1980s, Focus on the Family leaders realized that many of the issues it cared about had a public policy component, so it was instrumental in the formation of the Family Research Council and the Alliance Defense Fund (now called Alliance Defending Freedom). These organizations attempt to influence public policy, including federal legislation, both on Capitol Hill and in the nation's courtrooms. State legislatures often decide important public policy issues such as abortion and same-sex marriage. So Focus was instrumental in the formation of state-level Family Policy Councils. Today, more than thirty states have such organizations, and many of them have radio programs and monthly publications.

A recent and perhaps the most direct descendant of the statement issued by the Coalition on Revival is the Manhattan Declaration. The Manhattan Declaration, first published in 2010, has since been signed by more than five hundred thousand people. This document provides a robust philosophical justification for action by Christians to uphold the sanctity of life, biblical marriage, and religious liberty.

Some within the church are offended by such efforts. Jesus, though, said to his followers, "Do not think that I have come to bring peace to the earth. I have not come to bring peace, but a sword" (Matt. 10:34). Christians may be sure of peace in heaven and peace in our consciences, but peace in our worldly dealings is rare.

The sword brought by Christ is twofold: the sword of the Word eventually conquers (Rev. 19:21), but until then God's truth often provokes such a hostile reaction among non-Christians

that they apply the sword to believers. This effect of the preaching of the gospel is not the fault of the gospel, but of those who
do not receive it. Because of this backlash effect, it is a mistake
to think Christianity preserves its followers from trouble in
this world. Becoming a Christian is not the end of the battle,
but the real beginning.

The battle record of some established Christian publications
is not good. Some now are public relations vehicles for their
organizations, denominations, or peculiar beliefs. Some seem
devoted largely to keeping up appearances and smiles. Editors
who try to wield the sword on controversial issues sometimes
have found that readers and contributors have exceptionally
thin skins.

One of the pioneers in the revival of Christian journalism
is the *Minnesota Christian Examiner.* Founded in 1978 as the *Twin
Cities Christian (TCC)*, a biweekly newspaper, it is now a monthly
tabloid with a circulation of twenty thousand, considerable
advertising, and front-page coverage of issues that "soil the
breakfast cloth." For example, *TCC* gave front-page coverage to
a liberal church's sponsorship of a program for sex offenders
designed to help them "in the most important area of their lives,
that of intimacy." To show what those nice words really meant,
the story quoted charges from a responsible source that the
program included use of explicit films showing masturbation,
intercourse with animals, and a variety of homosexual acts—
the goal of the program apparently being not a consideration of
right and wrong, but how-to training. The program concluded
with a worship service featuring a pastor and his wife dressed
as clowns. One clown wore huge glasses with obscene words
written on the lenses.[3]

TCC went to bat for Christians facing discrimination. One
headline stretching across the top of the front page read, "Chris-

3. *Twin Cities Christian*, February 15, 1983, 1.

tian Students Suspended." According to the story's lead, "They weren't selling drugs, skipping class, or damaging school property. They didn't brawl in the halls or smoke in the bathroom. But last Thursday two Hopkins School seniors were suspended from classes." The students were "handing out religious literature. Their action violated a school board policy." The story explained that the students had deliberately handed out free copies of a Christian magazine before classes began in order to test the school board policy: "We need to fight for our rights," one student said.[4]

TCC used biblically sensational headlines in coverage of stories involving such abridgment of First Amendment rights. "Bible-reading Grandma Kicked out of Mall" was the headline on a story of a grandmother talking with a young man about the Bible as they sat in a shopping mall rest area. A security guard falsely accused the woman of selling religious literature, and escorted her off the mall property with orders not to return again.[5] When the Bible-reading grandma protested and *TCC* investigated the incident, the mall management backed down. "I'm not resentful," she said, "but people need to be warned about how our rights as Christians to worship God in public—even just reading a Bible—are being taken away from us." A loss of such rights can be more readily opposed when Christian journalists are present to blow the whistle.[6]

TCC also exposed Christians or Christian organizations engaged in unethical activity. The lead story in one issue

4. Ibid., April 12, 1984, 1.

5. Ibid., April 24, 1986, 3.

6. *Twin Cities Christian* also has reported the more severe intrusions on religious liberty that prevail in other countries. One front-page story, "Christian Woman Interrogated by KGB at Moscow Airport," told of a woman who "will never forget Mother's Day 1985. On that day she was arrested at Moscow airport, interrogated for more than six hours, strip-searched and later expelled from the Soviet Union. Her crime? Wanting to give gifts to Russian Christians—Bibles, copies of the Sermon on the Mount, Christian music tapes and clothing" (July 4, 1985, 1).

concerned an evangelist accused of faking miracles at healing crusades for his own purposes. An editorial criticized a local Christian television organization for soliciting funds but not providing information on how the money was being spent. Other stories decried the fundraising tactics of some Christian organizations.[7]

Founding editor Doug Trouten (now a professor of journalism at Northwestern College in St. Paul, Minnesota, and a former executive director of the Evangelical Press Association) defended his policy in a spirited editorial, "Why Write Bad Things About Good People?" He raised in print the questions he had been asked: "When a ministry folds and its leaders leave town with its assets, why report it? When the leader of a ministry dependent on donations seems to live in unnecessary opulence, why tell the world? When an elected official strays from the Christian principles that were a part of campaign rhetoric, does somebody need to blow the whistle?"[8]

Trouten noted that "the Christian press often becomes a willing partner in efforts to cover up wrong-doing by religious leaders," and argued that "this mentality runs contrary to Scriptural teaching. . . . Too often we are content to ignore unpleasant truths. Yet as Christians we worship a God of truth. We're not asked to follow our leaders blindly. The Bible says, 'I would not have you ignorant . . .' and 'My people are destroyed for lack of knowledge.' We need to know about those who lead us."[9] Today, the Minnesota Christian Examiner continues to provide knowledge. Current editor Scott Noble recently featured an initiative by Twin Cities churches to help the area's homeless teens—and highlighted the challenges churches face in dealing with governmental and secular nonprofit organizations.[10]

7. Ibid., May 8, 1986, 1; August 29, 1985, 18.
8. Ibid., May 9, 1985, 18.
9. Ibid.
10. Scott Noble, "Churches, Groups Come Together To Help Homeless Teens," *Minnesota Christian Examiner*, November 2012.

The original *Twin Cities Christian Chronicle* spawned many imitators, including the Christian Examiner chain of newspapers that purchased the Minnesota paper and changed its name in 2007. The *Christian Examiner* Newspaper Group now has six regional papers with a combined circulation of more than 180,000, making it the largest Christian newspaper group in the United States.

The owner of the *Christian Examiner* Newspaper Group, Lamar Keener, also plays a leadership role in the Association of Christian Newspapers (ACN), a group of about fifty newspapers with a combined circulation approaching one million. One of the oldest and best of the ACN papers is the *Kansas City Metro Voice*, started in 1988 and also inspired in part by the *Twin Cities Christian*. According to founding publisher Dwight Widaman, "We've grown from a table-top publication produced on a makeshift light table and the smell of burned wax of an old copy waxer, to a regional publication with two editions, state-of-the-art Apple computers and full color publication serving over 100,000 readers across two states."[11]

Widaman's publication is still "mom-and-pop" in the most literal sense of the word: The only employees are Widaman and his wife Anita, who after writing, editing, and laying out the publication, also help distribute the paper to more than 1,100 churches every month. But the paper makes good use of a large stable of freelance writers and goes well beyond cheerleading for Christian causes. The April 2012 issue had an article on Christians dealing with depression, and a profile of a Kansas teacher's organization that is a conservative alternative to the liberal National Education Association.[12]

11. Interview with author, September 2012.

12. Tim Challies, "Many Devoted Christians Get Depressed Sometimes Too"; Carolyn Cogswell, "Kansas Teacher Organization Offers Alternative to NEA." Both articles are from the April 2012 *Kansas City Metro Voice*.

These newspapers, in addition to the good work they do themselves, have left a legacy as a training ground for Christian journalists. At least two former editors of local Christian newspapers now work for *WORLD*.

Other examples of Christian journalism have emerged in recent years. Salem Communications is the largest Christian radio company in the nation. Unlike many other Christian broadcasters, Salem is a for-profit company whose stock is publicly traded. It owns about one hundred radio stations and produces hourly news broadcasts carried by more than three hundred stations nationwide. Salem Web Network includes more than a dozen news and information websites and claims to have more than one hundred million page views per month.

Despite the efforts and good work of the people mentioned in this section, we must also admit that such efforts are a mere drop in a very large bucket. Most regional Christian newspapers do not employ full-time journalists beyond the owners themselves. The news operation of Salem Communications, the largest Christian radio network in the country, is a fraction of the size of the news department of a big-city daily newspaper. It will take much more money and many more people to bring about the true revival in Christian journalism that is badly needed.

And likely much more sacrifice and courage. That's why more Christians should take lessons from a Kentucky editor of the 1840s, the original Cassius Clay. (Muhammed Ali was named after him, but showed his theology by making a change.)

The original Clay, born in 1810, was a Christian who published an antislavery newspaper in Kentucky. When proslavery partisans threatened to destroy Clay's printing press, he made a fort out of his three-story, red-brick newspaper office. Clay purchased two small brass cannons, loaded them to the muzzle with bullets, slugs, and nails, and stationed them at the entrance, while his friends stockpiled muskets and Mexican lances.

Those measures forestalled the attack. Then Clay took the fight to the opposition, going before hostile crowds to speak his piece. Once, facing his enemies, Clay held up a Bible and said, "To those who respect God's word, I appeal to this book." Then he held up a copy of the Constitution and said, "To those who respect our fundamental law I appeal to this document." Then he took out two pistols and his Bowie knife. He said, "To those who recognize only force . . ."[13]

Clay survived many fights and assassination attempts. Finally, he was seized by proslavery men and knifed. Gushing blood from a lung wound, Clay cried out, "I died in the defense of the liberties of the people," and then lost consciousness. He recovered, though, and helped to form the Republican Party during the 1850s. He had many political successes and personal adventures until he died in 1903 at age 93.

The secret of Clay's strength may have been his belief in the power of God's law and personal faith. Clay saw evenhandedness in the Bible: the rich should help the poor, and the poor should not envy or steal from the rich. Clay wrote, "Let true Christianity prevail, and earth will become the foreshadowing of Heaven." Clay also knew there is no neutrality in journalism. Knowing that all people, whether Christian or non-Christian, interpret the world through religious first principles, Clay openly acknowledged his beliefs and showed the willingness to fight for them.

The situation is a bit different now. In our daily business activities we can leave the Bowie knives home. Yet, the sword brought by Christ still flashes, and we need to be prepared to fight with our brains, pens, and computers. What keeps us from readiness to fight, often, is fear both obvious and subtle. Fear of ridicule and fear of audience are obvious problems; fear of

13. For this and the following, see Clay's autobiography, *The Life of Cassius Marcellus Clay* (Cincinnati: J. Fletcher Brennan and Co., 1886), and an essay he wrote, *Appeal of Cassius M. Clay to Kentucky and the World* (Boston: Macomber and Pratt, 1845). My thanks to the University of Kentucky library for allowing me access to several rare biographies.

distraction and, most crucially, fear of the Bible itself are the covert cripplers among Christians.

The Four Fears and Their Effect upon Journalism

How should we stand up to fear? First, Christian journalists must not be afraid of boldly stating the Christian view of reality, which includes both material and spiritual dimensions. We must subdue our fear of what materialistic colleagues will think of us, not only because of the realization that Christ has come with a sword, but because the biblical emphasis on truth-telling is fundamental to Christian journalism.

Some materialists will be tolerant of religious belief as long as it is privatized and equated with subjectivity: if it makes you feel good, believe it. Some also argue that heaven, if such a place exists, must be an equal-opportunity employer. Christians, though, know that subjective feelings are ephemeral. We need to gain an accurate picture of the cosmos and then act accordingly, or else we are lost.

The Bible always emphasizes reporting of what actually happened. Luke began his Gospel by writing, "Since I myself have carefully investigated everything from the beginning, it seemed good also to me to write an orderly account . . . so that you may know the certainty of the things you have been taught" (Luke 1:3–4 NIV). Paul told the Corinthians they should not believe in the doctrine of Christ's resurrection because it might be comforting for some. The important question was, did it happen? Paul insisted that either Christ rose from the dead or Christian hope is in vain. The entire book of Revelation is simply John's obedience to Jesus' command to "write what you see in a book and send it to the seven churches" (Rev. 1:11) We often describe the Bible as history, poetry, law, and story. It is all of these things, but much of it is careful, credible journalism. In short, when a Christian reports spiritual happenings as fact, not subjective impression, he will be ridiculed by some. That is the price to pay for worshiping the God who really is there, not just a psychologically soothing idol.

Second, Christian journalists must not be afraid of audience. We should not turn inward or be willing to accept a journalistic strategy that churches might find pleasant but the world will ignore. We should not be afraid of picking from the best of the methods of journalism, while always evaluating all means and ends in the light of God's Word (2 Cor. 10:5).

After all, the authors of the Gospels knew how to produce the same message but with different emphases for those with different backgrounds. Paul, in speaking to the Athenians, was willing to make contact with them by pointing out their worship of an unknown God (Acts 17). A successful Christian journalist must similarly attract attention in order to affect intentions.

Third, Christians must not fear that a new emphasis on journalism will distract from either concern for evangelism or the godly education of those already within the church. That concern is shortsighted, since both evangelism and education become more difficult when both non-Christians and Christians are bombarded by messages on "nonreligious" matters that assume materialism is true. Christian journalism is therefore vital pre-evangelistic work, needed to prepare individuals to accept the reality of God's grace.

Christian journalism also is postjustification work, helping those who have received God's grace to construct godly lives. It's important to remember that the Great Commission does not say we are to make converts. It says we are to "make disciples," teaching "all that I have commanded you" (Matt. 28:18–20). Christian journalists can play a central role in this disciple-making process.

Fourth, and most subtle of all, is the reluctance even among some Christians to acknowledge that all created things, including our own minds, are twisted by sin (Gen. 3:17–19; Rom. 8:20–22). Our minds are not capable of creating a sound set of guidelines from either observation or pure reason. Our only hope lies in learning biblical principles of thought and conduct, and trusting the Holy Spirit to help us make the right practical applications.

The Bible teaches that thought independent of God's special revelation is untrustworthy at best and eventually suicidal. Only the Word of God can give us principles for establishing a life pleasing to God. This vital concept is hard to swallow in a society with strong belief in existentialist creativity: individuals supposedly develop new ideas and ways of conduct *ex nihilo*, as if they were gods unto themselves. The Bible, though, stresses God as Creator and man as image bearer. We cannot create virtue or virtuous ideas apart from God's thoughts.

Sometimes, in short, Christians confronted by tough problems are afraid of biblical truth. Why not abortion when there has been rape? Why not divorce when husband and wife fight? Why write a story that could lose the journalist his job? There are biblical answers to such questions, but they require hard analytical and practical work. Sometimes even Christians fear the Bible because it does not give comfortable answers.

A Two-Pronged Strategy

If the four fears are overcome, Christian journalists will be strong enough, and will be receiving sufficient community support, to ask another question: Where can I best serve God? Some may now have a tendency to choose working at publications or media outlets owned and operated by Christians because those positions seem "safer," removed from contact with the world. A Christian journalistic revival, though, would mean that no place would be safe. Christian journalistic organizations would be aggressively reporting on the contrast between man's depravity and God's holiness, and non-Christian organizations would be prime mission fields.

Christian journalists sometimes seem tempted into arguments about whether explicitly Christian or secular media represent better alternatives for service. Such debates can be equivalent to Jesus' disciples squabbling about primacy on earth and seating arrangements in heaven. As bad as many public schools are today, a tough-minded, tenacious Christian teacher in the classroom can still be a Godsend to children. Similar considerations apply in journalism, where the influence of one person may be even more widespread.

Strong Christian publications and stations are vital, but salty Christians also are needed within today's influential, non-Christian media systems. As stories with overt theological dimensions continue to arise, and as the more subtle stories influenced by presuppositions cross newsroom desks, Christian reporters and editors should be at those desks and willing to speak up.

Christians in non-Christian media organizations can also serve as counselors and evangelists. Not only do the major media institutions have great power, but the individuals within them often have great problems. If we were to bring forward in time the series of mini-biographies in chapter 3, we would see that many apparently secure contemporary journalists desperately need help. Smiling anchormen and -women often are off-camera wrecks.

Christians who have thought through the nature of objectivity and sensationalism, and the ethical and legal problems of the field, can glorify God within such media outposts. Nor do well-prepared Christians necessarily have to choose between mealy-mouthedness and unemployment. As the discussions of objectivity and sensationalism in chapters 4 and 11 indicated, Christians do not have to *preach* in stories. Instead, Christians

273

can work toward honest selection of details, fair and ample quotation of biblical Christian spokesmen, and examination of the spiritual/material interface.

Still, a Christian reporter should realize that even a small movement toward true objectivity might anger an atheistic editor. In such circumstances, firmness is essential. As soon as a worldview conflict becomes apparent, Christian journalists working for non-Christians have to decide which of two roads to potential success to follow: the way of the tough and talented Christian, or the path of the presuppositional sycophant. These two roads tend to divide early. A reporter who writes of fundamentalists with appropriate sarcasm will be praised; a reporter who quotes not only Darwinian scientists but creation scientists will be questioned. And yet, a skilled reporter will have some value to his editors even if he refuses to play the game. He may not receive fast promotions, but he will not necessarily be fired, for real talent is in short supply.

The danger of slow career progress is clear. Yet, the prayer that Christ gives us as a model includes the sentence, "Give us this day our daily bread" (Matt. 6:11). The sentence is not, "Give us this day our daily steak." Nor is it, "Give us this day our daily starvation." We need bread: good, healthy sustenance, both material and spiritual. If a Christian's career is not as visibly spectacular—at least in the short run—as that of a person who is crafty and corrupt, that is a relatively small cross to bear.

Christians working for unsympathetic employers can make some practical intellectual and financial preparations while they are on the job. A Christian journalist must know that a news organization is not a home. We are wayfarers and sojourners here on this earth generally, and in newspapers or broadcast stations specifically. If God's providence has put the Christian in a high-paying job, he must immediately calculate what he needs to live on, not what he is temporarily able to live on. Any extra money is a special gift from God and should not be squandered. Some of that money might support the journalist if he is forced to resign. Furthermore, the goal should always be to develop skills that will allow the Christian to become his own boss, if the possibility arises. For, in the long run, Christian journalists will need Christian publications.

In that long run, it is clear that only news organizations owned and staffed by Christians will be able to practice journalism consistent with strong biblical faith. Only through independence can Christians make sure that the Bible is taken seriously in journalism.

That's why we think *WORLD* magazine, founded in 1987, is significant. *WORLD*, with a paid circulation of about one hundred thousand, is the most-read news magazine from a Christian perspective. With the 2012 demise of *Newsweek* as a print publication (it will exist on the web only), it is now one of the largest news magazines of any kind—Christian or secular. It also has a robust digital presence. It launched its website, www.worldmag.com, in 1997, and that first year had only a few thousand page views. By 2013, the site had two million page views a month.

One of the characteristics of *WORLD* that sets it apart from other distinctively Christian publications is its commitment to reporting outside the "Christian ghetto." Publications such as *Christianity Today* and *Charisma*, and online news sites such as the *Christian Post*, are all good in their own ways, but they mostly limit themselves to Christian or religious news. *WORLD* takes its Christian distinctives at least as seriously as do these publications, but *WORLD*'s beat is what its name implies: the world. On the masthead of every issue of *WORLD* is Psalm 24:1: "The earth is the LORD's and the fullness thereof, the world and those who dwell therein." Dutch theologian, statesman, and journalist Abraham Kuyper famously put it this way: "There is not a thumb's width of creation over which Christ does not say, 'Mine.'"

WORLD differs from secular media not so much in the events it covers but in how it covers them, with biblical objectivity. Here's the logic: Since God created and sustains the world, he knows the true, objective nature of his creation. The book he inspired, the Bible, presents the only objective and accurate view of the world. Journalists, therefore, should try to see the world as much in biblical terms as our fallen and sinful natures allow. The closer we get to the biblical view, the closer we'll get to objectivity.

Another characteristic that sets WORLD apart is its willingness to do independent journalism. We began this book with a discussion of the Jim and Tammy Bakker scandal, and noted that WORLD, a fledgling publication when that scandal broke, did not have the resources to cover it as founder Joel Belz thought it should. But that lost opportunity steeled the resolve of Belz and subsequent writers and editors. In 1997, WORLD published what is perhaps its most famous cover story, an expose of a major Christian publisher's efforts to bring out a gender-neutral translation of the Bible. The publisher, Zondervan, ultimately withdrew the Bible—and withdrew its advertising from WORLD at a time when the magazine was not financially healthy. Nonetheless, founder Joel Belz called the episode "WORLD's finest hour."[14]

WORLD has had other fine hours on subjects outside of the church. The magazine critically investigated plans to nationalize health care and pass out needles to drug addicts while harassing Christian anti-addiction programs. WORLD exposed Fidel Castro's license to kill and Chinese Communist use of U.S. technology to force women into aborting their children. It opposed the Clinton administration's booting of Christian homeless missions from the federal surplus food program, but it also criticized corporate welfare and crony capitalism.

14. Interviews with Joel Belz, 2012.

WORLD also exposed evangelical leaders who used ghost-writers without acknowledging them, pastors who were silent about abortion, ministries that refused to disclose their finances, Christian counselors who preferred psychobabble to the Bible, CCM musicians who dished out sugar rather than sprinkling salt, a popular radio personality who dealt in exaggeration, and a popular pastor who moved toward divorce while continuing to preach. *WORLD* publisher and founder Joel Belz acknowledged regarding that last story, "A number of readers have argued that we had no business mentioning the story at all," but said we were right to cover it for "it is a clear biblical principle that to whom much is given, much is required. . . . Such people are to be 'above reproach.' "[15]

WORLD criticized the left in stories like "Sex, lies, and audio-tape: Undercover tapes reveal that Planned Parenthood may be aiding and abetting statutory rapists." But the magazine also criticized the Bush administration for its inertia in fighting sex trafficking. In 2003 *WORLD* published a cover story headlined "It's not about hate, it's about debate: A U.S.-based Muslim public-relations group works hard to silence critics of Islam." But it also knocked the Bush administration for hassling Teen Challenge groups and ineffectively emphasizing bednets rather than insecticides in fighting African malaria.[16]

Editors preferred accentuating the positive through *WORLD*'s annual Hope Award for Effective Compassion, its Daniel of the Year award for Christian courage, and its Book of the Year awards, or its stories about marriages that have lasted for at least thirty-five years. But it also maintained the emphasis on exposing corruption that animated John Zenger in 1735 and many other Christians before and since.

15. Joel Belz, "About Accountability," *WORLD Magazine*, March 23, 1996.
16. All stories archived at www.worldmag.com. Search on key words.

Conclusion

Joshua in his old age told the Israelites, "Choose this day whom you will serve." The Israelites then promised they would obey God, for they had learned that "it was the LORD our God who brought us and our fathers up from the land of Egypt, out of the house of slavery, and who did those great signs in our sight and preserved us in all the way that we went, and among all the peoples through whom we passed" (Josh. 24:15, 17). The education of the Israelites, through God's grace, had enabled them to see events as they really occurred, with both material and spiritual dimensions.

Throughout the Bible, God's spokesmen and reporters constantly tried to explain to their listeners and readers the reality of his involvement in human history. Moses told the Israelites: "You have seen all that the LORD did before your eyes in the land of Egypt, to Pharaoh and to all his servants and to all his land, the great trials that your eyes saw, the signs, and those great wonders. But to this day the LORD has not given you a heart to understand or eyes to see or ears to hear" (Deut. 29:2–4). Seeing was not believing; reporters had to provide context, and then pray for God's grace on eyes and ears. Psalm 78 reported "the glorious deeds of the LORD," and Stephen testified before the Sanhedrin to God's continued working in human history (Acts 7).

Christian journalism, as history's first draft, should follow the Bible in depicting God's grace and man's sinfulness. Non-Christian journalism has led to attempts to make people happy, either by suggesting that things are right (the position of some non-Christian conservatives) or that man by his egotistical efforts can make all things right (the position of some liberals). Christians, though, know that things are not right, due to original sin, and will be made right only through Christ: "he is before all things, and in him all things hold together" (Col. 1:17).

"Be strong and courageous," God commands Joshua repeatedly. Avoidance of the four fears, through the strength and courage that only God can give, is vital for Christian journalists.

If Christians are willing to cover all aspects of life, to soil the breakfast table, to deal honestly with evil, to avoid intellectual trendiness, to meet communication demands of a fast-paced marketplace, to hit hard in a compassionate way that does not libel individuals—then we have done as much as we can, and we can pray with clear consciences for God to grant us success.

If Christians are willing to report faithfully that God is sovereign, that Satan is active but under control, that man pursues evil by nature but can be transformed, and that God does answer prayers in the way that is best for our growth in grace—then, with God's grace, Christians will have the most insightful and exciting news publications and programs in the United States.

Gloria in excelsis Deo.

Appendix 1
The Best of the Worst: Examples of Media Bias

The overwhelming majority of examples of media bias in this book come from 1988 or before. However, media bias didn't end then. In fact, it has accelerated. Documenting every example would be both impossible and—after a certain point—not very helpful.

However, Marvin Olasky has served as a judge for each of the past twenty-five years that the Media Research Center has produced an annual list of the worst examples of media bias. For many of those years, he's written a column for *WORLD* about that list. What follows are abridged versions of these columns, highlighting "the best of the worst" examples of media bias over the years.[1]

1996

First, instead of waiting to report facts, leading journalists frequently prejudged them. Newsweek's Eleanor Clift on February 10 said, "If Ken Starr is a credible prosecutor he will bring this to a conclusion and the Clintons will be exonerated." Even after Mr. Starr gained convictions, NBC's Jim Miklaszewski referred to "high-profile political witch hunts," and CBS's

---

1. These columns are archived at www.worldmag.com/topics/bias.

Dan Rather spoke of President Clinton "tied down as Gulliver was by the Lilliputians, by all this scandal investigation, ethics investigations that are bound to be unsuccessful."

Second, instead of trying to describe fairly what conservatives were trying to do, journalists frequently treated them the way medieval anti-Semites treated Jews. Time's Margaret Carlson said Republicans thought they had a mandate for "poisoning the water, tainting the meat, removing all these regulations." CNN's Bill Schneider was impressed to find in Jack Kemp "a rare combination—a nice conservative. These days conservatives are supposed to be mean. They're supposed to be haters."

Third, while most mediacrats avoided too-obvious bigotry, occasionally their view of the world became clear. Bonnie Erbe of NBC Radio/Mutual Broadcasting on August 16 said the Republican convention was appearing to be "pro-woman, pro-minorities," but "this is in sharp contrast to the delegates on the floor, 60 percent of whom are self-identified as conservative Christians." In media fantasies conservative Christians apparently are antiminority and antiwoman, in part because they oppose abortion, even though black babies are far more likely than white babies to be killed before birth, and even though abortion is more popular among men than among women.

Selection of heroes and villains also indicated typical Washington media mindsets. Hillary Clinton was a feminist heroine, and those who criticized her showed "pathological fear of Hillary and any other uppity woman," according to CBS. Al Gore was portrayed as an intellectual giant: Newsweek's Bill Turque described on September 2 what Gore "really loves: thinking about complexity theory, open systems, Goethe, and the absence of scientific metaphors in modern society."

The villains were conservative Republicans, responsible according to Time for the torching of some black churches, and talk radio hosts, who this year were once again linked by NBC's Bryant Gumbel and others to the Oklahoma City bombing. Christians who decried life in the fast lane were insufficiently tolerant, as was Bob Dole, whenever he showed mean-spiritedness by mentioning White House corruption.

Washington reporters' greatest wrath, however, was reserved for one of their own who bravely emerged as a whistle-blower: Bernard Goldberg of CBS stated in February that charges of liberal bias were "blatantly true. . . . [W]e don't sit around in dark corners and plan strategies on how we're going to slant the news. We don't have to. It comes naturally to most reporters." CBS News correspondent Bob Schieffer responded, "People are just stunned. It's such a wacky charge. . . . I don't know what Bernie was driving at. It just sounds bizarre."

The most bizarre defense of press evenhandedness came from *Time*'s Margaret Carlson, who on July 3—responding to a Freedom Forum poll showing that 89 percent of Washington reporters voted for Bill Clinton in 1992—said that her colleagues were not biased because some could bring themselves to vote for Republicans like Christie Whitman or William Weld (both of whom are pro-abortion).

1997

Time senior writer Richard Lacayo's October 27 sow's-ear-to-silk-purse analysis of the Clinton fundraising tapes: "Put aside for a moment the questions about what was illegal and what was just unseemly, and the overall effect is oddly comforting. If nothing else, the tapes prove that the most powerful nation on earth can operate on autopilot while the president chases campaign money."

Vice President Gore also avoided treatment as a Nixon-like rascal to be run out of town. Instead, *U.S. News* senior writer Timothy Noah fitted him out as a major thinker: "Gore's commitment to the world of big ideas is no pose. Unlike John F. Kennedy and

Adlai Stevenson, who became darlings of the highbrow set without fully earning the honor, Gore is truly engaged in the life of the mind." *Time* columnist Margaret Carlson asked on September 6, "Who would ever have thought that you doubt the probity of Vice President Al Gore?" Then she minimized his responsibility and said, "the system is corrupting people."

The villains, on the other hand, showed moral culpability. Newt Gingrich is "like Lenin," according to ABC's Sam Donaldson. "They both made a revolution by shooting people—Newt shot Democrats, Lenin shot everybody—and then they didn't have enough sense to stop shooting once they won." Republican congressional leaders, according to Robert Scheer in the *Los Angeles Times*, "would rather kill people than raise taxes."

Journalists also reminisced about oldies but goodies like "prescient" George McGovern, praised by *USA Today* founder Al Neuharth in his June 20 column: "What if Watergate had elected McGovern? . . . The Cold War would have ended in the '70s rather than in the '90s." (Neuharth is right, but the United States would have lost the war.) On October 1 *Los Angeles Times* reporter Elizabeth Mehren wrote about Anita Hill: "So, she was asked, does she sometimes feel like the Joan of Arc of sexual harassment? Sure, Hill replied, and here came the mirth the Senate never saw: 'I refuse to die, though.'" (Play the laugh track, quickly.)

Some media folks even showed nostalgia for communism. *CBS This Morning* cohost Jane Robelot reported on March 24, concerning barely hanging-on Cuba, "Under Cuba's communist form of government, a Cuban family's basic necessities, housing, education, health care, and transportation, are provided by the state for free or at very little cost." On October 2, Robin Wright of the *Los Angeles Times* looked at many countries and mourned "the transition from socialist governments, which sought to develop female as well as male proletariats. As those governments died, so went the socialist ideals of equality and the subsidies for social programs that aided women. In many countries, traditional patriarchal cultures resurfaced."

Headline comparisons are instructive. The *Los Angeles Times* on July 17 reported, "CIA Agent Says He Gave Huang Classified Data," and the *New York Times* that same day ran its headline, "CIA Officer Says His Briefings for Huang Were Simply Routine." We have a problem if classified information is passed on during routine briefings. *Newsweek*'s Jonathan Alter may have a deeper problem, judging by his recollection of models of missiles displayed at "one military meeting during the 1980s. . . . The American power phalluses were long and white; the Soviets', shorter and black. We were still safely ahead, but only by the margin of our machismo."

The deepest problem of all, however, may be that of Washington journalism generally: how the mighty have fallen! Think of the *Washington Post* twenty-five years ago as it exposed the Watergate cover up with some terrific investigative reporting and aggressive questioning. Then look at this question from *Washington Post* reporters to President Clinton, in an interview published January 19: "There's been a lot of talk lately, as you know, printed and so forth, about the Lincoln Bedroom and the people who stay here. And obviously a lot of them are your friends. And I don't think anybody would begrudge somebody having guests in their own house. Some of them, though, it seems apparently you didn't know quite as well. And we're wondering if you might feel let down a little bit by your staff or by the DNC in their zeal to raise funds?" That tame and lame line of questioning is a worthy contender for Embarrassment of the Year.

1999

Each year liberal journalists, instead of honestly acknowledging their liberalism, describe themselves as Dan Rather defined himself in an exchange on CNN's *Crossfire* on June 24: "an honest broker of information" whose motto is "play no favorites." But on May 26, Rather himself gushed about Hillary Clinton's "political lightning" and how she is a "crowd-pleaser." (Which crowd?)

I've seen repeatedly how the most influential newspapers play favorites while pretending to be objective. Ted Kennedy, according to *New York Times* reporter Adam Clymer, "deserves recognition not just as the leading Senator of his time but also as one of the greats in the history of this singular institution." Janet Reno, according to Juan Williams of the *Washington Post*, is approaching "Abe Lincoln status. People just assume she's honest, honest Janet Reno." (Which people?)

Mrs. Clinton won the most media plaudits this year, with Diane Sawyer one of many who crooned about her "political mastery." *Time*'s Lance Morrow swooned: "I see a sort of Celtic mist forming around Hillary as a new archetype (somewhere between Eleanor and Evita, transcending both) at a moment when the civilization pivots, at last, decisively—perhaps for the first time since the advent of Christian patriarchy two millenniums ago—toward Woman."

The worst bad guys made their appearance early in the year. According to *Newsweek*'s Eleanor Clift, the House managers who tried to convince senators that the impeached Bill Clinton should be convicted were like Ku Klux Klan "night riders," and "all they were missing was white sheets." A *New York Times* story about the impeachment trial opened with an analysis by psychotherapist Ellen Mendel of how she "feels the same despair that she did as a girl in Nazi Germany."

Each year those who parrot press attitudes receive lots of air time, but journalistic ventriloquism was never more evident than when Peter Jennings opened this year's February 4 *World News Tonight* by choosing one man to represent all. "We begin tonight with the voice of the people from the Senate gallery today," Jennings intoned, describing a spectator during the impeachment trial who had to be removed for yelling, "Take the vote and get it over with."

Newsweek's key players regularly identified their own preferred positions with those of "the people" or with wisdom generally. Eleanor Clift praised "Northeastern Republicans" who split off from their southern colleagues, showing "the aspect of the party that's still in touch with the people." (Which people?) Similarly, Jonathan Alter called a tax cut "one of the most irresponsible pieces of legislation to come down the pike in a long time. . . . Every economist of all stripes [sic] knows that it's just totally irresponsible!" (Many conservative economists favored the cut, but if they don't accept the conventional wisdom, maybe they don't count as economists.)

Time's Margaret Carlson did Alter one better. She attacked tax cuts as not only "irresponsible" but stupid: "The only thing that could explain this love of tax cuts is a lowered IQ." (Talking about IQ, here is her explanation of why tax cuts are a waste: "If I get $100 back, I can't go fix a school or clean a river.") In general, those who deviated from liberalism were either stupid or evil. On foreign policy, journalists labeled critiques of the Clinton kiss-up-to-China policy "witch hunts" (*Newsweek*'s Evan Thomas) or replays of McCarthyism (*Time*'s Tony Karon).

Never say that journalists don't have a sense of history. Ignoring all the revelations of John F. Kennedy's hyper-philandering, *Today* cohost Katie Couric wrote about "those golden years" of the Kennedy administration. But when tragedy ruined restoration hopes, *Newsweek*'s Alter wrote of John F. Kennedy Jr., "He was more than our 'Prince Charming,' as the New York tabs called him. We etched the past and the future on his fine face."

Such quotations by themselves suggest much but prove nothing. The Media Research Center, however, has done an array of statistical studies concerning selection of sources and interviewees, ideological labeling of groups, ways of framing stories, and so on. It has found a significant tilt to the left theologically and politically, and a refusal among many reporters to acknowledge that publicly.

Conservatives sometimes respond to that evidence by suggesting that media liberals should not present their views. But I'm pro-choice concerning media: Let ideas compete on all the pages of publications and on television news shows, so that readers and viewers have a choice. Here's my challenge to the editors of *Time* and *Newsweek*: We at *WORLD* have proclaimed our theology. Why don't you declare yours?

2001

In the movie *Field of Dreams*, James Earl Jones intones about the one constant in America over the decades: baseball. In the fifteen-year history of *WORLD*, amid liberal and conservative administrations, the end of one cold war and the beginning of another, we've also pointed out from time to time one more constant: liberal media bias.

We don't spend much space on this in *WORLD* anymore: it's so obvious, and we'd rather provide a positive alternative than harp on the negative. But for fourteen years now, the Media Research Center right after Thanksgiving has asked me to help select the winners of its annual awards for "The Year's Worst Reporting." I planned to say no this time, until I read a prophecy from the beginning of the contest year by *Newsweek*'s Jonathan Alter. Writing about George W. Bush in the light of last November's disputed election, he commented, "However agreeable and successful he turns out to be, the new president is doomed to be seen by many Americans as a bastard."

Newsweek thought that was clever; I think that's going too far, so it was time to wade into the muck once again and see:

- The usual anti-Christian bigotry. *Newsweek* bloviated thusly: "In John Ashcroft's America, he said in 1999, 'We have no king but Jesus.' . . . Can a deeply religious person be Attorney General?"

- The usual psychobabble. NPR's Nina Totenberg said the GOP and its "moderates" are "in an abusive relation-ship . . . the moderates are the enablers and the conservatives are the abusers."

- The usual kneejerk responses to problems. ABC's Elizabeth Vargas on July 31 breathlessly announced, "More trouble at the nation's amusement parks, two dozen people injured. Why won't Congress let the government regulate those parks?"

- The usual closed-mindedness on abortion. *CBS Early Show* cohost Jane Clayson announced at the beginning of one discussion, "First off, we should say we're not here to debate the right and wrong of abortion, just different generations' commitment to reproductive rights."

After September 11 I hoped to see a new maturity in the press, and initially some change was evident. Dan Rather made patriotic statements and Lance Morrow wrote in *Time*, "For once, let's have no 'grief counselors' standing by with banal consolations, as if the purpose, in the midst of all this, were merely to make everyone feel better as quickly as possible. We shouldn't feel better. . . . Anyone who does not loathe the people who did these things, and the people who cheer them on, is too philosophical for decent company. . . . This is the moment of clarity. Let the civilized toughen up, and let the uncivilized take their chances in the game they started."

Soon, though, the moment of clarity turned into weeks of fog, as the moral relativism and amoral multiculturalism taught at most universities, and cemented at most major media offices, reasserted themselves. Steven Jukes of Reuters wrote, "one man's terrorist is another man's freedom fighter." CBS foreign correspondent Allen Pizzy said on October 14, "freedom is a perception that lies in the eyes of the beholder." The rewriting of history also recommenced. The dean emeritus of the White House press corps, Helen Thomas, said, "Throughout his eight years in office, President Clinton warned us that the next great menace was international terrorism."

This is the same Bill Clinton who taught Wahhabi Muslims that American presidents are moral lowlifes who might lob a couple of public relations-guided missiles at tents left behind, but would not take any serious action.

Christian parents who raise boys learn the question to ask when meditating on the proper punishment for a transgression: "Is it boy or is it sin?" Boy nature—impetuous, adventuresome, sometimes ruled by the moment—can get young males into trouble. Parents need to help their charges become more responsible, but we should not assume the malice of sin unless direct disobedience is evident. Our response to secular liberal reporters should be similar: "Is it ignorance or malice?" Most journalists have grown up in nonbiblical homes and will naturally see people with biblical perspectives as weird. In my experience, patient explanation to most local reporters can at least educate them to the point where they are capable of writing a fair story—and that's what most desire. It's different with lots of the big boys.

I hesitate to assume malice, but I have no explanation other than hatred of Christ for some stories generated by CBS's *60 Minutes* and the *New York Times* in particular. That hasn't changed in the aftermath of September 11, and I shouldn't expect it to. As we celebrate the birth of Christ this month, it's vital to remember that Herod and his courtiers wanted to kill him, and they still do.

2002

Let's look first at press paranoia. CNN's Judy Woodruff on May 16 talked of purported "news from the White House that President Bush knew that al-Qaeda was planning to hijack a U.S. airliner and he knew it before September the 11th." The next day on ABC's *Good Morning America*, Charles Gibson asked, "Was the president really surprised" by news of the 9/11 attacks?

Dan Rather, also without evidence but blurting out his suspicions to Don Imus on May 22, broadened the conspiracy: "The attorney general of the United States, just before September 11th, started inexplicably taking private aircraft to places where normally the attorney general wouldn't take private aircraft." Seymour Hersh, formerly of the *New York Times* and now writing for the *New Yorker*, called John Ashcroft "demented," but folks who think TeamBush planned or anticipated the destruction that occurred on September 11 are conspiracy nuts.

Hatred of big corporations, particularly in the oil industry, has once again been a press theme. *New York Times* columnist Thomas Friedman wrote about "Mr. Bush and his oil-industry paymasters" and amplified that sneer in an October 17 interview with *Rolling Stone*: "These guys are bought and paid by Big Oil in America." *Time* on November 4 stretched far to bring in other guilt by association: "The military-style gun used in the sniper attacks—named, unfortunately for the White House, Bushmaster XM15—was manufactured by a company owned by Richard Dyke, a Bush fundraiser."

Juggling of cause and effect has been common. The *New York Times* reported on January 21, "Since the early 1970s, the number of state prisoners has increased 500 percent, growing each year in the 1990s even as crime fell." It seems more likely that crime has fallen because criminals have been locked up. CBS on July 16 offered investment advice based on two pieces of evidence: "Last week the president spoke, the market went down. Yesterday, the president spoke, the market went down. Should he be quiet for a while?"

Is a little knowledge a dangerous thing? Journalists know that the 1950s were "the McCarthy years," and that was bad. They don't understand the threat that prompted Sen. Joseph McCarthy's exaggerations and lies. The *New York Times* on February 24 complained "that the war on terrorism was starting to look suspiciously like the great American campaign—against Communism.... The McCarthy years in some ways were eerily similar to the present moment.... Communists were often conceived as moral monsters whose deviousness and unwavering dedication to their faith made them capable of almost anything." Sadly, many Communists were highly dedicated moral monsters capable of almost anything.

Liberal journalists' defenses against charges of bias often show how deep the bias goes. NBC's Tom Brokaw said on July 25 that he didn't see "a liberal agenda. It happens that journalism will always be spending more time on issues that seem to be liberal to some people: the problem of civil rights and human rights, the problem of those people who don't have a place at the table with the powerful." But those issues are not liberal: liberals have kept the poor on the government plantations, and compassionate conservatives are trying to free them.

I don't want to seem unduly critical of journalism in 2002. After all, CNN on September 3 narrowed down for worried viewers the possibilities concerning Osama bin Laden: "Experts Agree: Al-Queda Leader Is Dead or Alive." And the *Washington Post* offered good news in its October 4 front-page headline concerning the people of different races and ethnicities killed by the sniper in Montgomery County, Maryland: "County's Growing Diversity Reflected in Those Gunned Down."

I have to conclude, though, that some reporters are really weird. *Time*'s Joel Stein reported on July 29 his experience at a fundraising dance party for former Attorney General Janet Reno, who was trying to become governor of Florida. He wrote, "I leave my friends behind and rush the stage to try to dance with Reno, only to find myself in a small group of men living the same fantasy." Sorry, guys, I've never had that fantasy.

2005

I'd like to look at coverage about Hurricane Katrina that delayed rescues and prodded some politicians into making mega-billion-dollar promises.

You probably saw and heard reports of mayhem at the Superdome and the Convention Center, and on the streets of New Orleans. You may have missed the admissions weeks later by NBC, the *New Orleans Times-Picayune*, the *New York Times*, and the *Los Angeles Times* that, as the *Baltimore Sun* noted, stories about "murders, rapes and beatings have turned out to be false."

"Hundreds of armed gang members killing and raping people" inside the Dome—never happened. "Thirty or 40 bodies" stored in a Convention Center freezer—not one. Rampaging "armed mobs"—none. "Bands of rapists, going block to block"—never happened. Geraldo Rivera's "scene of terror, chaos, confusion, anarchy, violence, rapes, murders, dead babies"—well, that's Geraldo Rivera.

Orleans Parish D. A. Eddie Jordan said four murders occurred in the entire city during the week after Katrina hit, making it a typical week in a city averaging two hundred homicides per year. The Superdome had one shooting: Louisiana National Guardsman Chris Watt accidentally shot himself in the leg. New Orleans coroner Frank Minyard said he had seen only seven gunshot victims during hurricane week: "Seven gunshots isn't even a good Saturday night in New Orleans."

Why the hype? Official sources like the mayor and the police chief were hysterical, and some reporters merely became

megaphones for them. Crying and yelling made for better ratings than calm assessments of damage. Network stars wanted
to display what passed as compassion. Since few reporters knew
what was happening, a pack mentality kicked in as reporters
congregated in places of safety. Politics also played a role, with
liberals framing the story as one of rich people not caring about
poor people and whites not caring about blacks.

But media exaggeration was not a victimless crime. It delayed
the arrival of responders who, relying on press reports, had
to plan their missions as military rather than philanthropic
endeavors. Soldiers on hot days felt it necessary to don heavy
body armor, which also slowed them down. New Orleans police
stopped their search-and-rescue operations and turned their
attention to the imagined mobs of rapists. Two patients apparently died while waiting for evacuation helicopters grounded
for a day by false reports of sniper fire.

Bush-bashing of course came to the fore, with the typical
mainstream media view voiced well by former *New York Times*
executive editor Howell Raines: "The churchgoing cultural popu-
lism of George Bush" means that "the poor drown in their attics."
MSNBC, ABC, NPR, and *Newsweek* journalists were among the
multitude who took the disaster as an opportunity to campaign
overtly for higher taxes and bigger government. The international image of America, crucial to the war on terror, took an
enormous hit, as journalists described rampant heartlessness.

But the biggest loser may have been race relations. The picture that emerged was one of African-American masses of flood
victims resorting to utter depravity, randomly attacking each
other as well as the police trying to protect them and rescue
workers trying to save them. In reality, almost all were law-
abiding, but author Michael Lewis summarized the network
view this way: "Over and over and over again, they replayed the
same few horrifying scenes" and communicated this message:

"Crazy black people with automatic weapons are out hunting white people, and there's no bag limit."

My bag limit these days is a maximum of two columns a year on liberal press bias, especially since it's like shooting fish in a barrel. But Katrina coverage—oh, what a disaster.

2006

Each year for the past nineteen I've served as a judge for the Media Research Center's awards for the year's worst journalism. The winners will be announced any day now, and on my ballot MSNBC's Keith Olbermann and *Newsweek*'s Eleanor Clift are two of the leading candidates.

Olbermann said on September 11, at the site of the World Trade Center, "Who has left this hole in the ground? We have not forgotten, Mr. President. You have. May this country forgive you." On October 18 he announced that the Bush administration is "more dangerous to our liberty than is the enemy it claims to protect us from."

Clift, declaring on April 7, "There's nothing this administration won't do under the guise of battling terrorism," called for Americans to "stop Bush's imperial expansion of power." But Clift on July 15 said Russia's Vladimir Putin has "a commanding popularity among his own people, because he is perceived to be an effective dictator. What we have in this country is a dictator who's ineffective."

Imperialism and dictators: *Los Angeles Times* columnist Joel Stein wrote on January 24, "I don't support our troops.... When you volunteer for the U.S. military . . . you're willingly signing up to be a fighting tool of American imperialism." CNN's Jack Cafferty on May 11 said that Senate Judiciary Committee head Arlen Specter (R-Pa.), who had criticized the Bush administration, "might be all that's standing between us and a full-blown dictatorship in this country."

On the lighter side, former *Today* show host Bryant Gumbel on February 7 attacked the Winter Olympics: "Don't like 'em and won't watch 'em. In fact, I figure when Thomas Paine said, 'These are the times that try men's souls,' he must have been talking about the start of another Winter Olympics. Because they're so trying." NBC movie critic Gene Shalit reviewed on March 29 the cartoon movie *Ice Age: The Meltdown*: "Think global warming isn't real? Ask Manny the Mammoth, Diego the Tiger, or Sid the Sloth."

The good news late in the year was that a messiah comes. *Time*'s Joe Klein wrote on October 23 that Barack Obama "seemed the political equivalent of a rainbow—a sudden preternatural event inspiring awe and ecstasy. . . . He transcends the racial divide so effortlessly that it seems reasonable to expect that he can bridge all the other divisions—and answer all the impossible questions—plaguing American public life." ABC's Terry Moran said on November 6 about Barack Obama, "You can see it in the crowds. The thrill, the hope. . . . Is he the one?"

WORLD has covered the starvation in North Korea brought about by a real tyrant, but ABC's Diane Sawyer, reporting from a school there on October 19, said, "It is a world away from the unruly individualism of any American school. . . . Ask them about their country, and they can't say enough." The clip showed a North Korean girl saying, in English, "We are the happiest children in the world."

Later, Sawyer said to the class: "You know The Sound of Music?" Children's voices chorused, "Yes." Sawyer then sang with the class: "Do, a deer, a female deer. Re, a drop of golden sun . . ." Anchor Charles Gibson intoned, "A fascinating glimpse of North Korea."

Are such reports rare? Former *Washington Post* reporter Tom Edsall on September 21 said the proportion of Democrats to Republicans in "mainstream media" is "probably in the range of 15 to 25:1 Democrat. . . . There is a real difficulty on the part of the mainstream media being sympathetic, or empathetic, to the kind of thinking that goes into conservative approaches to issues. I think the religious right has been treated as sort of an alien world."

Even *ABC News* political director Mark Halperin on October 30 acknowledged that the dominance of the left in journalism "tilts the coverage quite frequently, in many issues, in a liberal direction. . . . It's an endemic problem."

2010

Chris Matthews has, with Keith Olbermann, firmly positioned MSNBC on the left. Matthews famously commented in 2008 about "this thrill going up my leg" that he felt when Barack Obama gave a speech. On September 7, 2010, he said it again in relation to the president: "I get the same thrill up my leg, all over me." Good for Rep. Michele Bachmann, R-Minn., who told Matthews on November 2, discussing that day's election results, "I think people are thrilled tonight. I imagine that thrill is . . . not so tingly on your legs anymore."

Some journalists grew pessimistic about the Obama administration but remained high on his new Supreme Court appointee, Elena Kagan. *ABC World News* correspondent Terry Moran reported her first day on the Court (October 4) this way: "You could almost sense or imagine some of the other justices and veteran court watchers kind of looking down the bench at Justice Kagan like a major league scout might say, 'You know, that kid's got some real pop on her fastball.' " Another hero is Eric Holder, because—according to CBS's Rita Braver—"Ignoring political pressure is Holder's constant message."

The Associated Press has departed from just-the-facts-ma'am style and moved toward analysis that often reveals the mindsets of reporters. Here's Paul Haven's September 24 dispatch from Havana: "Cuba's communist leaders mapped out a brave new world of free enterprise on Friday, approving a laundry list of small-time businesses." Haven worried that the changes "seem sure to create a society of haves and have-nots in a land that has spent half a century striving for an egalitarian utopia."

AP still claims evenhandedness, but *Newsweek* to its credit has abandoned hypocrisy and largely acknowledged its leftwardness. Sometimes it also seems ready to acknowledge its manufacturing of role models, as in its August 2 cover story about demagogue Al Sharpton: "He is out there all alone, still standing on the same principle he first enunciated in his housing project in Brooklyn: poor people have the same rights as rich ones to justice in the streets and in the court. If he didn't exist, we might, in fact, need to invent him." (Maybe we did.)

But surely the Public Broadcasting System provides high quality journalism, no? Hmm. Listen to this May 25 discussion of radical Muslims between author Ayaan Hirsi Ali and PBS host Tavis Smiley. Ali: "The idea got into their minds that to kill other people is a great thing to do and that they would be rewarded in the hereafter." Smiley: "But Christians do that every single day in this country." Ali: "Do they blow people up every day?" Smiley: "Yes."

The concept of having comedians present and discuss the news is spreading: Comedy Central is what it says it is in presenting Jon Stewart, but what's Joy Behar doing as cohost of ABC's *The View* and host of a CNN show? Her October 26 analysis of Nevada GOP Senate candidate Sharron Angle took my breath away: "She's going to Hell. . . . She's going to Hell, this bitch." When Behar interviewed President Obama on July 29, she went on and on about his political successes and then asked, "Where is your attack dog to come out and tell the American people, 'Listen, this is what we did?'" Obama responded, "Joy, that's your job." Her comeback: "I do it! But I'm only one woman!"

2011

For the twenty-fourth year in a row I'm a judge for the Media Research Center awards, and this year the ninety-eight finalists taught me a lot.

I thought President Barack Obama's popularity was evaporating, but ABC's Christiane Amanpour called him "full of sunny optimism, very Reaganesque," and Lara Spencer on the same network asked, "Is President Obama a baby whisperer? . . . Watch as the First Lady tries to quiet down the fussy little friend. . . . She then hands the bawling baby to the big man and, presto, the tot is simply transfixed."

I thought Middle Eastern demonstrators want basic human rights and Midwest state workers hope to retain above-average paychecks, but *New York Times* reporters Michael Cooper and Katharine Seelye equated Wisconsin with Tunisia, ABC's Diane Sawyer saw "Cairo moved to Madison," and ABC's Amanpour saw both efforts as "people power making history. A revolt in the Midwest and a revolution sweeping across the Middle East."

I didn't realize that Tea Party folks were terrorists, but *New York Times* columnist Thomas Friedman equated them to Hezbollah, and within a week fellow *Times* columnist Joe Nocera was writing that "Tea Party Republicans have waged jihad on the American people" and wear "suicide vests." MSNBC's Chris Matthews similarly observed that "the GOP has become the Wahhabis of American government."

Matthews didn't stop there. Last month he commented on Republican voters: "They hate. . . . Their brains, racked as they are by hatred, they lack the 'like' mode." He could have been describing himself when he complained about talk show hosts who "see the other end of the field as evil, as awful. Not just disagreeable but evil."

At least television pundits, unlike their print equivalents, sometimes have guests who talk back. Matthews fell into a rant when questioning Republican National Committee chairman Michael Steele: "You go to a Democratic convention . . . and black folk are hanging together and having a good time. . . . You go to a Republican event, you get a feeling that you are all told . . . 'Don't get together, don't crowd, you'll scare these people.' . . . Did you fear that if you got together with some other African-Americans, these white guys might get scared of you?" Steele replied, "No! What are you talking about?"

On the other hand, some guests (and listeners) don't talk back. In February another MSNBC host, Lawrence O'Donnell, was interviewing Michigan ex-governor Jennifer Granholm. He stated, "The Republican Party is saying that the president of the United States has bosses, that the union bosses this president around. Does that sound to you like they are trying to consciously or subconsciously deliver the racist message that, of course, a black man can't be the real boss?" Granholm replied, "Wow, I hadn't thought about the racial overtones."

And I hadn't thought, until *New York Times* columnist Maureen Dowd educated me, that GOP budget-cutters were "cannibals . . . vampires . . . zombies . . . the metallic beasts in *Alien*." (She mixed all of those metaphors into one memorable paragraph.) I also learned from Katie Couric that Americans will realize Islam is not a problem when we watch "a Muslim version of *The Cosby Show*."

But maybe the tilt of these mainstream opinion merchants isn't so important anymore. When Jill Abramson in June became *New York Times* editor, she said her rise was like "ascending to Valhalla. In my house growing up, the *Times* substituted for religion. If the *Times* said it, it was the absolute truth." Happily, almost no one has that kind of faith anymore.

And yet, people sometimes think they're getting facts in news reports. That's why a report by correspondent Ray Suarez on PBS's *NewsHour* astounded me. Suarez spoke of communist Cuba's "impressive health outcomes . . . no doctor shortage . . . care that's both personal and persistent." Right. In reporting from Havana in 2004 I talked with doctors serving as cab drivers and bellhops to get money for their families. Some churches hosted illegal clinics because parishioners couldn't get help through official channels. A pharmacy's shelves were mostly naked. A hospital had a BYOX policy: Bring your own X-ray film.

Happy new year, in a land that's still mostly free.

Appendix 2
Additional Resources

Whel *Prodigal Press* first came out in 1988, the study of media bias was the province mostly of academics. Since then, it has become a cottage industry. This appendix does not document examples of media bias (see Appendix 1 for that), but provides readers with resources that will keep them up to date on the most current and significant examples.

Media Research Center

For more than twenty-five years the Media Research Center has documented media bias in the mainstream media. The group publishes an annual list of the most egregious examples of media bias, and has regular updates to its website: www.mrc.org.

NewsBusters

Www.NewsBusters.org is a site maintained by the Media Research Center that provides daily examples of media bias.

Bibliography

A number of good to excellent books have come out in recent years on media bias and on the broader topic of how to be perceptive, discerning consumers of modern media. All of the books below are cited in one or more places in *Prodigal Press*, but they are collected here for the reader's convenience:

Russ Braley, *Bad News: The Foreign Policy of the New York Times* (Chicago: Regnery, 1984)

Herman Dinsmore, *All the News That Fits: A Critical Analysis of the News and Editorial Content of the* New York Times

(New Rochelle: Arlington House, 1969)

Bernard Goldberg, *Bias: A CBS Insider Exposes How the Media Distorts the News* (New York: Harper Perennial, 2003)

Tom Kelly, *The Imperial Post: The Meyers, the Grahams, and the Paper That Rules Washington* (New York: William Morrow, 1983)

Jim Kuypers, *Press Bias and Politics: How the Media Frame Controversial Issues* (Westport, CT: Praeger, 2002)

Philip Lawler, *The Alternative Influence: The Impact of Investigative Reporting Groups on America's Media* (Lanham, MD: University Press of America, 1984)

Marvin Olasky, *The Press and Abortion, 1838–1938* (Hillsdale, NJ: Lawrence Erlbaum Associates, 1988)

Neil Postman, *Amusing Ourselves to Death: Public Discourse in the Age of Show Business* (New York: Penguin Books, 1985)

Leopold Tyrmand, *The Media Shangri-La: Where Everyone is Free but Some Are Freer* (Rockford, IL: Rockford College Institute, 1975)

James Tyson, *Target America: The Influence of Communist Propaganda on the U.S. Media* (Chicago: Regnery, 1981)

Appendix 3
Public Relations, Theology, and Practice

This book up to now has not dealt with what is often the largest specialization within contemporary journalism schools: public relations. It is an important specialty, the occupation of more than one hundred thousand men and women in the United States and the major or concentration of more than twenty thousand college and university students each year. It is also a vital amateur activity for hundreds of thousands of other men and women, particularly leaders of small groups who have to deal with the press and cannot afford professional counsel.[1]

Non-Christian presuppositions dominate the upper levels of current public relations practice, much as they do the field of journalism generally. Yet, some public relations techniques may be put to godly use by Christians. This appendix has two parts. Part one discusses the theology of public relations at its highest government and corporate levels, through an examination of the ideas of the key founder of modern American public relations, Edward Bernays. Part one does not condemn all of public relations or suggest that Christians should not work in the field; it does suggest that Christians should prepare to oppose Bernaysian public relations by developing a biblical perspective. Part

---

1. Bureau of Labor Statistics figures quoted in Fraser P. Seitel, *The Practice of Public Relations*, 2nd ed. (Columbus, OH: Charles Merrill, 1984), 65.

two pulls out of one subset of public relations, "press relations," some useful advice for leaders of small Christian organizations.

Part One: Public Relations versus Godly Relations

Edward Bernays, known as America's number one public relations man from the 1930s through the 1960s, was an intelligent ideologue as well as a crafty campaign director. When I interviewed Bernays at his home near Harvard University in 1984, he was still mentally alert at age ninety-two, and willing to talk about the consistency of his atheistic beliefs throughout a long career.

The basis of Bernaysian thinking was clear: He acknowledged that he did not believe in God. Bernays believed in himself and his ability to "manipulate public opinion," as he put it forthrightly in the title of one of his articles. Without faith in God, Bernays wrote often of how chance ruled the world. He said that public relations was necessary because, without it, society would be controlled by "the fortuitous and whimsical forces of life and chance." He wrote, "There is something appalling to the ordinary business man in the fact that his business lies at the mercy of uncontrollable forces of whim and chance." He said he met a need by showing others how "to control by means of propaganda what otherwise would be controlled disastrously by chance."[2]

Bernays did not believe in God, but he did believe in the worship of human idols, idols he himself could fashion: "Human beings need to have godhead symbols, and public relations counsels must help to create them." Bernays saw his idol-making as vital to the salvation of society: "We have no being in the air to watch over us. We must watch over ourselves, and that is where

2. Edward Bernays, "Manipulating Public Opinion: The Why and the How," *American Journal of Sociology* (May 1928): 958–71; John T. Flynn, "Edward L. Bernays: The Science of Ballyhoo," *Atlantic Monthly*, May 1931, 562–71.

public relations counselors can prove their effectiveness, by making the public believe that human gods are watching over us for our own benefit." These human gods, created by astute public relations, would keep order by giving their followers reasons to live and goals to accomplish.[3]

Bernays also believed in the wisdom of his uncle, Sigmund Freud. Our interview was filled with comments such as "My uncle expressed this very well: People need sacred dances. Public relations counsels should be trained to call the tunes." Developing such power would not be difficult for those who understood human desires, because human beings are not individuals made after God's image, according to Bernays. They are rubber stamps, "the duplicates of millions of others, so that when those millions are exposed to the same stimuli, all receive identical imprints."[4]

This view of man as responder to stimuli led to Bernays's doctrine of "social responsibility." Powerful individuals with "the public interest" at heart must do whatever is necessary to preserve society from "reactionaries," or those with religious goals. Thoroughly modern social saviors are obliged not to abide by the ordinary demands of ethics that might apply to them as individuals. Instead, they must subordinate individual behavior and conscience to the "progressive" needs of society. Bernays's "elite," he declared, must manipulate "so as to bring order out of chaos."[5]

For sixty years Bernays was consistent with this message. He argued from the 1920s onward that "the conscious and intelligent manipulation of the organized habits and opinions of the masses is an important element in democratic society." Strange: a democratic society is normally considered one in which "the people" in general do rule. An authoritarian society is often

3. Interview with Bernays, conducted at 7 Lowell Street, Cambridge, MA, August 10, 1984.
4. Edward Bernays, *Propaganda* (New York: Liveright, 1928), 28.
5. Interview.

considered one in which a small group of people rule. Bernays was trying to square the circle by arguing, in effect, that we must kill democracy to save it. Strange: yet, without the presence of God's "invisible hand," there was no choice, according to Bernays; wise men such as himself had to "pull the wires which control the public mind."[6]

Bernays, developing the rationale for a public relations style which prized manipulation, also argued for a new methodology. A sound public relations specialist, Bernays wrote, "takes account not merely of the individual, nor even of the mass mind alone, but also and especially of the anatomy of society, with its interlocking group formations and loyalties." The individual was "a cell organized into the social unit. Touch a nerve at a sensitive spot and you get an automatic response from certain specific members of the organism."[7]

The social Pavlovian nature of this procedure was, for Bernays, no exaggeration. Whether or not he and others could manipulate so mechanistically was, and is, open to question, but Bernays claimed that he could "effect some change in public opinion with a fair degree of accuracy by operating a certain mechanism, just as the motorist can regulate the speed of his car by manipulating the flow of gasoline." The way to that goal was through working on the leaders, and through them their followers, sometimes called "herds" by Bernays: "If you can influence the leaders, either with or without their conscious cooperation, you automatically influence the group which they sway."[8]

Bernays argued consistently that "the special pleader who seeks to create public acceptance for a particular idea or commodity" is a hero. Public relations, for Bernays, no longer needed to be defended as what sinful men do in a sinful society. Public

6. Bernays, *Propaganda*, 9–10.
7. Ibid., 28.
8. Ibid., 37.

relations, Bernays thought, was the service which saviors of that sinful society would take upon themselves to perform. It was hard work to be continuously "regimenting the public mind every bit as much as an army regiments the bodies of its soldiers," but someone had to do it.[9]

Who? Bernays's vision of the future of public relations was most attractive to status-seeking practitioners. Certainly, Bernays wrote, "There are invisible rulers who control the destinies of millions," but those were not the political leaders or big businessmen of common paranoia. No, Bernays insisted, "It is not generally realized to what extent the words and actions of our most influential public men are dictated by shrewd persons operating behind the scenes."[10]

The behind-the-scenes operators were necessary to the operation of a society: "The invisible government tends to be concentrated in the hands of the few because of the expense of manipulating the social machinery which controls the opinions and habits of the masses." As to the job description and title of the behind-the-scenes operators, Bernays was precise: "There is an increasing tendency to concentrate the functions of propaganda in the hands of the propaganda specialist. This specialist is more and more assuming a distinct place and function in our national life. [He] has come to be known by the name of public relations counsel."[11]

"Public relations counsels"—leaders of the invisible government, taking upon themselves the responsibility of saving civilization from chaos. "Public relations counsels"—a brave new profession for a brave new world. Most low-level public relations specialists have never heard of Bernays, and many even in the highest reaches have never read his books; but those with

9. Ibid., 25. Also see Edward Bernays, "Molding Public Opinion," *The Annals of the American Academy of Political and Social Science* (May 1935): 82–87.

10. Bernays, *Propaganda*, 9.

11. Ibid., 37.

experience in major public relations offices (and a willingness to be candid) admit that Bernays' doctrine has become almost the official theology of elite public relations.

Bernaysian public relations has come in for its share of scorn. Judge Learned Hand called the Bernays-style public relations of his time "a black art," and others have been harsher. But Judge Hand admitted ruefully, "It has come to stay. Every year adds to the potency, to the finality of its judgments." There are some public relations managers, though, who persist in doing honest jobs. Some, with consciously Christian worldviews, stand against Bernaysian ideas.[12]

The Alternative

The biblical idea of public opinion, in one sense, is similar to that of Bernays. The Bible does not praise the rationality of either individuals and groups of individuals, or our ability to come to good judgments by following our natural tendencies. Rather, all of us are sinners, easily fooled by others or by ourselves, and ready to become a mob. Furthermore, our human tendency is always to proclaim ourselves autonomous, even though we know deep down that we are creatures and not Creator. Since the fantasy of autonomy can only be maintained when others go along with it, our human tendency, whenever we obtain power, is to attempt to manipulate public opinion in order to either make ourselves gods or create gods of our own choosing.

Even in the first book of the Old Testament, some individuals and groups attempted to publicize themselves as well as certain physical symbols. Genesis 11:1–9 relates the construction of the tower of Babel by people whose goal was to "make a name for ourselves." Since the builders cared more for their names

---

12. For more information, see Marvin Olasky, *Corporate Public Relations: A New Historical Perspective* (Hillsdale, NJ: Lawrence Erlbaum, 1987).

than for God's name, God responded by making understand-able naming more difficult by confusing the languages of the whole world. The babblers failed in the effort to spread their glory throughout the world; they ended up without even a com-mon name for themselves among themselves. So ended the first public relations campaign recorded in the Bible.

Other public relations campaigns followed, but one ran into stern opposition. In Genesis 14:21–24, Abraham showed understanding of the Sodomite strategy of image building by refusing to take the spoils of war offered by the king of Sodom, so that the king would never be able to say, "I have made Abram rich." Abraham realized that such a statement would be factually inaccurate, since it is God who made him rich. Abraham also avoided the possibility that others would perceive him to be in league with the Sodomites, either to the detriment of his own reputation or the building up of Sodom in the eyes of others who might think it innocent by association.

Throughout biblical history, tension between public relations and godly relations increased. King Saul was so concerned about the crowd chanting, "Saul has struck down his thousands, and David his ten thousands" (1 Sam. 18:7), that he tried to kill David rather than trying to follow God's commands, and eventually, lost his kingdom and his life. Later, a paid discrediting campaign was at first successful: Following the return from Babylon, oppo-nents of the Jews "bribed counselors against them to frustrate their purpose, all the days of Cyrus king of Persia, even until the reign of Darius king of Persia" (Ezra 4:5). Eventually the walls and temple of Jerusalem were rebuilt. Once again, public relations concerns won out in the short run, but not in the end.

The climax of the battle between public relations and godly relations came in the New Testament, with manipulated pub-lic opinion demanding the crucifixion of Christ. As Matthew Henry wrote in his commentary on Matthew 27, "The chief priests had a great interest in the people, they called them Rabbi, Rabbi, made idols of them, and oracles of all they said."[13] At the same time, though, the chief priests and elders knew how to incite a crowd, so that the mob sentiment—"Crucify him! Crucify him!"—was as much a function of the public relations men of that time, having "persuaded the crowd to ask for Barabbas and destroy Jesus" (Matt. 27:20), as it was of any uncoerced public opinion.

Bernays's ideas, innovative as they appeared to public relations managers in the twentieth century, were merely duplicating the strategies of the Pharisees: leaders first manipulate the crowd and then cite the crowd's voice as evidence of "the will of the people" before which leaders must bow. The cycle worked with particular viciousness when the only person standing in the way of the leader-mob alliance was Pilate. Pilate knew "it was out of envy" that the chief priests had handed Jesus over to him, but he nevertheless handed over Christ "to satisfy the crowd" (Mark 15:10, 15). For Pilate, public relations was more important than justice.

For Christ on the cross, however, public relations was so unimportant compared to godly relations that his dying words did not criticize Pilate, the priests and elders, or even the disciples who had abandoned him at the end. Instead, Jesus focused on the only crucial issue: "My, God, my God, why have you forsaken me?" (Mark 15:34). By following godly relations despite Pilate's emphasis on public relations, Jesus, through his shed blood, empowered his followers to do the same. They would no longer be rubber stamps. They would be able to take to heart God's words to Abraham after the patriarch rose above the public relations plans of Sodom: "Fear not . . . I am your shield; your reward shall be very great" (Gen. 15:1).

13. Matthew Henry, *A Commentary on the Whole Bible*, vol. 5 (Old Tappan, NJ: Fleming H. Revel, n.d.; orig. pub. in early 1700s), 416–17.

The Holy Spirit provides similar power to Christians today. Rationales for manipulation in the public interest are always available. The decision about whether to practice deception regularly, though, depends on our understanding of how the world works: through "the whimsical forces of life and chance," as Bernays believed, or through God's providence. If the former, then public relations officers who wish to avoid "social chaos" may feel self-righteous in taking whatever steps they consider necessary. They will often manipulate the public and then cite public opinion or even the public interest as reason for actions they take.

When we believe God's Word, though, we know it is not man who prevents chaos, but God. We do not need to act out of desperation and prestidigitate for the supposed public good, because God has the whole world in his hands. In practice, a consistent espousal of godly relations rather than public relations requires a deep belief in God's sovereignty, and an adherence to objective, biblical truth rather than an offering of incense to public opinion.

The starting point for a public relations person who desires to practice godly relations rather than Bernays-style public relations is a willingness to witness to God's sovereignty and justice by not hesitating to tell the truth about God's creation, come what may.[14]

Part Two: Practical Steps for Press Relations

If you are an officer of a small Christian organization you might be shocked if, for some reason, it comes under attack

14. Some current public relations managers distinguish between "fact accuracy" and "impression accuracy," occasionally upholding the former as the cleverest way of sowing misimpressions, but the Bible makes no distinction between the two. "Do not lie," we are told in Leviticus, and immediately after that, "Do not deceive one another" (Lev. 19:11 NIV). Psalm 62:4 condemns men who "take pleasure in falsehood. They bless with their mouths, but inwardly they curse," while Proverbs 6:17–18 notes that things detestable to God include "haughty eyes, a lying tongue . . . a heart that devises wicked plans."

from the press. You should not be. Whether you are involved in a "controversial" issue such as abortion, or are "just" doing traditional evangelism, you may be on the enemies list of a reporter or editor who perceives Christians as closed-minded.

You need to be prepared to deal with unsolicited media attention, and you need to realize that, with God's grace, even a negative story often will end up helping your organization. This part of the appendix, written in outline form, should help you to follow Mordecai's example and make better use of the gallows that may have been prepared for your organization (Esth. 7:10).

Some General Considerations

1. Reporting is a young person's occupation. The reporter writing a story about your organization often will be in his twenties.

2. This means the reporter covering a Christian organization's activities is probably inexperienced. The reporter may be interested in the Christian organization because of contacts with anti-Christian groups. He may think Christian organizations have something to hide, something he will investigate and disclose.

3. Newspapers and television stations rarely employ fact-checkers. If a story smells right to an editor or producer, he will go with it. Current journalists often develop story ideas based on preconceived notions of potential conflict or reader interest. These notions may be based on what they have read in national magazines or seen on network television news shows, even if situations described in those stories have little in common with the local situation.

4. Sometimes a reporter will have his story almost written before he ever talks to you. He is simply picking up facts and quotations to use as specific detail for the story already constructed, or a short piece of film to insert. Good writing with

apparently accurate detail generally will get the story past an editor, even if facts and quotations are wrong and the entire story is misleading.

First Steps

1. Your organization should prepare a basic "press kit." The kit should contain information describing what the organization does, who it serves, how it was started, how it is funded, etc. The press kit should include the name and telephone number of the organization's media representative, with indication of a willingness to be called for further information.

2. Your organization should designate a person as its media representative (hereafter, "M"). M should make sure that whoever answers the organization's telephone is instructed to tell the reporter to call him. There should also be back-up media representatives in case, in an emergency situation, M cannot be contacted. (For almost all organizations such circumstances are rare; in most cases, reporters can wait, even though they may not want to.)

3. M should prepare a "standby statement" containing questions and answers to frequently asked questions. Critical articles about other Christian groups, or criticism from local anti-Christian organizations, should be analyzed carefully to see what kinds of charges typically are made. Responses to those charges should be prepared.

When the Reporter Is on the Phone

1. At this point, assume the reporter has been put in contact with M. The reporter typically will say either, "I am doing a story on subject x and would like a comment from you," or "I want to do a story on your organization." If the standby statement is a good one, the organization's position on subject x will be covered; if

not, M should be careful not to give off-the-cuff answers. If the subject is one on which the organization wants to comment, the organization representative should ask the reporter about his or her deadline and state that he will call back before that time.

2. At this point, M should think through potential answers and discuss them with others. Then he should be sure to call back before the deadline. If the subject is one the organization does not wish to comment on, M can say so. Reporters often will try to push interviewees into making a statement of some kind, but organizations should oppose that pressure. Reporters may say, "I just want to know how you feel about this," or "Can you tell me why you won't answer?" M should be steadfast in biblical truth: "Let your yes be yes and your no be no."

3. If the reporter plans a story on the organization, M should find out if the story is so hot that the reporter is going to press immediately. That is unlikely. Assuming the organization is not involved in some scandal, M should set up an appointment with the reporter when it is mutually convenient.

4. The reporter may say, "I'd like to do this today," or in some other way push for an immediate response, but if the story centers on M's organization he needs an interview to make the story at least seem "objective." If M declines to be interviewed the reporter will print that in the story, but if the story is not explosive and M agrees to be interviewed within some reasonable period (say, several days), the reporter will have a hard time charging your organization with lack of cooperation.

Preparing for the Reporter's Visit

1. You and other leaders of your organization should choose a person to accompany M to the interview. The testimony of two witnesses is important, and it is easy to go off on a tangent in an interview; a second person can help steer the conversation back on track. Unless the reporter requests additional interviews or

there is some pressing reason to the contrary, it is not a good idea to have three representatives of the Christian organization at the interview. That will look like either organizational timidity or a desire to gang up on the reporter.

2. Always review and update standby statements. M should make an outline of important points. M and others might think of positive ways to answer negative questions. They might write out the answers to those difficult questions and show them to someone else. If M is unfamiliar with interviewing, he might want to role-play with another Christian, tape the role-playing interview, and listen to himself. He might practice keeping answers informative but concise: "He who holds his tongue is wise."

3. The organization should have a working recording device of some type ready for the interview. Not recording leaves no protection against misquotations. Interviews for television news shows generally will be short; but for print media interviews, be sure you are able to record twice as much as may seem necessary. M will not want to miss the crucial closing remarks because batteries ran low or the recording device was not functioning properly. The recording device should have a microphone that will pick up voices well, since many people during interviews tend to talk softly. A back-up recorder should be available.

4. If a hostile television interview is expected, you might think of videotaping the proceedings. (In normal situations, that might be considered overkill.)

Etiquette of the Newspaper or Magazine Interview

1. If the reporter is thorough, he will come with a recorder and ask permission to record. M should say yes as he brings out the organization's recorder. If the reporter does not bring a recorder, it is possible (although unlikely) that he will object to M's recording, perhaps asking, "Is this really necessary?" or "Can't we trust each other?"

Assure him that it really is necessary. Never submit to an interview with a potentially adversarial reporter without recording it.

2. If the reporter objects, do not go ahead with the interview; the reporter will be unable to write in his story that your organization refused comment, and he will be reluctant to write that he refused to ask questions with a recording device running.

3. If the circumstances of the interview are positive (such as a pattern of fair coverage of your organization in the news outlet requesting an interview), you must still take precautions; but this may be the occasion for a favorable story that could be immensely helpful. M should be ready to suggest to a sympathetic reporter several possibilities for a positive and truthful feature story on the organization.

4. If the reporter is writing an article based on criticism of your organization, M should find out what that criticism is at the beginning of the interview. For example, if M is representing a Crisis Pregnancy Center, he should ask the reporter, while the recorder is running, "How did you hear about the organization? Who made the complaints? How many complaints have there been? Will you investigate abortion businesses as well?" The reporter may say, "I'd like to start with…" It is perfectly appropriate to respond, "We will be happy to answer your questions, but we would first like to know…"

5. If the story is arising in a hostile environment, M and others should beware of a reporter's requests for extensive personal background concerning organization leaders. Tell the reporter about about professional credentials, but giving a testimony may backfire if the reporter wants to distort coverage by playing up in a sarcastic manner anything that sounds strange to him.

6. Following the interview, transcribe the recorded material immediately. You may never need the transcript, but if you do, the organization will be prepared. The transcript also will be handy for in-house use, since the Holy Spirit may have made M especially articulate during the interview. Questions from the reporter on

the transcript can be used to update standby statements. If some questions were answered poorly, M can learn from his mistakes.

Notes on Television Interviews

1. With television cameras, you are forced to make some kind of statement, or else your closed door probably will be filmed, with the reporter saying that your organization refused to talk to the press.

2. Television crews often have one camera shooting from behind the interviewer. The reporter will not be on camera during the interview. Following the interview, the crew will film the reporter asking questions. This means that sharp-edged questions during the interview, which might lead you to respond in kind, may be replaced by mellow questions, leaving you looking belligerent for no purpose. Therefore, answer every question in the positive way you want to answer it, regardless of the question's tone.

3. Remember that a press interview might last for several hours, while a television interview might last for ten minutes, of which thirty seconds might be used. You are at the mercy of the person who chooses which segments of the interview to use; so do not let down toward the end of the interview. An antagonistic editor may show you at your weakest.

4. Occasionally cameras may be at your door, unannounced. For example, if your pro-life organization is picketed by a pro-abortion group, and a television reporter interviews demonstrators, he is likely to engage in "balancing" by coming to your office to interview your spokesman. This should be no problem if you have prepared and if you follow steps in the section on interview etiquette above. Simply give concise statements based on your standby statement preparation.

5. Occasionally local stations taking after *60 Minutes* might burst into your office without warning. If your local television station acts in this way, make sure that whoever is in the office

is prepared to say, with a determined smile, "You are being extremely rude, and you are trespassing."

When the Story Appears

1. The story may be fair and helpful; if so, take advantage of the publicity. If it is a print medium story, tell others to read all about it, and reprint it in your newsletter. Show a videotape of the television story at your next general meeting. Coverage gives the organization legitimacy and, perhaps, added importance in the eyes of fence-sitters.

2. If the story is negative, examine your organization in its light. Is your organization being attacked because you and others are following in Christ's footsteps? Or were real weaknesses in the organization legitimately reported?

3. If the story is dishonest and defamatory, do not despair. It could be the beginning of a major victory. M and others will want to contact the news organization—but first, all evidence needs to be in order. A general discussion of slanting will get you nowhere, either in a news organization's office or (if it comes to this) in court. You have to have specific inaccuracies or misquotations to obtain a retraction, correction, or equal time/space.

Analyzing the Dishonest Newspaper or Magazine Story

1. Compare the quoted statements in the article with the statements M and the other organizational representative actually made. If a statement is enclosed in quotation marks, it should be exactly what was said. If any words are missing, the exclusion should be indicated by an ellipsis (three dots). If a statement is a paraphrase, it should accurately reflect the meaning of what was said.

2. Examine any charges or statements against your organization. Are they demonstrably inaccurate? Was M given a chance to respond to the specific charges?

3. An article on a controversial question often will have some paragraphs that can be labeled "pro" one side or the other. Count the paragraphs. Within the common mode of journalistic "objectivity," your side and your critics' position should have received roughly equal space.

4. Examine the way in which "neutral expert witnesses" or "third party sources" are used. In a controversy story, use of such third parties is designed to help the reader sort out who's right and who's wrong. Are the witnesses actually neutral? Is their viewpoint shown accurately? If you know the third party sources used, you might call to see if they were quoted correctly.

5. Only after determining that actual inaccuracies exist should you go on to the next steps. If the reporter has quoted M and others fairly, but you do not like the tone, and if he has taken facts out of context but has done so with subtlety, you have little recourse but a letter to the editor that probably will not be printed.

Analyzing the Television Story

1. The same general considerations hold. However, analyze not just the words, but the video segment, with great care, as indicated in chapter 8.

2. Observe reporters' and announcers' intonations and facial expressions. Raised eyebrows and a sarcastic tone are worth a thousand words.

Calling the Newspaper Office

1. A few words about organization: Typically, the publisher is a newspaper's CEO, with two people—a business manager and an editor-in-chief—reporting to him. The business manager handles finance, circulation, advertising, and other business aspects. The editor-in-chief (sometimes called executive editor or simply editor) is in charge of all the nonadvertising material in

the newspaper. Do not go to the publisher, except as a last resort. That is going over the head of the person in charge of editorial content, and is likely to waste time or produce resentment. Also, do not go to someone you know on the business side of the newspaper.

2. Typically, leaders on the editorial side are the editor-in-chief, managing editor (who is concerned with day-to-day news and features), news editor (who is responsible for national and international news, but also for writing headlines and copyediting stories), and city editor (who assigns stories and supervises local coverage generally). Titles vary, but you probably will end up talking with one or more of those individuals.

3. Reporters are under the supervision of editors. Do not call the reporter who wrote the offending story. With ego invested in the story, and with less maturity than most editors, he is more likely to be belligerent.

4. Be aware of the role of the "ombudsman" (reader's advocate, public affairs editor, Mr. Go-Between, reader contact editor) if your newspaper has one. Don't let titles fool you. Unless the person filling the job is extraordinary, the ombudsman is not a reader's advocate, but an employee of the organization that has treated you unfairly.

5. A few ombudsmen may be more independent. They may be individuals from outside the organization brought in temporarily, with a contract stipulating fixed terms of employment with no possibility of renewal. However, ombudsmen are selected by the newspaper's management and are likely to share the ideological presuppositions of that management. An ombudsman may be helpful, but he is not your friend.

6. In short, call the highest ranking person on the editorial side of the operation—not the business side. Do so with the expectation that you may end up talking with an editor slightly lower in the pecking order, but above the reporter. Remember to be careful with everyone you deal with in a news organization. Chances

are, if the news organization had better fact-checking and higher ethical standards, you would not be there in the first place.

Calling the Television Station

1. Organization charts in television news often are functionally similar to those of newspapers, but staffs are smaller and titles are different. A producer rather than an editor decides which stories to use and how much time to give them. Often there will be different producers for morning, early evening, and late evening news shows. At some stations producers report to a news director, who in turn reports to a "general manager" or "station manager."

2. Many people think the anchorman (or -woman) is tremendously influential. That is often not so. Within the studio his clout reaches only as far as his ratings. Organizationally on most local broadcasts, the anchor has little power. Only if he is so tremendously popular that his departure would cause ratings problems, can he throw his weight around effectively.

3. If you have a good complaint, do not call the anchor or the government. Call the news director or producer, if you know specific names and responsibilities. When in doubt, simply call the "general manager" or "station manager."

Preparing for Confrontation

1. After a defamatory story appears, you should meet quickly with your board of directors or other leadership group, if possible. Before the meeting you should prepare a memo noting the article's factual inaccuracies and misquotations. The memo should be free of church jargon, understandable on first reading or hearing, and succinct. The act of composing the memo will help your organization see whether it has a valid complaint. (At the end of this appendix are notes on journalism codes of ethics that you may wish to cite.)

2. If your board of directors (or similar group) agrees that there are factual errors or misquotations damaging to the organization, the board should pass a resolution that it will consider libel action if the news organization does not act to correct the record. Libel suits are tricky and hard to win. They are not to be entered into lightly. They must be considered, though, if only because the news organization will take your complaint much more seriously when dollar signs accompany.

3. Once your board acts, M will call the editor, station manager, or other appropriate person. M should be prepared to say enough over the telephone to provoke the editor's concern. M should note that he has a recording of the interview and a detailed record of misquotations, inaccuracies, etc., and that the organization is considering libel action. He should not say, "We feel the article was unfair." The editor probably does not care what the organization thinks. He cares if his staff messed up and if there is cause for legal action. M should end the telephone call by setting up an appointment.

4. Two representatives of your organization, at least one of whom was at the interview, should go to the appointment. If you have a lawyer on your board, it might be good to send him. Your representatives should be prepared to play the recording for the editor. (This is especially effective if his reporter did not record the interview.)

5. If the editor cannot listen to the recording that day, do not leave it with him, regardless of how many copies your organization has. Your representative should be present when the recording is played to point out specific problems. The representative also will want to see the editor's reactions when the quotations on the recording contradict the quotations in print.

Negotiating a Settlement

1. The news outlet probably will not make an offer at your first appointment. The editor or producer will want to discuss the troublesome matter with his colleagues and probably his lawyer.

2. If the news outlet, after some thought, will not offer anything, then you must consult a lawyer knowledgeable about libel. News outlets now are very concerned about possible litigation. The refusal to make an offer might mean that you do not have a case. On the other hand, the news outlet might be bluffing. See a knowledgeable lawyer.

3. The news organization may offer a retraction, a correction, an article to be written by you, or a letter to the editor. A retraction is an admission of error, generally combined with an apology. A correction is a restatement of the facts without explicit admission or apology.

4. Ideally, if you have been falsely defamed, there should be a prominent retraction and apology, in the same spot or time (preferably a better spot or time) as the original article or on-air story.

5. Since we live in a fallen world, and since editors—like the rest of us—hate to be publicly embarrassed, he may offer you a mild correction,, in which the news organization will correct specific errors but do nothing to remove the overall negative impression given by a skillfully biased article. In this situation, a mere correction might be as bad as seeing the story appear a second time, because it will remind readers of the initial charges. When the problems with the article are greater than a factual inaccuracy or two, be careful about accepting correction without retraction.

6. In such a situation, ask for space or time to present your own viewpoint, rather than a correction. You should have as much space and time to present your side of the story as the newspaper or other news outlet used to attack you.

7. If you are offered space on the editorial page, remember that such placement is not equivalent to space on a generally better-read news page. Negotiate on this point, at least asking for a boxed statement (in the same location as the original article) pointing readers toward your rebuttal.

8. Do not settle for a letter to the editor. If that is all you are offered, examine the libel route.

To Sue or Not to Sue

1. Jesus spoke of avoiding courts, and on this and other questions his words should be followed. As noted in chapters 6 and 7, the search for American libel justice in recent years has become grossly expensive, time consuming, and emotionally draining. Time spent on a libel suit could reduce your organization's effectiveness. Also, to defend themselves, news outlets might try to prove that your organization is as bad as they said it was. Complainants (and there are always some) will be pulled out of the woodwork.

2. On the other hand, if you have a strong case, and the news outlet is stubborn, allowing it to stomp all over you will just encourage it to stomp all over other Christian organizations. Keeping in mind the great suffering that is likely to result, contact your local lawyer or national Christian legal organizations that might be willing to take your case.

3. If you are forced into libel action, keep track of any harm caused your organization by the defamatory news report. If volunteers or contributions decrease immediately after the article appears, this can be powerful evidence for damages.

Counterattack

1. Take advantage of the publicity your organization is getting, even if it is bad. If a Christian radio station, TV station, or newspaper is in town, you need to bring them into the controversy right away. They will probably be interested in a story about how the paper was biased in a story about a Christian organization. A small organization against a big newspaper or television station makes for a good David versus Goliath story.

2. Try to get on talk shows or other forums where you can take advantage of the publicity and get your story across. Develop or activate your speakers bureau. Use specific detail from the

memo you prepared earlier in which you recorded instances of error or inaccuracy to show bias.

3. Discuss the article in your newsletter, and the steps taken to gain redress. Send out a fund-raising letter explaining how you were unjustly attacked. Remember that you are probably being attacked because you are effective.

Note on Journalistic Codes of Ethics

Journalism ethics codes are at best semi-serious. There is no policing by journalism organizations, and not much in the way of penalties for violations. The codes are generalizations. They say little about practical application of principles, and offer no means for enforcement. Still, they are statements worth quoting when journalists do not take complaints seriously. The Society of Professional Journalists (Sigma Delta Chi) Code of Ethics was adopted in 1973.[15] It states that "there is no excuse for inaccuracies or lack of thoroughness." It also stipulates, under the "Accuracy and Objectivity" heading, that:

> 5. Sound practice makes clear distinction between news reports and expressions of opinion. News reports should be free of opinion or bias and represent all sides of an issue. . . .

> 8. Special articles or presentations devoted to advocacy or the writer's own conclusions and interpretations should be labeled as such.

Under a "Fair Play" heading, the Code stipulates that:

> 1. The news media should not communicate unofficial charges affecting reputation or moral character without giving the accused a chance to reply. . . .

15. The Society of Professional Journalists (Sigma Delta Chi) Code of Ethics may be viewed at http://ethics.iit.edu/ecodes/node/3702.

4. It is the duty of news media to make prompt and complete correction of their errors.

5. Journalists should be accountable to the public for their reports and the public should be encouraged to voice its grievances against the media.

The Code ends with a pledge: "Journalists should actively censure and try to prevent violations of these standards, and they should encourage their observance by all newspeople." That means if the reporter or editor who has defamed you is not a member of Sigma Delta Chi, find someone who is. If he takes oaths seriously and a legitimate offense has occurred, he is bound to try to do something about it.

The other major code is the American Society of Newspaper Editors (ASNE) Statement of Principles. The particularly relevant sections of the statement, which was adopted on October 23, 1975, are as follows:

ARTICLE IV: TRUTH AND ACCURACY. Good faith with the reader is the foundation of good journalism. Every effort must be made to assure that the news content is accurate, free from bias and in context, and that all sides are presented fairly. Editorials, analytical articles and commentary should be held to the same standards of accuracy with respect to facts as news reports. Significant errors of fact, as well as errors of omission, should be corrected promptly and prominently.

ARTICLE V: IMPARTIALITY. To be impartial does not require the press to be unquestioning or to refrain from editorial expression. Sound practice, however, demands a clear distinction for the reader between news reports and opinion. Articles that contain opinion or personal interpretation should be clearly identified.

ARTICLE VI: FAIR PLAY. Journalists should respect the rights of people involved in the news, observe the common standards of decency and stand accountable to the public for the fairness and accuracy of their news reports. Persons publicly accused should be given the earliest opportunity to respond. Pledges of confidentiality to news sources must be honored at all costs, and therefore should not be given lightly. Unless there is clear and pressing need to maintain confidence, sources of information should be identified.[16]

16. The American Society of Newspaper Editors (ASNE) Statement of Principles may be viewed at http://ethics.iit.edu/ecodes/node/3588.

Index of Scripture

Index of Subjects
and Names

INDEX OF SUBJECTS AND NAMES